THAT'S RIGHT: YOU'RE FIRED!

THAT'S RIGHT: YOU'RE FIRED!

How Football Management Has Evolved Over 125 Years

Tim
Healy

Ballpoint Press

"I told the president,
Wilheim Neudecker,
'we need some changes.'
'That's right: You're fired,'
he replied."

Udo Lattek, Bayern Munich manager
in the difficult 1974-5 season

To the memory of Dave Billings

Published in 2017 by Ballpoint Press
4 Wyndham Park, Bray,
Co Wicklow, Republic of Ireland.
Telephone: 00353 86 821 7631
Email: ballpointpress1@gmail.com
Web: www.ballpointpress.ie

ISBN 978-0-9954793-3-3

Book design and production by Joe Coyle Media&Design,
joecoyledesign@gmail.com

All photographs: © PA Images

Printed and bound by GraphyCems

Contents

Foreword
John Giles

THE management of football teams has always held a fascination for those of us who love the game. Every era has had managers who stood out for their leadership abilities. This book provides a series of insights into managers from the earliest days of the game, not just in England, but across the football world. It details the evolution of the role from that of Secretary/manager through to the high-profile occupants of technical areas, today. Tim Healy's comprehensive study of managers from different backgrounds and nationalities makes for a truly enlightening read.

Acknowledgements
Tim Healy

WHILE it may be fair to describe writing as a lonely occupation, there are few writing projects which are carried out in absolute isolation. This book is certainly no exception and I shall always be grateful to the many people who were so helpful and encouraging during my time researching and writing.

In particular my heartfelt thanks are due to the following:

Dave Billings (RIP), John Clark, P.J. Cunningham, Pat Devlin, Paul Goldrick, Patrick Healy, Michael Kelleher, Gerry McDermott for advice directly related to the content of this book.

Gianfranco Agazzi, Johan Moritz Krobb, Peter Latz, and Peter Russell for their translation work.

Suzanne Bailey, Aodhagan Hurley, Joe Coyle, Dominic O'Keeffe, Andrew Rennicks and Paul Towell for their practical assistance in the design and marketing.

To those who were generous with their time in providing valuable insights during interviews:

Brian Glanville in London, Paul Courant in Brugges, Filippo Galli in Milan, , Eddie Gray in Yorkshire, Ruud Gullit in the Netherlands, Norman Hunter in Leeds, Danny McGrain in Glasgow, Peter Lorimer in Leeds, and Phil Thompson in Liverpool.

A special word of thanks to Liam Brady and John Giles for their time, assistance, support, encouragement and tremendous generosity of spirit — two of the finest players my country has produced and two of its finest gentlemen.

Introduction

IN the 21st century, managing successfully in professional football is a highly lucrative job. It is also a job in which the pressure is relentless. Media demands from twenty four hour news channels, dedicated television and radio stations and printed media can be insatiable. Players are paid enormous sums and chairmen/owners are, with some notable exceptions, impatient for success. And it is so much easier to sack a manager than an entire team of players.

A recent observation comes from author and journalist Simon Kuper, citing work carried out by Stefan Szymanski, economics professor at the University of Michigan. Kuper suggests that based on the evidence of exhaustive research into English football, which covered a period of thirty seven years: "Football managers are modern celebrities, yet the vast majority appear to add no value to their teams, and could probably be replaced by their secretaries or stuffed teddy bears without anyone noticing."

This may seem harsh but I am certain there are large numbers of football supporters who will identify with the comments. Szymanski's study concludes that the single biggest factor in determining success for a club is the wage bill. The clubs which succeed in winning championships, will, in general, be found to have had the highest wage bill while the bottom club at the end of a season is probably the one with the lowest player wage bill. Within this study the correlation between wages and success was found to be as high as ninety per cent.

The study showed Bob Paisley in first place with Sir Bobby Robson, Sir Alex Ferguson and Arsene Wenger the next highest achieving managers in England's Premier League or its predecessor, the First Division.

Brian Clough could not be assessed because Nottingham Forest did not file accounts as they were not a limited company. Meanwhile, at the time of the study Jose Mourinho had spent only three seasons in England and this was considered too short a period for assessment.

To further complicate comparisons, Ferguson had the benefit in the 90s of a crop of home-grown talent amounting to half of his team. Because they came through the club's youth system they may not have placed too heavy a strain on the wage bill in their early years benefitting the club and its manager in this type of evaluation.

And of course some clubs are better at developing players through their youth systems over time, thereby reducing not only transfer expenditure but also deferring the payment of massive wages until the players are firmly established in the first team. Most football people with whom I spoke felt that because there are so many variables in football, a good manager does not carry a guarantee of success. However, a bad one will always have an impact on the club unlucky enough or foolish enough to hire him.

The last word on how effective managers might be comes from the late Bela Guttman. When checking with Brian Glanville regarding an oft-quoted slogan of Guttman's 'the third year is fatal', Glanville not only confirmed that the legendary Hungarian had indeed used those words and had also told him that as a result of his sacking by A.C. Milan, he would include a stipulation in future contracts that he could never be fired if his team were top of the table, as Milan were at the time.

Glanville related a wonderful story which Guttman had told him on that same occasion in a Rome restaurant just after he had left Milan. Lucchese, who miraculously had been promoted to the top division, were due to play at Juventus and while making their way to what would be an inevitable thrashing their coach died.

They phoned all around the country but had great difficulty getting a replacement at short notice. Eventually they persuaded someone to take over in time for the game. This complete stranger sat on the bench while the team played. Then, quite amazingly, they secured a draw and proceeded to chair the replacement coach shoulder high from the field.

A study of the evolution of management in football provides one of the great ironies. England invented the game of football. More importantly, England provided the coaches and managers who took the game to many countries throughout Europe and South America. In the 21st century, the dearth of English managers in the domestic game was never more evident with only twenty five per cent of Premier League clubs having English born managers at the time of writing.

The first half of the 20th century produced some extraordinary, adventurous English coaches who became managers abroad, adapting to their new conditions and cultures, achieving success and earning enormous respect in the process. Because of a lack of demand for their services at home several of these imaginative coaches were forced to emigrate. While many earned great respect in their adopted countries their achievements often went virtually unnoticed at home. With the game becoming increasingly driven by money, perhaps some of Professor Szymanski's findings are not entirely surprising. In an age when money was less an influence and when there was a more level playing field, managers could have a greater influence on how their club and their team progressed. Wage restrictions applied for quite a long part of the game's history. While they were not always legally observed the divergence in wealth between clubs was nowhere as great as it is today.

Whether in football or in business, there is no predetermined personality for success in management but there are certainly traits and practices which enhance its prospects. The definition by John Giles of the football manager's function, is worth keeping in mind as we look at who made a difference: "The function of a manager is to provide an environment in which the best players will flourish."

No matter what era we choose, there were always certain football managers who were better at that.

1

Early Success at Home and Abroad

IN England, the home of football, there was little sign in the earliest days of anyone resembling the manager as we now know him. There were committees selecting teams and club secretaries making match-day arrangements and being in charge of the team.

By the late 19th century clubs were converting to limited companies. Some were run by boards of directors, a number of whom brought a business background with them, while committees continued to operate in many clubs. Eventually as the game progressed and as clubs grew there was an uneven pattern as to how management evolved.

In some cases the businessmen found it increasingly difficult to devote the necessary time to their hobby. Secretaries were appointed to handle the day-to-day aspects of the club's operations. Eventually, the position became known as secretary/manager but in most cases the committee still picked the team.

Being 'in charge' meant taking care of administrative issues because tactics and playing systems were still a while away. Sometimes, though not always, the secretary/manager was the one responsible for identifying and signing new players but this was usually subject to board or committee scrutiny.

In Europe, it appears greater responsibility was given to the manager or as he soon became known in Italy, the "Mister". Even in those early years there is plenty of evidence of clubs seeking to get the 'right man' in place.

George Ramsay

"Had the rough Scotsman not come across a practice football match (in 1876) between a bunch of ill-organised, inexperienced cricketers, it is unlikely that the name Aston Villa would be a household name today. In fact, the infant club would probably have spluttered out of existence within the year."

LMA League Managers Association Website

The F.A. Cup was first contested in 1872. It was a competition among amateur football teams, professionalism not yet having been imagined. The early cup winners included Wanderers, Oxford University, Royal Engineers, Old Etonians and Old Carthusians.

In 1883, Blackburn Olympic won the cup with what was widely recognised as a team containing professional players. This win brought about the end of an era, as no amateur team would ever again win the trophy. By 1885 the FA accepted that players, in limited circumstances, could be paid. As a direct result of the movement towards professionalism the Football League was created.

In 1888, William McGregor, the Chairman of Aston Villa, contacted other clubs seeking a meeting to discuss the organisation of regular fixtures. He had become frustrated at frequent cancellation of Villa games. The response to his request was astonishingly positive. Several clubs were feeling the pressure of having to pay players and were glad of the opportunity of more games and more revenue. The outcome was the inaugural League Championship played in the 1888-89 season.

McGregor, a draper by trade and a man with significant administrative skills, had been asked to become involved in Aston Villa by fellow Scot, George Ramsay, who had himself joined the club via an impressive audition when he fell into a game in Aston Park among Villa players in 1876. So good was the new arrival, he was soon asked to play for and to captain the Aston Villa team. Ramsay played until 1882 when injury forced him to retire. He remained with the club, was formally appointed secretary in 1884 and held that position until 1926.

Aston Villa won the FA Cup for the first time in 1887 and had their first League Championship win in 1894. Ramsay's long tenure was not due to some Scottish loyalty by McGregor but because of a remarkable record of success under his stewardship. Villa's victory in the FA Cup in 1920 meant that they had won that competition six times, a number which sat neatly with their six League titles.

Since then Villa have added one further FA Cup win in 1957 and a single league title in 1981, which was followed by the historic European Cup win of 1982. It was not until 1934 that the club decided to bestow the title of manager on an appointee. Sadly, the change did little by way of contribution to a return to winning. They never had a period of sustained glory like the one they enjoyed under Ramsay. That era of success places them among the historically successful English clubs.

Ramsay, the player, brought a level of skill quite uncommon in English football in those embryonic years. As secretary, he proved equally adroit when it came to replacing departing players. While still a player in 1876, he had recruited Archie Hunter from Third Lanark. Hunter was a sensation as a goal-scorer. The highlight of his career was the 1896-97 season when leading Aston Villa to their first FA Cup triumph, he scored in every round of that competition, becoming the first player to do so. Within three years Hunter collapsed while playing against Everton. The heart attack he suffered brought an abrupt end to his career and sadly, its effects were so bad that within four years he died aged only thirty five.

Ramsay brought a succession of scoring forwards to the club. Charlie Athersmith was signed in 1890; John Devey a year later. Nor was he shy about procuring the right players. He created controversy in 1893 when signing two of West Bromwich Albion's best in Jack Reynolds and Willie Groves. Villa's local rivals were furious and while protests resulted in fees having to be paid, the two players would become key members of Villa's team as league titles and cup victories were racked up over the following years.

The high point for Aston Villa and George Ramsay was the completion of the double in 1897. The Cup Final was won at Crystal Palace when Villa came from behind to beat Everton 3-2.

In 1899, having had to replace three of their best players following the double two years earlier, Ramsay led Villa to their fifth title in seven years. It was his and Aston Villa's glorious period. Successes would continue under the Scot, but never with the same frequency.

Tom Watson

"Mr. Tom Watson, who has done such a very great deal for the Sunderland football club, has undertaken the secretaryship of the Liverpool Football Club. This is undeniably a good stroke on the part of the Liverpool management and it would appear that now, at any rate, the Anfield Roaders will not figure in test matches for a very long time."

Liverpool Review, 1st August, 1896 – Ref: "Red Men" by John Williams. Note: Test matches were contests to avoid relegation

Where the secretary/manager's authority extended to signing players Tom Watson provided a good example of how successful this could be. Known as the Geordie Messiah he had achieved much in the game before he set foot on Merseyside. Starting with Newcastle West End, he made a name for himself as secretary and was soon lured to the rivals at Newcastle East End, the club which would later become Newcastle United.

His predilection for the "Scottish game" and the north east's proximity to Scotland facilitated the arrival of several Scottish players, first to his Newcastle side and later to his next footballing home, Sunderland. At twenty nine he helped Sunderland achieve league status in 1890 before taking them to levels of success the like of which they have never known since.

The fat bowler-hatted and universally popular secretary/manager led Sunderland to the league title in 1892, 1893 and 1895 while they came second in 1894 and lost only once at home in the six-year period of his stewardship. He was said to have fallen out with the board over money, leaving the door open for the newly promoted and ambitious Liverpool to tempt him south with an attractive salary of £300 per annum. At that time the average weekly wage of a working man was around £1 although someone with specialist skills could earn up to two pounds and ten shillings, or £125 per annum.

Having arrived at Liverpool in 1896 Watson took a few years to make an impact but in 1899 the club came close to winning the league. Their final game that season was away to Aston Villa where a draw would do Liverpool while Villa needed a win to secure the title. By half-time Villa had scored five goals and wrapped up another championship.

When Liverpool finally won their first title in 1900-1901 it was with a team largely assembled by Watson. They finished just two points above Sunderland with Notts County third and Nottingham Forest fourth. Liverpool's strength was their defence, built around the brilliant Alex Raisbeck who was as potent an attacking weapon as he was a defender. A second title was won in 1906.

Tom Watson became the most astute transfer market operator of his time. His 1898 signing of Raisbeck from Hibernian looks an inspired move from any distance. The acquisition of forward Sam Raybould from New Brighton Tower spoke volumes for Watson's judgement of a player. Raybould had seemed quite ordinary until his arrival at Liverpool. His goals proved vital in those first two championship wins.

Watson had many responsibilities as secretary/manager although it is doubtful that he had complete autonomy when it came to team selection. He did have what seems a fairly free hand in identifying and buying players. Above all, he had oversight of the finances of the club and in this area he excelled.

Despite signing a large number of players he was famous for getting value for money and Liverpool Football Club was profitable every single year Watson was in charge, just as Sunderland had been during his time there.

Watson's ability to rebuild is evidenced by the fact that only four players remained from the 1901 team when the title again was won in 1905-6. In between those victorious seasons, the club had gone through turmoil following the death of its founder and principal benefactor, John Houlding. His death created issues concerning the ownership of the ground. Amid the disruption Liverpool were relegated but returned as Second Division Champions and went on to regain the league title.

Liverpool made it to the Cup Final of 2014 only to lose by the only goal to Burnley. Sadly Watson died of pneumonia on 5th May 1915. In 1910 he had been awarded the Football League's Long Service Medal for twenty one years in football management. He had taken Sunderland to three league championships and Liverpool to a further two titles, the first man to lead different teams to the championship.

Ernest Mangnall

"Manchester City are making big changes. Their Secretary, Mr. Ernest Mangnall, formerly with Burnley, whom he left in season 1904-5 to become secretary of Manchester United, terminates his engagement."
Lancashire Evening Post 3rd May 1924

In the years immediately after Liverpool's second league title win another Lancashire club would make its mark. Any assessment of Ernest Mangnall is coloured by the success of the club he helped establish as much as by his personal achievements which include leading Manchester United to their first two league championships.

Today Manchester United is a world famous club. The success

under Sir Alex Ferguson can create the illusion that the club has never known failure but only three managers have ever led the club to league titles. Ferguson won thirteen. Sir Matt Busby won five league titles and the first successful leader, Mangnall, presided over those initial two wins in 1908 and 1911 adding an FA Cup in between in 1909. Mangnall was the secretary/manager and appears to have been in sole charge of transfer activity, the factor which had the greatest influence on those early successes. After Mangnall, United's wait for their next league title would take all of forty one years, until 1952.

Arguably the most surprising aspect of Mangnall as United secretary/manager was that he was ever appointed. He began in football as a director of Bolton Wanderers, before becoming secretary/manager at which point they were relegated from the First Division in the 1898-1899 season. He then moved to Burnley in 1900 again as secretary/manager. It was late in the season but he was in time to lead Burnley to relegation to the Second Division.

Within two years they would finish bottom of the Second Division being forced to apply, successfully, for re-election. His appointment to Manchester United came as quite a surprise in those circumstances. But his impact was to be far greater and longer-lasting than could have been expected from his previous record.

Founded in 1878 as Newton Heath LYR Football Club by the Carriage and Wagon Department of the Lancashire and Yorkshire Railway at the Newton Heath Depot, by 1892 they were in the Football League. But within ten years the club was the subject of a winding-up order. Four local businessmen, including John Henry Davies, who was to become the influential Club President, came to the rescue, saving the club before changing the name in 1902 from Newton Heath to Manchester United.

The vacancy at United which Mangnall filled had come about because a director, Harry Stafford, and the secretary/manager,

James West, were suspended for making illegal payments to players. Stafford, a former player for Newton Heath said: "Everything I have done has been in the interests of the club."

Up to then, Manchester City had been the dominant team in the area but following an investigation their best player, Billy Meredith, was found guilty of attempted bribery and banned for a year. The Aston Villa captain claimed Meredith had offered him £10 to throw a vital game at the end of the 1904-05 season as City chased the league title.

When Meredith was suspended there was no indication of any assistance coming from his club so he decided to make the matter public. His declaration had a cataclysmic effect as it was an open admission that City had been breaking the rules on payments to players. He said, in reference to the official maximum wage limit of £4 per week, the secret of Manchester City's success was, "the club put aside the rule that no player should receive more than four pounds per week......the team delivered the goods, the club paid for the goods delivered and both sides were satisfied."

From 1902 City had been managed by a Scot, Tom Maley. Their passing game which was uncommon in England at the time proved highly popular, with crowds of over 20,000 attending games at their Hyde Road grounds. In 1904 Maley led City to their first ever trophy, the FA Cup, but sadly for him, the Meredith statement would derail his career and the club's progress.

Maley had a life ban imposed and seventeen City players received a one-year ban. Maley claimed he was following what appeared to him the standard practice of ignoring the maximum wage. So a career that could have seen him as the man who established Manchester as a great football capital was ruined. While his ban was later lifted, the damage had been done.

Mangnall was the main beneficiary of these developments. With a transfer war-chest thanks to John Henry Davies, he signed four of the best Manchester City players. Billy Meredith, Sandy

Turnbull, Jimmy Bannister and Herbert Burgess became the backbone of the first league-winning Manchester United team in 1908, with Turnbull the leading scorer. The suspension imposed on the seventeen players applied only to playing for Manchester City. An auction was to be held to dispose of all seventeen but Mangnall got in ahead of that auction to secure the four who would transform Manchester United into a championship winning side for the first time in their history.

Apart from the subsequent victories in the first ever Charity Shield, the 1909 FA Cup and the second championship in 1911, Mangnall showed his administrative vision and capability in overseeing the development of the Old Trafford Stadium. The new stadium opened in early 1910 with a capacity of 80,000. Originally it had been planned to provide for 100,000 but costs began to escalate and it was trimmed back to have standing on three sides of the ground and seating at one end.

Mangnall then did the unthinkable — he moved to City in 1912 as secretary/manager, a position he held until 1924. This term was severely interrupted by the war but in his absence United went into decline. He came desperately close to following Tom Watson by winning league titles with two different clubs. In 1920-21 City finished runners-up in the league, the nearest he came to a trophy during his eight full seasons at that club. He then became the driving force behind a stadium move, as plans were put in place to construct what City announced as an "English Hampden." In 1923 City moved to the new stadium at Maine Road, which would shortly host crowds of up to 76,000.

Uniquely, Mangnall's legacy may be seen at both Manchester clubs as, to this day, he is the only one to have managed both United and City. He was certainly a capable administrator.

In addition to his managerial successes and the development of two massive stadiums, he was responsible for the founding of the Central League as well as the Football Managers Association.

Herbert Kilpin

"Herbert Kilpin 24.1.1870 — 22.10.1916
Sociofondatore e Capitano
Milan Cricket and 1899 Football Club
Con Riconoscenza."
**Inscription on grave no.162 in gallery
XV Cimetero Monumentale, Milan**

All of football's leaders did not remain in the English game. The first three to make an impact on the game in its infancy in Italy came from diverse backgrounds and found themselves abroad for quite different reasons. They provide early examples of English managerial success abroad.

The first football club in Italy, Internazionale Torino, was founded in the late 1880's by Edoardo Bosio, an Italian-Swiss gentleman who had strong links with a Nottingham-based lace manufacturer. Indeed the first Englishman to play abroad was a native Nottingham lace-maker, Herbert Kilpin, who played in two losing championship finals with that Torino team.

Before emigrating, Kilpin had begun playing for a team called Garibaldi, formed by Italian immigrants in Nottingham. Having initially settled in Turin he later moved to Milan and along with businessman Alfred Edwards was a founding member of the AC Milan club in 1899. Kilpin won three championships there, first as a player and then as player-manager, in 1901, 1906 and 1907, before retiring in 1908. That last win makes him the first Englishman to manage a foreign team to championship success.

His legacy is a club which shares with Boca Juniors the record for the most international trophies, with eighteen officially recognised UEFA and FIFA titles. But it was certainly not glory all the way. After Kilpin led Milan to their third title in 1907 there was a gap until 1951 before AC Milan could again call themselves champions of Italy.

Little is known of the remaining years of Kilpin's short life up to his death in 1916. His fondness for whiskey and cigarettes hardly helped. It was said that his only drink was whiskey and that he drank it before and after games. "Before" and "after" was a cause for concern but when he managed to add "during" he really did have a problem. But sadly, Kilpin found a way to prevent his participation in games from interfering with his whiskey drinking. He was known to have hidden his bottle in a hole in the ground behind the goal- line for easy access. It was little wonder he lasted no more than eight years after retiring.

It can be inferred that his marriage to Maria Capua, an Italian lady described as "beautiful and aristocratic" did not work out well either. Had they been together at the time of his death, such a relatively short time after the marriage, he would have been buried in or near his wife's family tomb instead of in an unmarked grave which remained thus for more than ninety years. Italian historian, Luigi La Rocca, discovered Kilpin's grave and with full support from the AC Milan club, he was re-interred at the Cimitero Maggiore, on 2 November 2010, with an appropriate headstone.

James Richardson Spensley

"Here lived the English doctor, James R. Spensley, sportsman – great friend of Italy – a football pioneer with the Genoa Cricket and Football Club, founder of Genoese scouting."

**Inscription on a plaque mounted on
a house in the Marassi region of Genoa**

While Kilpin was making his name in Turin and Milan, football was gaining a foothold in Genoa, the third city in that north Italian triangle. Expatriate British residents founded the Genoa Cricket & Athletic Club in 1893, using the anglicised name rather than Genova. Three years later football was introduced to the club by Dr. James Richardson Spensley who had arrived to serve as doctor to the crews of British ships in the port. Spensley, as well as being a club director and a referee was also said to be a "goalkeeper of questionable ability" who nonetheless managed to accumulate six Italian Championship medals with Genoa.

He had been player-manager during some of his time at Genoa and continued as manager for a year after retiring as a player. He went on to cofound the Boy Scout movement in Italy before becoming a Lieutenant in the Royal Army Medical Corps during the First World War. Sadly he died in 1915 aged forty eight, from injuries incurred on the battlefield at Mainz, as he was compassionately tending the wounds of an enemy soldier.

While Dr. Spensely was involved as player and sometime secretary/manager of the early Genoa teams, participating in those first six championship wins, both he and Kilpin were really accidental managers who fell into the role as their playing days were nearing an end, and who in all probability had little competition for their managerial positions.

It was another Englishman, William Garbutt, who led the Genoa club to titles number seven, eight and nine. The last of these was in 1924 and while subsequent championships were lost amid stories of heartbreak and allegations of corruption, now in the 21st century, Genoa still seeks its 10th championship title.

William Garbutt

"Garbutt has gone coaching at Genoa."
The Athletic News, 26th August 1912

Born in January 1883 into a working-class background in Stockport, William Garbutt became a professional footballer, first with Reading of the Southern League and later with Woolwich Arsenal and Blackburn Rovers. His career lasted from 1903 to 1911 and ending prematurely when he incurred a groin injury for which there was no remedy.

In an era and a region of high unemployment, Garbutt initially joined the army and it was while playing for Royal Artillery that he caught the attention of Reading, leading to his career as a footballer.

He was quite an impressive right winger earning representative honours when playing for the English League against their Scottish counterparts in February 1910. But sadly for Garbutt who took some heavy punishment from fullbacks because of his reputation for skilful play, once that final injury struck, his career as a player was over at twenty nine years of age. Careers ended by injury were a common enough occurrence in those days. The absence of adequate or indeed any kind of insurance as well as the lack of opportunity to stay in the game made such events devastating for the affected players and their families.

Garbutt was a keen student of the game, learning from each trainer with whom he came in contact, particularly at Blackburn under Bob Holmes who arrived there as trainer in 1905 around the same time as Garbutt. His training methods and emphasis on high levels of physical fitness were to prove valuable lessons.

His playing career over and with virtually no employment prospects in England and a young pregnant wife, Garbutt headed for Genoa to take up work there in the docks. There are two quite different versions of how he then came to be appointed manager of Genoa Cricket and Football Club. The first, and generally regarded as the less likely is that Vittorio Pozzo recommended him for the job.

The more likely route is thought have been a recommendation from one Thomas Coggins, an Irishman, who was in charge of the youth teams at Genoa C.F.C. and whose brother had come across Garbutt in England. Indeed the Gazzetta Dello Sport goes so far as to describe Coggins as a friend of William Garbutt (Un suo amico, l'Irlandese Thomas Coggins, tradduttore a responsabile dei ragazzi del Genoa, lo segnala al club ligure.)

He is regarded as the first professional manager in Italian Football, having been appointed in July 1912 only a short few months after retiring as a player. To this day, a manager in Italy, regardless of his nationality, is referred to as the "Mister", a description that originated with William Garbutt at Genoa.

Garbutt is listed as having managed Genoa from 1912 until 1927. There was, however, a notable interruption to this period, the First World War. The Italian championship was decided in those years by a round robin tournament, the Girone Finale, among the top four teams at the end of the regular season. War had broken out in 1914 and in May 1915 Italy became involved. The Girone had not been completed. Football was abandoned and it was not until 1919 that the decision was taken to award the title. At the time of the suspension of games, Genoa had led the Girone table and although they could conceivably have been overtaken, the Italian Football Federation decided to award them the championship, Garbutt's first.

An understanding and appreciation of the calibre of person and character of Garbutt can be gleaned from looking at his army record. Returning to England in July 1915 to sign up for military duty he enlisted as a private. Inside two months he had twice been promoted, first to Corporal and then Sergeant.

Within a year his Division was posted to battle in the Somme where he suffered a leg injury. He returned home for treatment before re-joining his colleagues at the front. By 1917 he had been identified as officer material and was sent home to train for what would eventually be a commission as Second Lieutenant. At the end of the war he had the British War Medal, the Victory Medal, and to quote his biographer, Paul Edgerton: "The ribbon of which he was entitled to adorn with two silver oak leaves, as a result of being 'mentioned in despatches' in the London Gazette by Field Marshall Sir Douglas Haig for 'actions deserving of special attention.' "

Once the Great War had ended, he was contacted by Genoa C.F.C. about returning. His new contract paid 8,000 lire per annum, a substantial sum in 1919. Garbutt had a belief in high levels of fitness, something which was quite new to the Italian game at this time. Above all, as his wartime record shows, he had qualities which made him an ideal leader of men.

The loss of four key Genoa players in the war, meant Garbutt had to re-build. Steadily and systematically he did so, taking Genoa to further championships in 1923 and 1924. The first of these titles featured going unbeaten for an entire season, something which had never before been achieved and which would not be achieved again until 1978-9 when Perugia lost none of their thirty games but freakishly drew nineteen, managing to deprive themselves of a championship in the process.

Having been cheated of the 1925 championship, losing a play-off to Bologna in utterly bizarre circumstances, William Garbutt's final two seasons fizzled out at Genoa whose board was made aware well in advance of his intention to move on. His standing was extremely high within Italian Football and once he had decided to depart Genoa the next offer was not long in coming.

The amalgamation of three smaller teams in the capital in 1927 saw the creation of Associazione Sportiva (A.S.) Roma, with Garbutt as the new club's first manager. As with all such developments at the time, this had to have the approval of the fascists, who were increasing their dominance and control in all walks of life. In his two seasons at Roma, Garbutt led the newly-formed team to cup success in 1928, winning the Coppa Coni — forerunner to the Coppa Italia and to third place in the Championship in 1929, ensuring the young club would be guaranteed a place in the new format Serie A which came into being the following year.

The next move for Garbutt, his wife Anna and their son was to Napoli. He spent six years there and while Napoli did not claim any titles in that time Garbutt took the club to third place in the league in seasons 1932-3 and 1933-4. While living in Bagnoli Irpino, in the hills outside Naples, the Garbutts adopted a local girl, Maria. Various legal issues arising from their staus as foreigners prevented the final formalities but the young poverty-stricken girl became the fourth member of their family

The political situation in Italy was not getting any better with the continuing rise of the fascists and their antipathy to all things foreign. Genoa Cricket and Football Club was instructed to change its name to Genova 1893 while Internationale had to merge with Unione Sportiva Milanese and operate under the new title of Societa Sportiva Ambrosiana.

Realising he had taken Napoli as far as he could, Garbutt acceped the offer to manage Athletic Bilbao, already a successful club with a history of employing English coaches. With his family temporarily still in Naples, he threw himself into quite a different challenge. At Genoa, Roma and Napoli, Garbutt had to build teams. At Bilbao he inherited an established side and immediately led them to become champions of Spain in 1935-6.

In July, while Garbutt was back in Naples to collect his family for their relocation to Bilbao, General Franco and his colleagues began their military uprising and Spain saw the beginning of its bloody Civil War. The Garbutt family had to change plans. William took the lucrative salary offered by AC Milan. Their son had already returned to England to enlist in the army while Anna and their young adopted daughter, Maria, remained near Naples.

Milan had finished no higher than eighth in the four seasons prior to Garbutt's appointment. Indeed the club was in 10th place when Garbutt took charge. It is a measure of his ability that in these circumstances he guided the club to a very respectable fourth place as well as taking the team to the cup semi-final.

The remainder of the William Garbutt story is more like a war novel than a football tale. When Churchill came to power in 1940 he decreed that Italians in Britain be interned. The Italians reciprocated. Garbutt was jailed in Genoa. His wife Anna, ironically, was untouched as she was an Irish citizen and not subject to the same treatment. She played her part, appealing his case and eventually having the family interned in the village of Acerno in the hills above Napoli. Later they were moved northwards to the Abruzzo region to another small village, Orsogna.

By 1944, a further move had the family of William, Anna and Maria in Imola. By now he had suffered and partly recovered from a stroke while Anna continued to be plagued by along-standing asthma affliction. Their bank savings in Genoa were sequestered, leaving them under financial strain. Though under no obligation to do so, the Genoa club paid a small pension to their former employee and this was critical in the family's strained circumstances. But on 13 May 1944 allied bombers, mistaking Imola for another town, dropped the bomb which killed Mrs. Anna Garbutt and left Maria with severe hearing difficulties.

After the war, William was eventually prevailed upon, to try to lift the Genoa club to its former glory. In bad health, he was unable to serve as before and announced his retirement in 1948. Garbutt and Maria, his adopted daughter, returned to England where he died in 1964. His death, like his life and his successes went unnoticed in the English papers and within the still isolated world of English football. Meanwhile, there were eulogies in the Italian sports papers but also in the Genovese and Neapolitan daily papers.

Fred Pentland

"Get the simple things right and the rest will follow."

Fred Pentland

The second and third decades of the 20th century provided several examples of former players from England moving to Continental Europe where they found work as coaches or managers. The cessation of organised football at the outbreak of The Great War (1914-1918) brought about enforced emigration of football men, in many cases to coach and manage outside the war zones.

When Fred Pentland took control at Athletic Bilbao in 1922 he became their fifth English leader. Born in 1883, the same year as William Garbutt, there were certain parallels to their careers and Bilbao was not the only club where they each gave service. Pentland, a native of Wolverhampton, played for Blackburn Rovers between 1903 and 1906, prior to Garbutt who arrived there in 1908. Fred earned five England caps but a persistent knee injury led to the premature ending of his career. His initial attempts to carve out a life in coaching took him to Halifax Town in 1912 and Stoke in 1913.

By the following year, showing a sense of adventure which could only be described as ill-timed and unfortunate, he was on his way to Berlin to take charge of the German Olympic Football team. Within a few months of his arrival Germany was at war and Pentland was confined to an internment camp in Berlin, where he would spend the entire war. But he made the most of this unfortunate development, managing a team within a civilian camp of some four thousand men, several of them, like himself, international footballers.

In contrast to Garbutt, Pentland did not have a wife or child to worry about during that time, which must have contributed to his ability to accept his conditions and get on with life. Upon returning to England after the war he spent some time recuperating in hospital and it was here he met a war-widow nurse who was to become his wife. By 1920 he was coaching the French Football team at the Olympics in Belgium where having beaten Italy, France were eliminated by Czechoslovakia.

An immediate move to Racing de Santandar lasted a year before he was poached by Athletic Bilbao. Pentland's first act was to show the players how to tie their bootlaces correctly. His motto was: "Get the simple things right and the rest will follow". Phil Ball, in his accoumt of Spanish football, "Morbo", says he was not merely eccentric but barking mad, with an insistence on wearing a bowler hat at all times, a habit which earned him the nickname "El Bombin".

He was devoutly committed to the 'ball at feet approach to football.' He won two Leagues and five Cups with Bilbao and he was an advocate of neat passing football. How mad is that? He was the first manager to win the double in Spain and his Athletic Bilbao team inflicted on Barcelona, their worst ever defeat, 12-1, a record that still stands. And he managed two national teams when the Olympics was the primary competition in the years before the World Cup.

As far back as the 1920s Fred Pentland was one of several English football coaches who wanted to play a game based on simple passing, keeping possession and letting skill prevail. It is clear that to coach and manage in this way meant only one thing — a move away from England and the English game. These ideas were as unwelcome in English football then as their absence has been bemoaned in more recent times.

Patrick O'Connell

"He changed everything at the club........his professionalism was amazing, his fitness and tactical ideas ahead of his time."
Julio Jimenez Heras — PRO Real Betis

No one knows for sure why a former Manchester United captain became the only Irishman to manage Barcelona. What is known about Patrick O'Connell is not all good — but he had a couple of very significant achievements. His breakthrough into senior football was with the legendary Belfast Celtic. From there he moved to Hull in 1909, to Sheffield Wednesday in 1912 and on to Manchester United two years later.

He is yet another player whose career was badly disrupted by the war although he remained a Manchester United player throughout those years. His six Irish caps included participation in a team which won the 1914 British Home Championship. He ended his playing career in 1922 with Ashington, then of the Third Division, whom he went on to manage briefly before departing to Santander where he managed from 1922 until 1929.

O'Connell was deeply involved in a notorious betting scandal when on April 2, 1915 relegation-threatened United defeated mid-table Liverpool 2-0. In his book "The Ball is Round" David Goldblatt offers the hypothesis that as a group of players from both sides knew the war would severely limit their earnings they decided to make a killing on this game, agreeing in advance that United would win 2-0 and betting on this outcome.

Only days before that Old Trafford game, Colonel CF Grantham, commander of the 17th Battalion, known as the Footballers' Battalion made his feelings known in no uncertain terms pointing out that only 122 of a possible 1,800 players had thus far enlisted. It was even alleged that every football club which continued to pay a player was actually bribing someone to stay out of the army. With such a climate prevailing it is easy to understand how this theory makes sense.

The April 1915 game was quite an extraordinary, indeed farcical spectacle. There were actually two games going on, one in which the players involved in the fix did everything possible to achieve the necessary 2-0 outcome. At the same time others from both sides strove to do their best to win. The young Elisha Scott stood in Liverpool's goal and was the busiest man on the field during the first half as United attacked incessantly, finally scoring just before half-time. Some Liverpool players were so upset at their corrupt colleagues that they threatened not to return for the second half.

After O'Connell had quite disgracefully kicked a penalty the proverbial mile wide, George Anderson scored his and United's second goal. The Manchester United manager, John Robson, was so disgusted by what he was seeing that he left the ground before the game ended. So obvious had it been that something was awry, the Football League launched an immediate enquiry.

But in less than three weeks an announcement was made heralding the suspension of all football until such time as the war would end. The inquiry then dragged on until December when a conclusion was reached that a conspiracy had existed to defraud bookmakers but both clubs were completely exonerated.

Seven players in all were issued with lifetime bans by the Football League. Jackie Sheldon of Liverpool who had previously played for United, winning a Championship in 1911, was identified as the organiser. In all, three Manchester United players were given lifetime bans, among them Enoch West who would go on to work alongside Patrick O'Connell in the Ford Motor Works at Trafford Park during the war. But first he took unsuccessful court actions for libel against the football authorities and several newspapers.

O'Connell gave evidence and when questioned about his penalty miss responded, quite incredibly, that "I have missed dozens in my time."

Sheldon, by now fighting in France, eventually confessed to the conspiracy having initially denied all knowledge. Clemency was later extended to all seven guilty players although only six of them would be in a position to play football again.

When Patrick O'Connell left Britain in 1922, he left behind a wife and four young children. It has been suggested that this was what was known at the time as 'an Irish divorce' (or to give it its correct name — desertion). In a TV special "Don Patricio O'Connell" made for the TG4 Irish network, O'Connell's grandson, Michael, talked about his grandmother, the woman deserted by Patrick, and expressed lifelong astonishment at how she never had a bad word to say against him, despite the desertion which left the family in poverty.

His spell at Racing de Santandar was followed by two years at Real Oviedo before O'Connell moved to Real Betis, managing that club to the League title in 1935. Even this achievement was tarnished as O'Connell was accused of trying to persuade their opponents in the final game, his former club, Santander, to lose that game. But in Sevilla he was greatly respected as a coach who brought discipline and order and of course the ultimate success to Betis. In any event Betis won that final game 5-0 and O'Connell was soon on his way to Barcelona. That 1935 title remains the only one ever for Betis and a sculpture honouring the team and its manager can still be seen in the city.

At Barcelona he took over a team which had not been competitive for several years. His approach was respected. He believed in correct diet, in thorough preparation and in proper rest. His team immediately won the Championship of Catalonia, a very important competition in those years. They also made it to the Cup Final losing 2-1 to Real Madrid. Despite this defeat, the outlook was good. It was that of a young team showing a lot of promise for the years ahead.

In the summer of 1936 O'Connell was in Ireland but would have been aware through the media that war had broken out in Spain. The Board of Barcelona wrote to him advising that everything had changed and that if he choose not to return it would be understood and accepted. Barcelona as the capital of Catalonia suffered deeply at the hands of Franco and his supporters. The Club President who had been instrumental in bringing in O'Connell was himself murdered by Franco troops.

One of the reasons O'Connell is remembered with respect and affection in Barcelona is that he returned to his post. But the club's very existence was now threatened for economic as well as political reasons. Players took pay cuts and the manager, in solidarity, did likewise reducing his monthly salary from fifteen hundred pesetas to a thousand. These gestures were welcome but insufficient to save the club from possible extinction. The second reason for the respect afforded to O'Connell in the Catalonian capital was what happened next.

In 1937 O'Connell led the summer tour to Mexico and the United States which had been underwritten by a former Mexican Basketball star, Manuel Mas Soriano. The tour provided a financial lifeline for the club and a very real lifeline for the players who were feeling increasingly unsafe as the civil war proceeded. O'Connell is held in high regard to this day for the manner in which he conducted matters on that tour which was originally planned to last two weeks but actually went on for two months.

While only four players returned to war-torn Spain at the end of the tour, the financial rewards were such that the club's survival was assured. While O'Connell deserves credit for taking charge of the venture, the club secretary, Senor Calvet, certainly needs to be remembered with gratitude. It was their shared decision to wire the tour proceeds to a bank account in Paris that ensured those funds were safe from Catalonia's fascist enemies.

Upon returning to Spain, O'Connell left Barcelona, going back to Real Betis for two years before crossing town to manage Sevilla from 1942 to 1945 then ending his time in Spain back at Santander until 1949. Strangely, as little is known about the type of football he espoused as about his motivation in heading for Spain in the first place. He focused on diet, discipline, rest and fitness and he certainly had some managerial ability because he came so close to completing league success with both Seville clubs by taking Sevilla to the runners-up position in the league championship of 1942-3.

During his first spell in Sevilla he developed a relationship with another woman. She was Irish as was his deserted wife. She looked like his wife and she actually had the same first name, Ellen, as his wife. She worked as a nanny for a British diplomat when she was introduced to O'Connell. As far as she knew he was a single man and it is believed they were married there before moving to Barcelona.

His grandson, Michael, summed up the contradiction between O'Connell's life in football and his disastrous private life. "He was a hero who was also a swine because he deserted his family, leaving them in poverty. In fact he condemned them to poverty, loneliness and emptiness." Meanwhile, Sue O'Connell, Michael's wife and the biographer of Patrick O'Connell, summed up his football career — "He was involved in some of the greatest clubs on the planet. He captained Manchester United and his country and he managed Barcelona, in between taking Betis to their only Championship."

Arguably his greatest contribution to football was his role in the saving of Barcelona in 1937 — something which most lovers of football in the 21st century will probably consider a worthwhile act. He returned to London with his second wife in 1958 and died there, destitute and alone on February 27, 1959.

2

Three Giants and the World's First Great Coach

THE evolution of football management continued to be an uneven process. The 1920s saw the emergence of a few hugely capable people, each of whom brought new levels of professionalism, organisation, even genius, to the practice.

The period between the wars proved a fruitful time for the development of the game of football across Europe. New powers emerged internationally and among clubs. Three of the greatest managers of this era were Hugo Meisl, Vittorio Pozzo and Herbert Chapman, all of whom shared an obsessive love of football and an ability to manage at the highest level.

Pozzo and Meisl, especially the latter, benefitted from their inguistic abilities. When Arsenal Chairman Denis Hill-Wood spoke glowingly of Herbert Chapman, he did not say Chapman could have been Prime Minister, he said he should have been Prime Minister. Hugo Meisl was the creator of the world's first international competition between clubs, the Mitropa Cup. He was the instigator of Europe's first tournament for national teams, the Dr. Gero Cup, and he coached and developed the Austrian Wunderteam of the early 1930s.

Jimmy Hogan who worked closely with Meisl, has been described as a manager but in reality he was a coach — probably the greatest coach of that or of any era. While Meisl, Pozzo and

Chapman each achieved a high degree of autonomy, this was most untypical of the time. Managers having control over their clubs and teams was still a long way off at most clubs in Britain and Europe.

Jimmy Hogan

"Jimmy Hogan taught us everything we know about football."
Sandor Barcs, President of the Hungarian Football Federation at the post-match press conference after Hungary had beaten England 6-3 at Wembley on 25 November 1953 before a crowd of 105,000

Born in Burnley in 1882 to an immigrant Irish Catholic family, Jimmy Hogan would graduate to play senior football for Burnley in 1903 before moving south two years later to Fulham and happier times. From an early age he showed he knew and appreciated the significance of money. This caused him to fall out with Burnley whose board refused to pay him the then maximum wage of £4 per week. Their justification was that he had another job and unlike several teammates, he lived at home with his parents.

Fulham's secretary/manager was Harry Bradshaw who had begun his career in football as secretary of Burnley. Despite never having played himself, he was highly respected and led Woolwich Arsenal to salvation from near bankruptcy in 1904 and on to promotion to the first division. He believed in the passing game which made Fulham an attractive destination for Hogan: "My football knowledge improved tremendously at Craven Cottage where I found myself amongst the great Scottish players who were playing in the style I had been longing for."

From his earliest days playing football Hogan had shown an appetite for learning and had constantly bemoaned the lack of coaching and the indifference towards the development of what he saw as the vital skills of the game. Practicing what he preached, he effectively became his own coach, proving a talented and skilful player. He played his part in Fulham's two Southern League Championship wins in 1906 and 1907 and their F.A. Cup run in 1908 when they reached the semi-final for the first time.

Although the team played in a style liked by Hogan, there was at this time the widespread belief, frequently voiced, that footballers should be kept away from the ball during the week so that they would be all the more hungry for it come Saturday's game. Hogan railed unsuccessfully against this school of thought. Training consisted of running and more running.

Hogan moved from Fulham via Swindon to Bolton Wanderers for whom he appeared intermittently from 1908 until 1913. Not lacking in self-esteem, he had hoped despite a chronic knee injury to move from Swindon to a big club. Bolton Wanderers were in the second division but going there held the attraction of a return to Lancashire. The club provided him with rail tickets so he could live at home in Burnley and commute to Bolton. These years were interspersed with his first ventures into coaching with Dordrecht in the Netherlands in 1910 which led to a brief stint coaching the Netherlands national team and some time with FK Austria Vienna in 1911-12.

At just twenty eight years of age he was the youngest British coach ever to practice on the continent. By 1912, still hoping to continue a playing career and still technically a Bolton Wanderers player, he returned home briefly for what proved to be a frustrating experience in playing terms.

His initial coaching role at Dordrecht had arisen through his friendship with leading referee James Howcroft who recommended him for the job. Howcroft was a frequent visitor to continental Europe, officiating at games and making widespread contacts. During a visit to Austria he was asked by Hugo Meisl to recommend a coach who would work with the national team as well as with selected club sides. Howcroft had no hesitation in putting Jimmy Hogan's name forward, an act which was to have a great and positive influence on the development of football in Austria, Hungary and Germany.

During the English close season, Meisl had Hogan work with the Austrian team in preparation for the 1912 Stockholm Olympics. The Austrian Association had little by way of funds so Hogan's main income came from the club sides where Meisl placed him. Hogan clearly had a busy schedule but after some initial local scepticism towards his methods the players responded. The team performed indifferently at the Olympics and Hogan returned to tidy up his affairs with Bolton Wanderers.

By 1913 he was back in Austria where Meisl offered him a role as coach to the Austrian national team, doubling up once again by coaching leading club sides. When the First World War broke out Hogan underwent some real hardship. He was arrested and interned along with every other British citizen in the region. His pregnant wife and their two young children managed to get back to Britain with the assistance of the American Consul.

While Hogan was soon released into the care of two British brothers who ran a business in Vienna, it was 1916 before he got out of Austria. His hope was to return to England to be reunited with his family but instead he found himself deposited in Budapest. It later transpired that the Cambridge-educated Hungarian, Baron Dirstay, had worked to get Hogan out of Austria and before he had time to adjust to his new surroundings Jimmy Hogan had an office in a stadium which contained the best facilities he had ever seen. He was now the trainer of MTK Budapest, a team which was financially supported by among others, the aforementioned Baron Dirstay.

Under his tutelage, MTK embarked on a glorious streak in 1917 winning every Hungarian Championship through to 1925. Jimmy Hogan gained enormous respect for his ability to find young players and bring them through to become internationals. There was real appreciation of his coaching methods which were heavily biased towards the development of skills and for the fact that he retained the ability to demonstrate exactly how players were to perform the different skills of the game.

He clearly kept himself fit and nimble to the extent that many years later when he returned to Britain, to Celtic and Aston Villa, he could still teach through demonstrating exactly what each skill required. His personal fitness levels were to stand him in good stead because despite a long-time smoking habit and an eventual battle with emphysema, Jimmy Hogan lived to the age of ninety one.

The football climate in England at the time of Hogan's entry to coaching is best understood through reference to the Football Association and their approach to life and to a game which, while it had been invented in England, was showing signs of rapid growth in popularity much further afield.

In 1903 the Union des Societies Francaises de Sports Athlet-iques wrote to the F.A. seeking their assistance in creating what would become F.I.F.A. The reply indicated that the F.A. saw no reason for such a development. In 1904 F.I.F.A was created by Belgium, Denmark, France, The Netherlands, Sweden, Switzerland, Portugal and Spain (represented by Madrid Football Club as the Spanish federation had not yet been formed). The first World Cup competition took place in 1930 and none of the "home" nations participated. The 1934 and 1938 competitions again were held without British participation or interest. Because of the 1939-45 war, it would be 1950 before England would take part in a World Cup.

Following his success with MTK Budapest and his contribution to the general progression of Hungarian football, he had spells in Switzerland and with Dresdner in Germany before returning to work with Hugo Meisl and the Austrian "Wundermannschaft" (Wonderteam).

The words "Hungary" and "Wembley 1953" bring to mind England's most dramatic home defeat — a revelatory moment for English football and its belief in its own position of superiority. The result was a shock. The manner of the defeat and the 6-3 score-line created bigger shocks. At the post-match press conference Mr.Sandor Barcs, President of the Hungarian Football Federation must have caused further alarm when uttering the words: "Jimmy Hogan taught us everything we know about football." The great Hungarian player and coach, Gustav Sebes, went further. "We played football as Jimmy Hogan taught us. When our football history is told, his name should be written in gold letters."

Hogan's legend would have grown even greater in Hungary, if such were possible, when six months later Hungary defeated England 7-1 in the return game in Budapest. Another "great" who held Hogan in high regard was Helmut Schön who led what was then West Germany in three World Cups, finishing third in 1966, runner-up in 1970 and winner in 1974. Schön was the first national manager to lead his team to success in both European Championship and World Cup.

In his formative years, at Dresdner, he had been coached by Hogan. His letter of condolence to Hogan's son in 1974 showed how much he had revered his old coach. Almost fifty years since Hogan's time at Dresdner, Helmut Schön wrote: "In my lectures to coaches today, I still mention his name frequently." It speaks volumes for the regard in which Jimmy Hogan was held and for his enduring legacy.

Hugo Meisl

"The organising intelligence behind the growth
of Viennese football was Hugo Meisl."
David Goldblatt, "The Ball is Round."

The man with whom Jimmy Hogan's career is most closely associated is Hugo Meisl who was born on November 16, 1881, at Maleschau in Bohemia, then a part of the Austro-Hungarian Empire. Today it is called Malešov and is in the Czech Republic. The two men's backgrounds could hardly have been more different, but their common love of football brought them together. Meisl's was a well-to-do Austrian Jewish family whose business was textiles.

At twelve he was sent to Vienna to be educated. However, the young Meisl demonstrated an almost complete lack of attention to his studies, preferring to play football and cricket, becoming a member at fourteen of the Vienna Cricket and Football Club. This was at a time when the popularity of football was exploding in Austria. In 1897 Vienna had seven clubs but within three years this number had risen to forty five.

By the time he was seventeen his father, in frustration, organised special tuition for the young man who had by now become convinced that his life would be in football. Within a year, his father insisted he get a proper job and arranged a form of apprenticeship to merchants with whom he himself did business.

During a year divided into spells working for merchants in Paris, Venice and Trieste it transpired that Hugo had a phenomenal linguistic aptitude. This was to become a key factor in his career. Although he was regarded as a skilful, intelligent inside forward, Meisl, believing his football skills would never reach the levels of his linguistic ability, decided at twenty three to become a referee.

Within a year he had progressed to refereeing a game between Sparta Prague and AC Vienna. Two years later he had become secretary of the Austrian Football Association and had refereed an international between Austria and Hungary. His managerial and administrative abilities were becoming clear and having checked the translations of the rules of football on behalf of FIFA in 1911, he succeeded in placing himself where he really wanted to be, at the head of his national football team. Following a 1-1 draw between Austria and Hungary, frustrated at the shape and structure of the Austrian team, he became convinced that a better way was possible.

It was against this background that Meisl sought the help of his refereeing colleague James Howcroft, which led directly to Jimmy Hogan's arrival in Vienna. Hogan joined Meisl and in 1912 they led the Austrian team to the Olympic Games in Stockholm. Preparations for this tournament went badly wrong when Meisl's squad of players was reduced to just twelve fit men immediately before the tournament. However, despite the inevitable elimination Meisl took to the local people and in no time was fluent in Swedish and contributing articles on football to Swedish journals.

The last international game played by Austria before the First World War was a 2-0 win over Hungary after which all football was suspended until 1918 while Meisl was drafted into the Austrian army for the duration of the war leaving him in no position to assist Hogan or plead his case once war had broken out and all instructions were coming from Berlin.

There is no doubt that Hogan and Meisl formed an ideal partnership. Exposure to Meisl's thinking was of great benefit to Hogan in that he got affirmation of his beliefs and the confidence to proceed with the teaching of technique to all his charges, club players as well as the national squad.

Hogan was a devotee of the Scottish game — neat short passing and keeping possession. Their times together saw them work on evolving systems and overall improvements. Between them they were said to have created "the first modern training programme in football".

The outcome of the shared approach was a refinement of the Scottish game, the emergence of a style which became the method used by Austrian teams of the twenties and thirties and which required high levels of concentration and quick passing.

Team structure and tactics were still the preserve of the few great thinkers in the game. The earliest tactical formations had one defender, two midfielders and seven forwards (1-2-7) before Scottish teams changed to two defenders, two in midfield and six forwards (2-2-6). Preston North End, the winners of two League titles and an FA Cup at the end of the 19th century, devised the 2-3-5 formation which was in general use for several decades thereafter. Within this system the centre half was a creative attacking player. In the 1920s the great Herbert Chapman adopted what was known as the WM formation which amounted to 3-2-5 with the centre half now in a more defensive role than previously. This formation was used universally for the following thirty years.

Chapman's Arsenal team aimed to move the ball as quickly and accurately as possible from defence, effectively turning defence into attack quicker than the opposition could react. The team formation favoured by Meisl was based on Herbert Chapman's WM system with very minor changes. Meisl did not have at his disposal the midfield maestro, Alex James, around whom Chapman built his Arsenal team.

After the 1914-18 war, Meisl continued as head of the Austrian FA. He forged contacts across Europe with such figures as Herbert Chapman and Vittorio Pozzo. Such was his regard for the Englishman that Meisl called his first-born son Herbert and had Chapman as godfather to the child.

One of the attributes he shared with Chapman was the willingness and ability to see the big picture. He, was instrumental in the creation of the Mitropa Cup in 1927. This was a European inter-club competition, a forerunner by some thirty years of The European Cup. Initially it involved teams from Austria, Hungary, Czechoslovakia and Yugoslavia, later supplemented by entries from Switzerland, Italy and Romania expanding the idea of Mitropa or Mid-European Cup.

Following serious illness and surgery in 1929 Meisl returned to manage Austria and achieve that for which he is most fondly remembered — his leadership of the "Wonderteam". This team, playing a quick-passing game emerged as a major force in 1931 when they went unbeaten in fourteen games and became favourites for the 1934 World Cup.

This run included beating Italy 4-2 in the 1932 final of the Central European Cup, the predecessor to the European Championships. The undefeated run which included beating Germany 6-0 and 5-0, Switzerland 8-1 and Hungary 8-2, ended in spectacular circumstances when Austria with Meisl and Hogan at the helm, played England in Stamford Bridge. Some 42,000 spectators witnessed one of the greatest games ever seen with England prevailing 4-3.

There are two tragic footnotes to that game.

Matthias Sindelar, Austria's best player then (and still voted so in a 1999 poll) would die in mysterious circumstances in Vienna in 1939. Having refused to play for Nazi Germany, which by now had annexed Austria. Sindelar, nicknamed "Der Papierene" (the paperman) because of his slight build and an uncanny ability to glide through defences, died in a Vienna apartment along with his girlfriend. The cause of death was carbon monoxide poisoning but whether this was accidental or suicide became the subject of inconclusive debate. Mnay years later a close friend of Sindelar said that the report had to show an accidental cause or the Nazis would not have permitted a normal burial — the suggestion being that this was a verdict of convenience, hiding the real cause.

Ironically, Jimmy Hampson of Blackpool, a two-goal hero for England in that great game, would never again play for his country and in 1938 was lost at sea on a fishing trip, his body never recovered.

A more pleasant story was told by Willy Meisl, Hugo's journalist brother, who years later was scheduled to attend a game at Stamford Bridge. A friend had arranged that a ticket in his name would be left for collection. At the ticket office he made his enquiry and was beginning to spell his somewhat unusual surname when the official turned to him and said, "I know how to spell it, how could I ever forget that name?"

The Wonderteam had the great misfortune to peak between World Cups. Too late for the 1930 competition, by 1934 they were beaten in the semi-final. Meisl led Austria to a Silver medal in the 1936 Olympics losing the final to Vittorio Pozzo's Italy. In 1936, they had the consolation of finally getting one over on an England team powered by six Arsenal players, winning 2-1 before a crowd of 60,000 in Vienna. Within a year, Meisl would die of a heart attack, at the age of 56.

The enduring legacy of Hugo Meisl and Jimmy Hogan was what became known as the Danubian School. It was their trademark football style with an emphasis on short, quick interchanges and a game in which skill was valued above all other elements. Their influence would be felt for decades as the style was propagated by coaches and managers some of whom worked under Hogan and Meisl and others who bought into the beauty of the concept

Herbert Chapman

"Goal judges must come. I am convinced referees need their help if they are to avoid mistakes and injustices."

Herbert Chapman in 1934. Note: They were introduced in 2009

While Meisl and Hogan were creating beauty on the continent, an extraordinary man was making his way in the English game.

Herbert Chapman was born on 19 January, 1878 at Kiveton Park, a mining town between Sheffield and Worksop, into a family of six boys and one girl. The Education Act of 1870 had changed the world making school attendance compulsory up to twelve years of age. It also created the climate for further education and Chapman availed of this at Sheffield Technical College where he studied mining engineering. He played football for various teams in the Sheffield area but he saw his future in mining engineering throughout this time.

From Sheffield Chapman moved to Stalybridge Rovers in Lancashire then on to Rochdale and Grimsby. The tour continued, taking Chapman to Worksop, Northampton, Sheffield United and Notts County. A managerial vacuum at Grimsby and the constant pointless changing of the team at Notts County were to have a lasting influence. During all these footballing changes he was pursuing work in engineering while continuing to study.

His brother Harry was much more successful as a player, signing for Sheffield Wednesday in 1901 and going on to win two league championships and an FA Cup.

In early 1904 Herbert visited Northampton with a Notts County side with whom he was rapidly falling out of favour as a player. He returned to Northampton for almost a season before being signed by Tottenham Hotspur of the Southern League. By spring of 1907 his very mediocre playing career was coming to an end. He was contacted by some of his Northampton friends and asked to persuade his about-to-retire Tottenham colleague, Walter Bull, with whom he had also played at Notts County, to come to Northampton as a replacement for their recently sacked secretary/manager.

Chapman looked forward finally to embarking on a real career in mining engineering. Bull initially accepted the offer to manage but at the last minute decided to play one more year at Tottenham and suggested Chapman take his place at Northampton. The twenty nine year old Chapman offered to come as player-manager, purely on a temporary basis until they filled the post permanently. He was appointed in April 1907, the month in which the Daily Reporter described a game played elsewhere as "a match to decide which team is nearly as bad as Northampton."

Undaunted, Chapman brought in new players, introduced tactics and saw to it that players were selected in roles best suited to their abilities, a particular hobby horse of his. Within two years of his appointment Northampton were Southern League Champions, with a record number of wins, a record number of points and a record number of goals scored.

Meanwhile the reserves won the Northamptonshire League Championship, supporting a strong Chapman principle that all of the club teams were important and that all should play a similar system and win their competitions. Chapman left Northampton a better team, with better support and better accommodation for supporters and they had become a significantly more profitable club.

He moved to Football League side Leeds City in 1912 as secretary/manager. Leeds had spent eight years in the Second Division of the Football League. Chapman took Leeds to sixth place and the following season to fourth, just missing promotion.

A combination of events including the First World War and its massive disruption of football affairs and a scandal at Leeds City which resulted in the suspensions of several club members including Chapman were the predominating features of the rest of the decade.

Out of football and happy at last to be working as an engineer in what he regarded as his real career calling, he suddenly found a new difficulty as the company which employed him was sold, effectively leaving him without work. He was approached by Huddersfield Town in 1921 and this encouraged him to right the wrong which had been visited upon him in the Leeds City affair.

The penalty had been imposed for illegal payments to players but Chapman established he had not been at the club when the offence occurred and had the suspension lifted. He was appointed to the position of assistant to Ambrose Langley, the secretary/manager at Huddersfield Town. Within months of this appointment Langley, believing Chapman was too talented and too impatient to remain an assistant for long, choose to resign, leaving Chapman in control.

Huddersfield had been founded in 1908 and first entered the League in 1910. They had hit major financial difficulties in 1919 and at one point, when Leeds City had been wound up, it had been proposed to move the Huddersfield club to Elland Road in Leeds. In 1920 a successful cash appeal to supporters and the sale of a player resolved these issues and saved Huddersfield who went on to gain promotion in that same year while also reaching the Cup Final only to lose to Aston Villa at Stamford Bridge.

One of Chapman's many attributes was his judgement of a player. The catalyst for the emergence of Huddersfield as a major force was the signing of inside forward Clem Stephenson from Aston Villa. Chapman had got a close-up view of Stephenson who had turned out for Leeds City during the war — many players were allowed play for whatever team was nearest to their base during those years, the normal rules of engagement, contract, and indeed competition, being suspended at the time.

What made the signing notable was that Stephenson was thirty three at that point and had spent ten years at Villa. Newcastle born, he insisted on living there and this was causing friction with the midlands club. Chapman became aware of this and intercepted Stephenson on his way home to Newcastle before making what was considered an astonishingly high offer for a player of his years. Villa received £4,000 which was not far off the then record fee of £4,600.

Chapman, meanwhile set about improving all aspects of the club. What would be termed a holistic approach in the 21st century was then a highly revolutionary and enlightened way to develop a football club. Better changing facilities were provided for the players. Better press facilities were built. The pitch was completely re-sodded. The second team and a third team were developed with trusted lieutenants put in charge and with Chapman making it his business to see these teams in action and to monitor the progress of every young player on Huddersfield's books.

Chapman's assumption of a more managerial role, as we know it today, appears to have occurred during his time at Huddersfield. Initially, his role as assistant and subsequently as secretary/manager did not come with complete autonomy. His assumption of power appears to have come from a combination of influences but mainly through directors who had hitherto held all the power requiring to commit more time to their own businesses.

The running of a club had become more difficult, Huddersfield Town being an extreme example because of its notoriously cantankerous players. The Football authorities reduced the maximum wage from £10 to £8 in 1922. While this was widely accepted, albeit reluctantly, given the prevailing economic conditions in post-war Britain, the Huddersfield Town players had been an exception, threatening strike action.

All of these facts, from the economic pressures of running their own businesses to not wanting to deal with bolshie players were set against the awareness that in Chapman they had someone who clearly had the capability to assume control. The fact that he had trained as a mining engineer and had worked in managerial or quasi managerial roles in industry gave him a level of credibility which coupled with his football knowledge made him a unique candidate to manage a club.

Chapman's first major trophy with Huddersfield was the 1922 FA Cup while the team finished in quite a low league position, just avoiding relegation through some sterling performances towards the end of the season on the back of the Cup win.

At this point he stated publicly that the league championship was the next objective. In 1923, with some astute signings, Huddersfield finished third in the League and went out of the Cup to eventual winners Bolton Wanderers. The second and third teams also performed well reflecting a general improvement at every level within the club. By the final day of the 1923-24 season, Huddersfield had won their first championship, defeating Nottingham Forest while Cardiff their rivals were held by Birmingham. The achievement was all the more praiseworthy as Huddersfield had been seriously affected by injuries and an illness epidemic early in the season.

The following year the championship was retained. Chapman had now established the club as a force in the land. They completed the hat-trick of championships in 1926 becoming the first club to do so. His judgement of players, his knack of getting the balance between taking care of players' needs yet maintaining strict discipline was exemplary. His awareness and vision of what it was that would make a club attractive to supporters and the need to attract those same supporters was decades ahead of the times.

But Huddersfield's third title would be won without Herbert Chapman.

In May 1925 Arsenal were seeking a secretary/manager. Chapman was approached and offered £2,000 per annum, a relatively high salary for the position at that time. Huddersfield did everything they could to keep the man who had transformed their club into the most successful in England, even offering to match Arsenal's salary.

But the lure of London was too great. He saw it as a big opportunity for his family and he saw Arsenal as having much greater potential than Huddersfield because of its location in the capital. At times like this Chapman seemed to think like a marketing manager, seeing that with such a huge population on the doorstep Arsenal could become something much bigger than a provincial club like Huddersfield. At that time Arsenal were finding it difficult to maintain first division status.

A recurring theme in Chapman's managerial career was the fact that consistently he built excellent relations with his employers. The basis of his working relationship would be that he would deliver the results, they would trust his judgement in the transfer market but he would take sole responsibility for team affairs. All of this was revolutionary. Committees and later Boards of Directors had adopted a hands-on role at every football club. It had been unheard of that an employee would be given such authority. In this respect he was fortunate to encounter such people as the enlightened Denis Hill-Wood who said: "Why pay experts to do a job if non-experts are going to be allowed to interfere?" To put in context the assumption of such power by one man, bear in mind that the national team would follow suit in 1963 some thirty eight years later.

Upon his arrival at Arsenal he issued the warning that it would take five years to gain success. Chapman set about the task of team building. In his first season 1925-26 Arsenal finished runners-up to Huddersfield Town who were completing their three-in-a-row of league titles. In 1927 Arsenal reached their first ever FA Cup Final where their conquerors were Cardiff City.

Chapman paid Bolton a record fee for David Jack. However the fee was still short of the £13,000 which Bolton had been demanding. How this transfer was concluded made a great story for Bob Wall as he related his first experience of transfer negotiations when the Bolton management were eventually invited to London's Euston Hotel. Wall was an administrator who would later become Secretary and later still General Manager of Arsenal, his only employer in a career that lasted fifty years.

"We arrived at the hotel half an hour before our appointment. Chapman immediately went into the lounge bar. He called the waiter, placed two pound notes in his hand and said: 'George, this is Mr. Wall, my assistant. He will drink whiskey and dry ginger. I will drink gin and tonic. We shall be joined by guests. They will drink whatever they like. But I want you to be careful of one thing. See that our guests are given double of everything, but Mr. Wall's whiskey and dry ginger will contain no whiskey and my gin and tonic will contain no gin.'

When the Bolton pair arrived, Chapman ordered the drinks. We quickly downed ours and he called for the same again. The drinks continued to flow and our guests were soon in gay mood. Finally, when Chapman decided the time was opportune for talking business, they readily agreed to letting him sign Jack — and for £10,890, which we considered a bargain. Never did ginger ale and tonic water leave two persons so elated. When we were safely in our taxi on the return journey to Highbury, Chapman exclaimed: 'Well, that's your first lesson in football. You know how to conduct a transfer.' "

Chapman caused a surprise when going after Alex James of Preston, an out and out goal scorer. James himself was in for a shock when he was informed of his completely new role after signing. Arguably only Chapman had the courage to even attempt such a move. The result was that James became the fulcrum of the first great Arsenal team, the inspirational midfield genius through whom virtually every attack was channelled as Arsenal's exciting counter attacking football took them to the summit of the game in England. Chapman wrote about Alex James: "His mind was big enough to allow him to sink much of his individuality in his play, in order to fit in with the schemes of the team."

The signing of Cliff Bastin from Exeter completed the picture for Chapman. Bastin was training as an engineer and like the young

Chapman saw his long-term future in that career, but was eventually persuaded to move to north London.

Although Chapman's official title at Arsenal was still secretary/manager, he had control over all major aspects of the club. And he knew how to exercise this control. The new West Stand was built and a plan to replace the East Stand with something more fitting of a modern successful club was put in place as was a plan to cover the North Terrace. One story sums up everything that was positive about Chapman's approach to life as the leader of Arsenal Football Club.

The underground railway station opposite the entrance to Highbury was called Gillespie Road Station. Chapman called a meeting with the Railway Authorities and insisted they change the name to Arsenal. The obvious excuses were offered such as the enormous inconvenience and considerable costs involved in changing signage, printing of maps and tickets etc. Chapman was nothing if not persuasive and his powers of persuasion extended beyond convincing players to come and play for him. Gillespie Road Station would soon have a new name — "Highbury".

One of his many strengths was his tactical ability and the change in the offside rule in 1925 was regarded as a significant factor here. The rule change meant that two rather than three players had to be nearer the opposing goal line when the ball was played. It must be remembered that Chapman's success at Huddersfield preceded this change but his grasp of the opportunities presented by the new rule was immediate.

He discussed the tactical implications with Charles Buchan who felt the centre half would need to become a defensive rather than an attacking figure. Chapman agreed but also decided that another forward should drop back strengthening the mid-field.

The WM system came about as a direct result of their deliberations and experiments. The long established 2-3-5 formation now looked more like 3-2-2-3. Chapman's real strength in introducing a revolutionary tactical change was that he knew he had the players capable of understanding and implementing his ideas. The outcome was a team that could counter attack with breathtaking speed and devastating results.

In 1930 the five-year forecast was fulfilled when Arsenal won their first ever major trophy, the FA Cup. This was followed in 1931 by a first league championship. Not only were Arsenal the first southern club to win the title but their total of 66 points would not be equalled until 1961 by the Tottenham double winning team.

The team's method was to turn defence into attack with astonishing speed. Clearances were invariably channelled through James, now revelling in his new role. He would quickly release a forward with a devastating pass. In 1932 Arsenal's onslaught on a double faltered when James was injured three quarter's way through a league campaign in which they had been in a two-horse race with Everton. His absence was also a factor in a cup final where Newcastle won 2-1.

A shock exit to Walsall in the 1933 FA Cup was a severe blow to Arsenal and Chapman. But by the end of that season, the league title had been won for the second time. An incident in the Walsall cup defeat had involved an Arsenal player, Tommy Black, who had become involved in a running feud with an opponent, eventually conceding a penalty for Walsall's second and decisive goal.

Chapman had dealt with such indiscipline before when promptly transferring Ernie Islip out of Huddersfield for a breach of discipline. Black discovered the hard way how Chapman reacted to serious indiscipline and would have found time to reflect on matters as he soon arrived at his new club, Plymouth

In 1932 Chapman had a forty five minute clock installed at the north end of the ground so everyone could see, at a glance, how much time was left to play. This was outlawed by officialdom who felt it interfered with the referee's authority. Chapman had it replaced with a twenty four hour clock which remained in place as long as the stand on which it was mounted — until the 1990s.

The Arsenal jersey had been all red but Chapman felt that the jersey design of the country's leading club, Aston Villa, was more distinctive. So he had the Arsenal jersey changed to red with white contrast sleeves.

Another Chapman innovation was the concept of the two FA Cup Final teams coming on to the pitch together, an accepted part of the ceremony these days and indeed something which has become part of football today, but it was seen for the first time in 1930 when, appropriately enough, Arsenal played Huddersfield Town.

The use of numbers on players' shirts was prohibited but Chapman tried to break this rule by introducing numbered jerseys for a league game in 1928. The Football League objected at the time and it was 1939 before numbers were made compulsory.

Chapman arranged with the railways to establish an exclusive Arsenal carriage for away trips. This carriage would always be an addition to a regular train so it would be the first or last carriage, and separate from other passengers.

On one of his frequent visits to Europe Chapman saw floodlights working satisfactorily and on his return set about arranging for lights at Highbury. These were duly installed on the West Stand but the FA were unhappy with the idea and banned their use for official games. It wasn't until until 1955 — a quarter of a century later — that floodlights were allowed into the English professional game.

Eleven years ahead of his time with the numbering of shirts and twenty five years ahead on floodlighting, Chapman could still do better. Supporters of football will have noted the innovation first seen at the 2009-10 Europa League, wherein two additional assistant referees are added to the game, positioned behind the goal line. In "Herbert Chapman on Football" published in 1934, he expressed the view that such a development would come, making him seventy five years ahead of his time on that one.

Team talks were unheard of before Herbert Chapman's arrival at Leeds City. It is difficult to imagine in an age of detailed DVD analysis, monitoring systems, statistics, written reports on opposing players etc. that the most basic team talk did not exist until Chapman introduced the practice.

Herbert Chapman was the first manager to talk and think in terms of making a plan which improved the chances of success. This all seems so logical and rational now but his thinking was revolutionary in the 1920s. And these team talks had a big impact at Arsenal: "The weekly team talks improved their motivation and heightened their involvement, and weekly rounds of golf helped them to relax. He set great store by what he regarded as the dignity of the athlete, treating his players as human beings instead of mere paid servants, which was how they were regarded elsewhere."

In 1931 in an FA Cup replay at Villa Park, Chapman had his Arsenal players use rubber studs for the first time to overcome the icy surface conditions. This was considered a vital contribution to a 3-1 win. Chapman's expressed belief that the England team needed to meet and train together regularly was ignored until it became common practice twenty years later.

A notable aspect of his understanding of football as a business is that despite unprecedented levels of spending on players at both Huddersfield and Arsenal, both clubs were profitable during his time as manager. The expensive signings were to bring about improved performance leading to on-field success and improved gate receipts leading to profitability.

On transfer expenditure, it should be recalled that as well as spending big on star players, Chapman also spent smaller sums on what were to prove astute signings such as Eddie Hapgood for £250 from Kettering and Cliff Bastin for £2,000 from Exeter. Both players became part of Arsenal's history as well as full internationals.

Having won the FA Cup in 1930, and League titles in 1931 and 1933 Arsenal were on the way to a further league championship in 1934. However, tragedy struck when on New Year's Day Chapman caught a chill while watching a game at Bury. Undaunted, he insisted on going to Sheffield the next day to take a look at Arsenal's next visitors, Sheffield Wednesday.

On his return he was advised by the club doctor to rest but instead he went to watch the Arsenal reserve team play. By now pneumonia had set in and in the early hours of 6 January 1934, he died just two weeks before his 56th birthday. The seriousness of his illness had not been realised, least of all by Chapman himself, while the Arsenal players would learn the terrible news on their way to Highbury from newspaper vendors' billboards reading: "Herbert Chapman Dead".

His team went on to win the league title and complete three-in-a-row in 1935, followed by the FA Cup in 1936 and another league title in 1938 as World War II and a cessation of competitive football drew ever nearer. Hugo Meisl sent his condolences in the most emotional, grief-stricken terms to Chapman's widow, and Meisl himself would suffer his fatal heart-attack just three years later.

Chapman's name was known to those of us in later generations as the second man, after Tom Watson, to manage two different teams to league titles, an achievement later equalled by Brian Clough and then Kenny Dalglish. However, to this day Herbert Chapman is the only manager to manage different clubs to both league and FA Cup success.

One of his golden rules was: "It is never safe to be satisfied. No matter how good a team may be, there should always be an attempt to improve it." Perhaps it could be said that no matter how great a manager may be there will always be another who is better. In this case, we may still be waiting.

Vittorio Pozzo

"If my dog had not died in that period, I would not have come back to football."

Vittorio Pozzo explains what led to a change of heart that brought Italy two World Cups

In a time when travel was much more difficult and communications more primitive, it is striking to consider the friendships which existed between the great managers of the time, Meisl, Chapman and the Italian, Vittorio Pozzo, the football manager with the most appropriate first name, given the scale of his victorious achievements in the game.

He was born in Turin in 1886, the year before football was first played in that city. In the earliest days, attendances were low but legend has it that the twelve year old Vittorio was present at the first ever Italian championship final in which his native Torino lost to Genoa by 1-0 with a Mr. Savage scoring the decisive goal.

The young Pozzo was hooked on football. In a pattern similar to that followed by Hugo Meisl, he travelled extensively in Europe once he had finished high school. He then took a commercial course of study in Switzerland and while there, played for the Grasshoppers club.

His most formative period was the time spent in England beginning at the London Olympics of 1908. He attended tournament games at White City and was greatly impressed with how everything was done. Vittorio was there to study and to learn English. His main field of study was football, however, as he travelled to games in Newcastle, Manchester, Birmingham, Sheffield and Blackpool.

To fund his continuing stay in England he gave Italian lessons at the Berlitz School. Once his studies were over his family sent him a one-way ticket from Bradford back to Turin to ensure he would attend a family wedding. Although never using the ticket, he kept it with him throughout his life as a memento of an important time in his youth.

While abroad Pozzo became fluent in English, French and German and worked for the Turin based newspaper, "La Stampa", for which he wrote articles and reports on sports topics. At twenty five he was appointed Federal Secretary of the Italian Football Federation, FIGC (Federazione Italiana Gioco Calcio). He resigned within a year citing a wish to avoid a world of hypocrisy and compromise.

In 1912 he was appointed trainer of the national team for the Stockholm Olympics. This may not have been the great achievement it would seem at first reading. Pozzo was chosen for his experience abroad and his knowledge of languages. But it should be noted that in a pattern more usually reflected in later Italian politics, there had been seventeen different trainers in the twenty two months prior to his appointment.

After those Olympics, Pozzo resigned but his observations on the experience give an excellent insight into the kind of man he was and how he was developing.

"It was useful to learn a lot of things. On the contrary, I taught nothing. The Olympics was a school for me, I was a student again. And I understood that one person with practical and sane concepts is better than the sum of many peoples' ideas, even if each one idea is a good idea. This is not ambition, this is to be practical, to be straight. That Olympics was not a duty but a sort of mission."

One of the many with whom Vittorio Pozzo spoke and from whom he learned was Hugo Meisl, who was in Sweden with his own national team but also to referee.

"He was the referee of our game against Finland. During the match, Meisl spoke Italian with our team. As he saw me in difficulties, he took me to one side and as a teacher with a pupil, he told me that the trainer of a national team is the most difficult and thankless task for a man. Meisl was a great man, capable of foreseeing what will happen in the future. He was not only interested in the techniques of football as I was, but also in the politics of the sport. During the Olympics we organised the first match between Italy and Austria for the following year."

Pozzo and Meisl maintained their friendship right up to the latter's untimely death. After his Olympic experience he returned to Turin, taking charge of the Torino club, arranging an enlightening and lucrative three-month tour of South America in 1915, as per Meisl's suggestion.

During the First World War he served as a Tenente (Lieutenant) in the Alpini, an elite group of soldiers founded in 1872 whose mission was the protection of Italy's northern mountain border with

Austria and France. They became widely known during that war when they fought against the Austro-Hungarian Kaiserjager and the German Alpenkorps for three long years in what became known as "The War on Ice and Snow."

Pozzo's biographer, Mauro Grimaldi, described him as possessing the characteristics of moral rigidity, loyalty and modesty all of which he later applied to his relationships with players. He returned to Turin after the war to the football club where he resumed as trainer until 1924. Meanwhile, he went to work as a manager for Pirelli.

He was again asked to take charge of the national team at the 1924 Paris Olympics. This time, his acceptance of the role was on condition that he had sole charge of the team. He declared: "Italy was previously led by technical commissions formed by many people wherein compromises were always made in order to get a final agreement and this is the worst way to lead a team." This concept of a manager taking sole charge of a national team and team selection would take several decades to reach other parts of the football world.

He started the process of changing the Italian approach to football introducing a rational, studied and measured way of playing to replace what had been described as "heat and instinctive fire" with little evidence of planning or thought.

He introduced the idea of a secluded place for the team before each game. He spoke with each player individually in private. He spoke about moral and ethical values applying psychology to these conversations. Players got comfortable with him and saw him as a man to whom they could talk and whom they could trust. Pozzo took care of all arrangements including transport and choice of hotels, with a fine attention to detail.

After the Olympics of 1924, now back at Pirelli in Milan, Pozzo's wife became terminally ill and upon her death he resigned from all involvement with football and the national team. He placed his children in schools and spent weekends walking his beloved mountains with his dog for company. Eventually Pozzo resumed following the football games on Sundays. He explained: "If my dog had not died in that period, I would not have come back to football."

By 1929 the political situation was changing with the rise of the fascists. Arpinati, a fascist leader had also become head of the football federation. In that capacity he approached Pozzo and asked him to return to take control of the national team. It was clear that fascism wished to use the national team for propaganda. Pozzo accepted the task and endured criticism for many years from those who insisted he must himself have been a fascist to have accepted the job at that time. However, Vittorio Pozzo denied such accusations in the strongest terms.

Once again showing his abundant man-management abilities he created a cohesive unit. His strategy was to study each player and help him resolve any issues that were causing him concern or inhibiting his ability to perform within the team. He resolutely defended his players as individuals and as a group against anyone who proffered criticism.

The story is told of how a Juventus player and a Roma player got into a heated quarrel during a championship game. Pozzo dealt with the problem by ordering that from then on, whenever there were two beds in a room, that room would be shared by a Juventus and a Roma player. While the players were silently absorbing this instruction, Pozzo further added that he wanted the door always left open — "so I could see if one of the two has been strangled by the other". Later still he toured the rooms handing out chocolates to "sweeten their bitter tongues". It is a lesson in how to diffuse a situation.

The result was victory in the World Cups of 1934 and 1938 with an Olympic Gold in Berlin in between. On two separate occasions, following shock defeats in 1930 and in the run-up to the 1934 World Cup, he dropped the respective team captains each time.

In a parallel approach to that of Herbert Chapman, he saw the potential benefits arising from the change to the offside law. While

Chapman's WM was a 3-2-2-3 formation, Pozzo's was what he considered a more defensively secure 2-3-2-3. His system came to be known as the "Metodo" and while it offered a counter-attacking capability along with that little bit more defensive security, we were still a long way from catenaccio.

Pozzo continued to manage the national team until 1948 albeit with a long interruption during the Second World War. He resumed his journalistic work for "La Stampa" for whom he reported on the 1950 World Cup. The final time he saw Italian success was when he watched the Azzurri win the 1968 European Championships, the competition which succeeded the Central European International Cup which he had twice won while managing Italy.

On one of those victorious occasions Italy received a massive trophy of Bohemian glass. Not long afterwards, this was dropped on a tiled floor, shattering in tiny pieces. The second memento Vittorio Pozzo carried with him all his life, after the unused ticket home from England was a piece of glass from that once-fine trophy. Pozzo died on 21st December 1968 in the small town of Ponderano, in the hills north of Turin. At 82, he had enjoyed a much longer life than his contemporaries, Meisl and Chapman.

3

British Managers

THIS chapter looks at ten British managers, starting with Major Frank Buckley who managed either side of the Second World War. The others, mostly had their playing careers interrupted by war, before going on to manage at the highest levels. While Herbert Chapman was capable of imposing discipline, Buckley and some of those who followed him, placed discipline at the centre of their approach to managing.

Bill Struth was a noted disciplinarian as was Stan Cullis who followed Buckley at Wolves. Without exception, these managers had a hard streak. Some choose to hide it better than others. Their treatment of players who had served them with great distinction often left much to be desired. Among those who could be subjected to such an accusation were Cullis, Busby, Shankly and Catterick.

Although Alf Ramsey was a very successful club manager at Ipswich Town, it is as England manager that he is best remembered. He appears elsewhere with other World Cup winners while Brian Clough and Alex Ferguson are each given a full chapter.

The position of secretary/manager and later manager had become important in terms of newspaper coverage of clubs' activities. Directors considered it beneath them to deal with journalists. Players were precluded by contract from doing so. This left an obvious conduit of club news to the newspapers — later to a wider range of media channels. It suited both sides. Journalists got their information and managers got to promote their own names becoming in many cases the face of the club.

The point was also reached where the manager became the expendable person, the one who took the blame when things did not work out. Such an occasion is perfectly illustrated in Stephen Wagg's "The Football World": "There is no reason to doubt the sincerity of Coventry Chairman Derrick Robbins when he described (Billy) Frith in 1961 as one of the best six managers in the country, nor when a few months later he had sacked Frith and been asked if he still rated him in the top six he replied: 'I really felt he would do it.' More and more directors now genuinely did expect big things from a manager, and if he failed to produce them they would expect big things from the next one."

Major Frank Buckley

"I'm going to make you lot walk through the town to let supporters see what a lot of rubbish you are and the first man to break into a run gets the sack."

Major Buckley

While Herbert Chapman stood head and shoulders above every administrator or secretary/manager of his time, there was one other individual who brought purpose and order and military discipline to football. Major Frank Buckley was born in Urmston near Manchester in 1882. Having attended a Jesuit school where he greatly enjoyed sports and physical activities, he signed up at eighteen for a twelve year stint with the King's Liverpool Regiment. He was posted to Ireland and played in an Irish Cup Final for his regimental team against the Lancashire Fusiliers.

Three years after signing up and following trials with Aston Villa, Buckley bought himself out of the army to join the midlands club. Having failed to break through at Villa he spent a short time at Brighton & Hove Albion before joining Manchester United. He again found difficulty breaking into a team that contained Sandy and Jimmy Turnbull and Billy Meredith.

A spell at Manchester City was only marginally more fruitful but the determined Buckley moved back to the midlands to Birmingham City. Three years at Birmingham were followed by his most productive move to Derby County where he and Steve Bloomer were credited with leading County to the Second Division title and promotion. In 1914 while at Derby he obtained his one England cap in a 0-3 defeat to Ireland.

Once war broke out and the Football Battalion was created, Frank Buckley was first to enrol. His previous experience in the army helped him up the ladder as he eventually rose to the rank of Major. The Football Battalion took heavy casualties at the Somme with Buckley himself coming near to losing his life. He was shipped back to England for surgery to remove shrapnel from his lungs.

He returned to the Western Front but coming in contact with German poison gas was disastrous for his damaged lungs and he was again forced back to England.

The war over, he became manager of Norwich City in the Southern League and then spent three years out of football before returning at Blackpool where he is credited with changing the team colours to tangerine for a "bright and vibrant" appearance. Buckley's military background shone through as he became known for strict discipline with a strong emphasis on physical fitness. He is also credited with introducing physiotherapy to Blackpool and he gained a reputation for getting injured players back in action in a short time.

Wolverhampton Wanderers secured Buckley as manager in 1927. One of his strengths had been player recruitment and he had a reputation for unearthing good players who cost little, from all over the country. The secret here was his military connections. He had maintained contact with several of the Football Regiment who were now acting as scouts for the Major.

At Wolves he imposed the same strict regime as he had done at Blackpool. Not only were players given written notice of how they must behave, the public were informed of this and invited to report any player seen out socialising or breaking the rules.

His most notorious reaction to a defeat was when Wolves had been beaten in a cup game by Mansfield Town in 1929. The players were paraded through the town in their kit on the following market day, as a ritual humiliation.

Wolves won the Second Division in 1931-32 and in the following five years Buckley continued to secure bright young players at little or no cost. However, there were regular sales of players who had performed well and this drew unfavourable reaction from supporters. It was believed the board of the club were simply intent on making money rather than taking a serious shot at winning the league. In the 1936-7 season a minor riot broke out after a home defeat to Chelsea. Goalposts were uprooted and it was reported that over 2,000 people had taken part in the protest against Major Buckley.

Buckley came across a pharmacist who proposed to him a treatment for players which involved a course of twelve injections. The Major initially was unsure of this 'gland treatment' but claimed to have tried it himself and to have found it highly beneficial. Two of the players declined to participate when it was put to them by their manager that this 'gland treatment' was the answer to all their problems. Word soon began to circulate that Wolves were having their players injected with 'gland extracts from animals.'

After some startling performances where they racked up seven goals against Everton and ten against Leicester, the matter was raised in the House of Commons by the MP for Leicester, who called for an inquiry. This was ruled out but not before a Labour member suggested the Conservative Government ministers could do with a course of these injections. The football league carried out its own investigation. The outcome was no ban on such treatments but a notice was posted in all dressing rooms of league clubs stating that players could avail of such treatments on a voluntary basis. In the run-up to the outbreak of war in 1939, Wolves began to show signs of greatness, finishing second in the league in the two final years before the enforced break.

They also lost the Cup Final of 1939 to Portsmouth becoming the first team to take the runners-up spot in both major competitions in the same year.

In 1944 Buckley terminated his contract at Wolves, moving to Notts County for an enormous annual salary said to be £4,500. Two years later he moved on to Hull City for a further two years. His next and final management posting was at Leeds United from 1948 to 1953 where his most notable achievement was the signing of the young John Charles.

For a man who never won a major trophy he is regarded as an innovative manager who did spectacular work especially at Wolves. He is credited with laying the foundation for the success that followed in the fifties when three league titles were won along with two FA Cups. He brought through such legendary players as Stan Cullis and Billy Wright and was credited with introducing psychologists to football.

Bill Struth

"His team was ageing, there was talk that he had lost the dressing room, and it was clear – most of all to Struth – that he had to resign. He did so on 30th April, 1954. He had been manager of Rangers to the age of 79."

The Management, Michael Grant and Rob Robertson

While Chapman and Buckley were the best known leaders in football south of the border, in Scotland a true giant of the game presided over phenomenal success during an historically long career. Bill Struth managed Rangers from 1920, when Chapman was at Leeds City, until 1954 just a year before Alf Ramsey took over at Ipswich Town.

And Struth's time in charge saw Rangers dominate. Eighteen championships and ten Scottish Cups were his main achievements. Two League Cups were added when that competition was introduced. In Glasgow, the Glasgow Cup and the Glasgow Merchant

Charity Cup were considered important and Struth's teams won a combined total of thirty six of these local competitions. Rangers were the dominant force in Scottish football during his long spell at the helm.

His most frequently quoted words are, 'we will welcome the chase'. The full quotation indicates a man with a keen sense of perspective even in an era of dominance, an awareness of the need for competition coupled with the realisation that dominance in football is never permanent. "Our very success, gained you will agree by skill, will draw more people than ever to see it. And that will benefit many more clubs than Rangers. Let the others come after us. We will welcome the chase. It is healthy for us. We will never hide from it. Never fear, inevitably we shall have our years of failure, and when they arrive, we must reveal tolerance and sanity."

He was a powerful figure whose influence extended to all aspects of the club. The main stand at Ibrox was designed by the famous Archibald Leitch with input from Struth. In recent times, quite appropriately, it was named after the manager who presided over its creation.

An Edinburgh man, he had been a professional athlete before becoming involved in football as a trainer. He came from Hearts to Rangers to train and act as assistant to the man in charge in 1914. Six years later, when that man, William Wilton, was tragically killed in a boating accident, Struth was asked to take over. He went on to win fourteen league titles in the nineteen years up to the war.

Struth was a disciplinarian who insisted that players wear shirt and tie to training as well as on match days. He is regarded as the man who set exceptionally high standards of behaviour for Rangers players. Players were treated well, travelling first class to games when this was unheard of, but they were acutely aware of what being a Rangers player meant. A player caught walking with his hands in his pockets would be reprimanded by this man of his times who set the standards against which Rangers managers and players would be judged for decades after.

Stan Cullis

The night Stan Cullis got the sack
Wolverhampton wandered round in circles
Like a disallowed goal
Looking for a friendly linesman.
The Stan Cullis Blues, by Martin Hall

The British game saw the emergence in the 1950s and 60s of a cohort of very strong managers which included Stan Cullis at Wolves, Matt Busby at Manchester United, Bill Nicholson at Tottenham, Bill Shankly at Liverpool, Harry Catterick at Everton, Don Revie at Leeds and north of the border, Jock Stein at Celtic. And the manager who achieved the greatest success in the international game, Alf Ramsey, had shown his undoubted ability at club level with Ipswich Town.

Stan Cullis was very much a protégé of Major Frank Buckley. In his own words: "Buckley spent many hours drilling me in the precious art of captaincy, telling me in no ambiguous terms that I was to be the boss on the field. No youngster of eighteen could ask for a better instructor than the major, who laid the foundations of the modern Wolves during his sixteen years at Molineux."

Born and raised in Ellesmere Port, Cullis grew up playing local football alongside Joe Mercer. Both players attracted scouts when playing for the representative side, Ellesmere Port Boys. But Cullis' future was already planned by a father who was a fanatical Wolves supporter and who declared his son would sign for Wolves when the time was right. The Major clearly saw leadership qualities in the young Cullis because it was unusual, indeed remarkable, for a twenty year old to be given the captaincy of a First Division team.

By 1937 at the age of twenty one he had secured his place in the England team. The arrival of war put an end to his haul of international caps after just twelve appearances for his country. However, a severe head injury during the 1938-39 season had already placed his long-term career in jeopardy. The medical prognosis was that so serious had been the trauma, a further concussion could be fatal. Having served in the army as a Physical Training Instructor, Cullis played only briefly after the war before accepting medical advice and retiring.

In 1948 he was appointed manager of Wolves and immediately introduced a fitness programme which by his own reckoning would take eighteen months to bear fruit. Players were given minimum target times for 100 yards, 220 yards, 440 yards, 880 yards, one mile and three miles and further targets for the height they had to jump. Wolves won the FA Cup in 1948, their first trophy since 1908. In 1953 they finished third in the League. In 1954 Wolves were league champions and runners-up in 1955. Further titles were won in 1958 and 1959 with the FA Cup added in 1960. Many would place asterisks beside those two latter league titles because of what had happened to the Busby Babes at Munich.

The Wolverhampton Wanderers of Stan Cullis had a method of playing and some decent players to implement that method. They were direct, with an emphasis on switching to attack as quickly as was possible.

His goalkeeper was then England international, Bert Williams. Team captain Billy Wright went on to hold the record for England caps at 105 and led the Wolves team to three leagues as well as the FA Cup, retiring in 1959 before the cup again was won the following year. Pacey wingers Jimmy Mullen and Johnny Hancocks gave the team an attacking edge. Mullen was handed a debut at sixteen by Frank Buckley and was a one-club man. Hancocks was top scorer as the 1954 Championship was won and scored 158 goals in 343 appearances, an impressive total for a winger.

From 1955 to 1963 Cullis had Jimmy Murray, another outstanding goalscorer, who managed 199 goals in 273 games for Wolves. He made a bold move in 1950 when paying Brentford £10,000 for the seventeen year old Peter Broadbent who became one of Wolves best ever signings.

In between their league wins, Wolves became the focus of attention for games against continental opposition in the mid-1950s. Those floodlit games caught the imagination of football supporters across the nation as full houses saw Racing Club of Argentina, Dinamo Moscow, Spartak Moscow, Honved of Hungary and Real Madrid all visit Molineux.

Just as Major Buckley had managed to swell the coffers with regular sales of players, Cullis was now bringing in big revenues that would further strengthen the club. The fact that the players were not being paid anything other than a win bonus, where applicable, was also a financial boon to Wolves. This lead to controversy and threatened action by the players but a compromise was reached which cost the club relatively little.

By 1964 Wolves form had dipped and Stan Cullis was fired. How players saw this strong man is summed up wonderfully when John Giles asked a Wolves player what Cullis was like. "Describing Cullis to me, he tried to find the words that would adequately convey the mixed feelings he had about the man. 'He was the biggest c**t I have ever met in my life.' He then added, with genuine warmth: 'Great manager though.' "

For supporters, it is simpler. Cullis was a hero and his sacking was a blot on the record of their club, something with which they were saddened, even embarrassed. Wolves fan and poet, Martin Hall summed up his feelings in "The Stan Cullis Blues" a poem in the eponymous collection.

Matt Busby

"Winning isn't everything. There should be no conceit in victory and no despair in defeat."
Matt Busby

Matt Busby's was a life in which he experienced the greatest of triumphs and the most ghastly of tragedies. The very mention of his name evokes affection, sadness and respect. Here was a man who built a brilliant young team containing the greatest player of his generation and saw it wiped out in horrific circumstances. That the Munich air-crash occurred during a journey towards European glory made it all the more poignant and made the eventual successful pursuit of that glory a bitter-sweet fairy tale of modern times.

Busby came from the mining village, Orbiston, Bellshill, in Lanarkshire. Born in 1909, he came from a family more cursed than most by the events of the First World War. His father, a miner, went to serve his country and died by sniper's bullet, at Arras, in April 1917 leaving a widow and young Matt, a month short of his eighth birthday. Three of his uncles were also killed in France during that war. His mother later re-married and planned to re-locate to the United States but delays in processing papers led to a reprieve for Busby.

By then he was working in the mines while playing football for a local side. He was signed by Manchester City in 1928 and his debut came in November of the following year. In 1930 Manchester United sought to buy the Scot but found they could not afford the £150 fee. In March 1936 he transferred to Liverpool for a fee of £8,000. By then he had played on a losing team in the 1933 Cup Final before returning with City the next year to win the FA Cup. Having made over 200 appearances for Manchester City he went on to make a further 115 for Liverpool, eventually captaining the team and earning a single cap for his country.

With the advent of war, many Liverpool players, Busby included, signed up with the King's Liverpool Regiment. It was fitting that Busby should be asked to train and coach footballers within the army rather than follow the fatal route of his family's previous generation.

Following the war, Liverpool proposed to appoint him assistant manager but this was still the era of boards of directors selecting teams and Busby had learned enough to have developed his own ideas. A board of directors picking the team was not one of them. Instead, in February 1945 he agreed to manage Manchester United, taking up the post in October of that year. In between those dates, still in the Army Physical Training Corps, he took an army team to Italy where he came across and was very impressed with Welsh international Jimmy Murphy whom he persuaded to join him at Manchester United in the role of Chief Coach.

Busby's appointment was attributed to Louis Rocca, the pair having come in contact at the Manchester Catholic Sportsman's Club. Rocca was instrumental in bringing crucial finance into the club in the early thirties when he prevailed on local businessman, James Gibson, to invest £2,000 in the impoverished club. As Chief Scout, Rocca had recruited among others Johnny Carey who would captain United to FA Cup success in 1948 and later to League Championship success, becoming the first non-British player to lift both cup and league trophies.

It seems that Catholicism was good for one's football career at that time at United. Carey was a tremendous leader and captained a European Selection against a Great Britain team at Hampden Park in 1947. By then he was back at United having served in the Middle East and Italy during the war. It was a war that, being Irish, he could quite easily have avoided. Carey's attitude was that if he earned a living in England, he had an obligation to serve England.

The Old Trafford ground had been subjected to German bombing during the war and was in bad shape. The structures such as the main stand and changing rooms were destroyed as was part of the terracing, and the pitch itself while not cratered was scorched and unfit for purpose. United were forced to play at Maine Road for the four years it took to complete repairs. City profited from the arrangement to the tune of £5,000 per annum and ten per cent of all gate receipts.

United had finished in fourteenth place in 1939, the last year before the war. This was their best placing in ten years. Along with Jimmy Murphy, Busby set about raising standards and had Manchester United challenging for the big prizes almost immediately. They finished second in the League in 1947, 1948, 1949 and 1951.

Finally the League Championship was won in 1952 to add to

the FA Cup of 1948 but the team was showing its age and it was becoming clear that rebuilding was the next big task. There was an expectation that the club would plunge into the transfer market but Busby had other ideas involving the introduction of young players, some of them still in their teens. He had quite ingeniously circumvented the rule limiting the number of apprentices by employing them as groundstaff or under any other convenient heading. It was the beginning of what forever would be known as the 'Busby Babes'.

Busby was blessed with great judgement, not only of players but also of people. He possessed an innate intelligence and leadership ability, qualities which were fundamental to his success at Manchester United. With Murphy as his assistant he also had Tom Curry, described by Busby as "the best trainer in Britain," with Bert Whalley as coach.

Whalley had played for United, his career curtailed by injury and as well as coaching was a Methodist lay preacher, giving the lie to the notion that one had to be a Catholic to work at the club. Whalley was meticulous in his approach and particularly in his dealings with young players.

Whalley issued a weekly written report to each player, outlining how he had performed. He was very much the conduit between the club/management and those young men and was invaluable to Busby, creating a family atmosphere, and encouraging players in their ambitions. Led by Murphy, this coaching team set the standards of hard work, intelligent application and respect for the club and for colleagues and above all was the team ethic. What Busby and Murphy were doing was creating a culture which would stand to them and to the club for years to come.

United actively scouted and sought the best young players and the best young players wanted to go to Old Trafford. Roger Byrne was from Gorton in Manchester, while other local boys included, Albert Scanlon, Geoff Bent, Dennis Violet and Eddie Colman. Bill Foulkes was a St. Helens man. David Pegg came from Doncaster,

Bobby Charlton from Ashington, in Durham. Duncan Edwards, from Dudley, was snatched from under the noses of the big midlands clubs with Stan Cullis of Wolves said to be particularly displeased, accusing United of offering inducements for his signature.

Mark Jones came straight from schoolboy football in Barnsley while the arrival of the second Barnsley man, Tommy Taylor, was the result of a rare plunge into the transfer market by Busby. So exceptional was Taylor that Manchester United paid £30,000 for him in 1952. He was everything required in a centre-forward, the one position United needed to fill. Taylor was strong, brave, great in the air, could strike equally well with either foot, would guarantee goals and was unselfish if a teammate was better placed.

The Irish came from Belfast in the case of Jackie Blanchflower, while Liam Whelan was a Dubliner. Whelan followed the path of Johnny Carey to Manchester United, setting a pattern for many more young Irish players who were to enjoy great success at a club to which they were brought by Dublin scout supreme, Billy Behan.

John Giles is a man who played for United in that era, winning an FA Cup in 1963 before going on to a great career at Leeds United. He is no worshipper of Busby but gives him enormous credit for how he handled the young players and for his philosophy of encouraging a positive approach. He never criticised a player when some attempt at positivity might have backfired. Busby was always thinking ahead and as Giles put it: "He knew that encouragement rather than criticism would work better in the long term."

At a time when the players were not quite ready for the first team and the Central League was felt to hold physical dangers because of the profile of many of its inhabitants, United were blessed with a solution provided by the Football Association, the FA Youth Cup. Introduced in 1952 to bridge the gap between school-going youths and adults, it was tailor-made for United. With their emphasis on signing the best young players it was no surprise that they owned the competition in its infancy, winning the first five finals.

While Busby was often described as "avuncular," and possessed an inherently gentlemanly demeanour, he could be as determined and ruthless as any, when the occasion demanded. And the ruthlessness could also extend to not treating players fairly, when it suited him. In this respect he shares a particular background and an unexpected lack of empathy which manifested itself most often in mistreating players who had outlived their usefulness.

The term "Busby Babes," was first used in 1951, the creation of the Manchester Evening News journalist, Tom Jackson. Late in that year supporters caught their first sight of eighteen -year-old Jackie Blanchflower and Roger Byrne who was already twenty one. The process continued with four more of the "Babes," Pegg, Violet, Foulkes and Duncan Edwards making their debuts during the following season. By 1956, Manchester United delivered their second championship under Busby and they retained the title in 1957.

Of the regular starting eleven in 1956 only two players remained from the 1952 team, Roger Byrne and Johnny Berry. Busby had completely rebuilt a winning side with an average age of twenty two. An extraordinary statistic from the 1957 league winning team was the goals scored or rather the scorers. Tommy Taylor scored twenty two goals while a youthful Bobby Charlton scored ten but midfielder Liam Whelan finished as top scorer with an amazing twenty six goals.

In the same year, the team came close to winning the double, losing the Cup Final 2-1 to Aston Villa having had to play with ten men for most of the game as their goalkeeper Ray Wood went off injured in an age when substitutes were not allowed.

With such a young and strong team, Busby and Manchester United seemed set to dominate English football for the following decade. Busby's thoughts though ran beyond the English game. His dream was to take part in European competition. And to win.

The European Cup was introduced in the 1955-56 season. French football magazine L'Equipe selected the participants, their intention being to have a tournament among the most prestigious

clubs in Europe. It was editor, Gabriel Hanot, who at the UEFA Congress in April 1955 successfully proposed the introduction of the competition.

Chelsea, as league champions of England were duly invited to participate in the inaugural European Cup in 1955-56. The FA banned Chelsea from participating, fearing this competition would simply be a distraction from domestic football. It was an immediate success, with Real Madrid beating Stade Reims 4 -3 in the final at Parc des Princes, Paris, on 13 June, 1956.

The following year the holders managed to overcome a young Manchester United team 5 -3 on aggregate on their way to retaining the cup before 124,000 in their home stadium.

United and Busby had now seen at first-hand what it took to win this new and exciting competition. And winning it had become a matter of pride and honour for Busby. Having retained their domestic title they could return to the European Cup and this time, go all the way. That was the dream. And it was certainly a realistic achievable dream.

By now the European Champions, Real Madrid, were once more invited in as champions with Seville qualifying as Spanish league winners. East Germany, Northern Ireland and the Republic of Ireland were represented for the first time in an increasingly popular competition.

In a preliminary round, Manchester United beat Shamrock Rovers 9-2 on aggregate. In the First Round they took a 3-0 lead to Dukla Prague and although they lost the away leg 1-0 they were through to the quarter-finals. The first leg of their quarter final against Red Star was played on 14 January 1958 before the same size attendance as for the Dukla Prague game — a full house of 60,000. Goals from Bobby Charlton and Eddie Colman gave United a slender 2-1 lead for the return in Belgrade.

United had spluttered in the league as they sought a third consecutive title. Some poor results, the worst a 4-0 defeat at Bolton saw them slip behind leaders Wolves. Busby made changes, dropping a handful of his established players, showing no sentimentality towards those who had won him two championships.

David Pegg and Johnny Berry lost out to Albert Scanlon and the young Welshman, Kenny Morgans. In addition, Liam Whelan and Jackie Blanchflower were replaced by Bobby Charlton and Mark Jones. The other major change, the fifth one wrought by the manager was the purchase of goalkeeper Harry Gregg from Doncaster to replace Ray Wood. League form improved immediately with a series of wins including the most satisfactory 7-2 thrashing of Bolton Wanderers which well and truly avenged the earlier defeat.

United progressed through a couple of rounds of the FA Cup. They were in hot pursuit now of Wolves and there was the second leg of that European Cup quarter-final in Belgrade. Before heading to Yugoslavia they had the difficult task of playing a strong Arsenal team at Highbury with league points critical if they were to keep pressure on Wolves who would visit Old Trafford on the Saturday after the Red Star game. Talk was of a treble involving League, FA Cup and European Cup. Highbury hosted a dramatic event with United winning 5-4 in an absorbing game. Now to Red Star on Wednesday and back home to take on Wolves and close that gap to four points while denting Wolves confidence.

Having experienced difficulties on previous trips, United decided to charter a plane for the Belgrade game. Their Monday morning departure was delayed over an hour because of fog at the local Ringway Airport. The necessary re-fuelling was scheduled for Munich and that went without a hitch. The weather at Belgrade was horrendous and it transpired the team plane was the only one to land there that day.

Next day things looked a lot better in the sunshine and despite some patches of snow remaining on the pitch, it was deemed playable. A crowd of 52,000 saw a really good game in which United led after two minutes through Dennis Violet. Bobby Charlton scored twice to put United three up. In a reprise of the previous week's

Highbury game, United came out for the second half and soon allowed their opponents back into the game.

On this occasion, a referee who appeared determined from the outset to favour the home team whenever possible, had a bearing on the game's progress. The second half had hardly begun when Red Star scored after what appeared a foul on a Manchester United player was ignored by the official. This was followed by a dubious penalty. Two minutes from time, they scored from a free kick. But Manchester United saw out the remaining time and again were through to the semi-finals.

Next day, 6 February, 1958, the flight took off, bound for Munich for refuelling. Temperatures were sub-zero at the airport in Bavaria but the plane landed at lunchtime without crisis. The re-fuelling complete, the plane was given clearance to take off. In freshly falling snow two take-off attempts were abandoned. The third attempt, which should never have happened, ended fifty four seconds after the throttles were opened, in the most sickening and catastrophic event in the history of Manchester United.

The plane never got off the ground, ploughed through the airport perimeter, struck a house and then a shed used for storing oil drums. The first obstacle caused the fuselage to break up, the second led to a conflagration of the tail section. Goalkeeper Harry Gregg was a hero as he pulled several people from the wreckage, returning time and again with no concern for his personal safety. When it was over, the dead included one of the co-pilots and the cabin steward, eight journalists, among them Frank Swift of News of The World, the former England and Manchester City goalkeeper who had won a league medal alongside Matt Busby.

Walter Crickmer the Manchester United Club Secretary was among the dead as were the two loyal servants and great stalwarts of the training ground, Trainer Tom Curry and Coach Bert Whalley. The players who perished were: Captain Roger Byrne, Geoff Bent, Eddie Colman, Mark Jones, David Pegg, Tommy Taylor, Liam Whelan and after a fifteen day battle, Duncan Edwards.

Matt Busby was seriously injured and in the days after the crash there was a daily vigil and constant monitoring of the conditions of both the manager and the stricken young genius, Duncan Edwards. The descriptions of Edwards by those who saw him or knew him are consistent. He was the greatest footballer England had produced with every quality imaginable. When the plane was delayed after the second failed attempt to take off, Edwards courteously sent a telegram to his landlady informing her the flight was cancelled and he would not be home that night.

Those who survived the tragedy included the pilot, the radio officer and the two stewardesses, four other passengers including a Yugoslavian mother and child, both pulled from the wreckage by Harry Gregg, and from the newsmen, Peter Howard of the Daily Mail, Frank Taylor of the News Chronicle and telegraphist, Ted Ellyard of the Daily Mail.

Jimmy Murphy had been excused the trip to Belgrade as he was on duty in Cardiff, managing his national team. It was the night Wales beat Israel to qualify for World Cup Finals, for the first time. He returned from that game oblivious to what had happened in Munich and went to the ground to meet the squad on their return. His only concern was that any new injuries picked up might impact on the coming game against Wolves. He learnt the news upon his arrival at Old Trafford.

The surviving players were Jackie Blanchflower and Johnny Berry, neither of whom would ever play again, Kenny Morgans whose loss of form from the trauma was so bad his career too was over, Harry Gregg, Bobby Charlton, Bill Foulkes, Dennis Violet, Albert Scanlon and the second goalkeeper Ray Wood.

Matt Busby remained in a German hospital with multiple injuries, too ill in the opinion of doctors to be told the truth about what had happened. He left hospital nine weeks after the crash but did not have the strength to return to work. Murphy had the task of putting a team on the field once United were obliged to play again, the Wolves game being the only league match postponed.

He had no Matt Busby with whom to discuss plans and his two most loyal servants, Bert Whalley and Tom Curry were lost to him forever. Even the ever-efficient and astute Secretary Walter Crickmer was no longer there to offer counsel. Somehow, amid the personal unbearable sadness, Jimmy Murphy got down to work. Their Cup tie was also put back but only from Saturday 15 February to the following Wednesday. As for finding replacements Murphy paid Blackpool £8,000 for Ernie Taylor and promoted some of the many talented young players from the club's youth and second teams. So just thirteen days after Munich, on a wave of raw emotion, Manchester United won through to the FA Cup quarter finals, beating Sheffield Wednesday 3-0 before 60,000 distraught onlookers.

The remaining league games to the end of the season brought only a single victory but the makeshift team seemed to achieve a focus for the one-off cup days. West Bromwich Albion and Fulham were duly eliminated and miraculously Manchester United were in the Cup Final of 1958. By then Busby was well enough to attend but would not be back on duty until the beginning of the following season. But there was no fairytale ending to this campaign and United were beaten by their old adversaries Bolton Wanderers. They still had a European Cup semi-final against A.C. Milan. Surprisingly, they managed to win the home leg 2-1 but predictably lost the return in Milan 0-4.

Busby's inclination was to walk away from football but his wife, Jean, persuaded him to continue out of respect for those who had perished at Munich. He returned to set about re-building a team, bringing players through and making clever and sometimes high-profile signings.

Youth player Nobby Stiles came into the team in 1960. Two years later the British transfer record was shattered when Denis Law was brought back from Torino for £115,000. It was money well spent as Law was a brilliant signing spending eleven years at Old Trafford in one of which he scored forty six goals. Pat Crerand was signed from Celtic in 1963. Also in 1963, George Best made his league debut.

The FA Cup was won in 1963 when Leicester City were beaten in the final. By 1965 Busby had a team good enough to bring his fourth and United's sixth League title. Busby made it five to his name when Manchester United were crowned champions in 1967. The European Cup was a difficult competition to win, having thrived and developed since the early days. Celtic set the trend with their first success by a British team in 1967. United were well equipped to try to emulate them the following year when the final was fixed for Wembley Stadium.

Their first opponents, Hibernians of Malta presented little difficulty and with two goals each from Denis Law and David Sadler, United took a 4-0 lead to Malta where they strolled through a scoreless draw. In that same first round, Glentoran of Northern Ireland came close to causing a sensation when they drew their home leg 1-1 with Benfica before getting a 0-0 draw in Lisbon, the former winners going through only by virtue of their away goal.

The second round draw was hardly welcomed at Old Trafford as the team was drawn to travel to Yugoslavia. It cannot have been an easy place to go to for Busby and those who had come through Munich. This time the opponents were Sarajevo and after a scoreless draw in that first game, United won through by 2-1 their goals coming from George Best and John Aston. The quarter final draw paired United with Gornik Zabrze from the Polish mining town.

In front of a 63,000 crowd, an own goal and a Brian Kidd goal gave United the advantage but the second leg was no cakewalk as Gornik pulled a goal back with twenty minutes remaining. United held out and were again through to a European Cup semi-final where they would play Real Madrid, winners of the first five European Cups and still a power in the game.

David Sadler, who had arrived at the club in 1963, summed up the feelings within United towards the European Cup: "There was a desire to win the European Cup and we all felt it. Europe had come to mean so much to the club. The crash came about because United went into Europe against the judgement of many people in football. It was about Matt's and the club's desire and forward thinking to where football was going to be, which is where we are now with this fantastic Champions League."

The approach to the game was less than perfect with Manchester United feeling they had thrown away the league, to, of all teams, Manchester City.

A single George Best goal was all United could take to Madrid by way of a lead. In a packed Bernabeu it soon looked inadequate. Madrid tore into their foes, scoring three times in the first half to lead 3-1 on aggregate. An own goal almost on the stroke of half-time gave United a glimmer of hope. The half-time whistle could not come soon enough for a battered and traumatised Manchester United.

Amidst the shock and forebodings, Busby calmly addressed his team before they returned to action. His message was simple to the effect that he could accept losing if the team played like Manchester United but this had not happened in the first half. As the second half progressed they began to get a foothold in the game and with seventeen minutes left, Sadler got on the end of a free kick to scramble a goal. Within five minutes, in a moment of the sweetest irony, team captain and Munich survivor, Bill Foulkes, had pushed forward and was perfectly placed to glide a George Best pull-back to the Real net.

It was 3-3 on the night and 4-3 to United on aggregate. Wembley and a clash with Benfica beckoned and people began to believe Manchester United's name was on this cup.

While Benfica and the great Eusebio would have other ideas, Busby's choice of Stiles to mark the great man was masterful. With Eusebio closed down, Manchester United took a second half lead through Bobby Charlton. Benfica were not lying down and on seventy three minutes they equalised. Extra time was necessary. And it is that period of extra time that will forever be remembered as United suddenly appeared inspired. Shackles thrown off they scored first through Best, audaciously rounding the goalkeeper as if he were playing in a five-a-side on a Belfast street. Then Brian Kidd made it 3-1 before that great Munich survivor Bobby Charlton scored his second and United's fourth.

Finally, Matt Busby had taken his club to a European Cup. The team that died was the second he had built and this was his third. In a year he could retire with the satisfaction of having reached the summit of European football. Busby's achievements go away beyond five league titles and eventually winning the European Cup. He rebuilt a club and that is his enduring legacy. In marked contrast, when the all-conquring Torino team perished at Superga in May 1949, it was the end of an era. Torino never managed to recover in the manner of Manchester United under Jimmy Murphy and Matt Busby.

His treatment of players such as Shay Brennan and Nobby Stiles does not reflect well on Busby. It is well documented that Brennan, a hero of Manchester United's first European Cup win was treated abysmally when his time came to retire. Nobby Stiles was transferred to Middlesbrough for £20,000 — a substantial sum for someone at that stage of his career.

This was an era when players did not earn big money and the usual way to assist a player who had given stellar service was to allow him leave on a free transfer or for a low figure. The player could then negotiate a signing-on fee. But if clubs choose to ignore this protocol by extracting the maximum fee, it left little room for the departing player to make any kind of a bonus from the move.

It was acknowledged by Bobby Charlton that when United trailed 3-1 at half time in the European Cup semi-final in Madrid, as he himself was fit to throw in the towel, Matt Busby's words apart, Nobby Stiles was the one who brought belief back into the half-time dressing-room. Essentially Stiles did what Roy Keane would do in Turin some thirty one years later. But when the time came for Nobby to leave, there was no sentiment, no generosity, no indication of respect for his incredible service. For this Busby, sadly, stands indicted.

Jock Stein

"John you're immortal now."

Bill Shankly to Stein immediately after Celtic had won the European Cup in Lisbon in 1967

Jock Stein wrote himself into the history books with the exploits of his Lisbon Lions in 1967. Celtic full back and European Cup winner Jim Craig reflected on the club's good fortune that saw Stein appointed boss at Parkhead.

"There is no doubt in my mind that without Jock, we would never have achieved our potential. He was the driving force behind our success, the human catalyst who fused the various personalities, the perfectionist who raised our standards."

When Sir Alex Ferguson retired and David Moyes was appointed to replace him, former Scottish International, Pat Nevin, was asked about the extraordinary number of Scottish managers in the English game at that time. His answer was that there is a common thread which links them all — they all go back to Jock Stein. In an article on Jock Stein by Ewing Grahame, published in The Telegraph in October 2012, he wrote: "Sir Alex Ferguson claims he was the biggest influence on him and Craig Brown, Walter Smith and Jim McLean say much the same." Bill Shankly also worshipped Stein. Indeed the quote from the victorious Celtic dressing room in Lisbon — "John, you're immortal now" was Shankly's famous tribute to his great friend whose ground-breaking team he had travelled to support.

Stein was born on 5 October 1922 in Burnbank, South Lanarkshire. His father and family were committed Rangers supporters to the extent that when Jock played for Celtic his father would head off to the Rangers game. His playing career began in earnest in

1942. He worked in the mines during the week, playing for Albion Rovers at the weekends. Being a miner was a reserved occupation during the war so he was able to continue playing while working.

After a mixed spell at Albion Rovers including a promotion and relegation, in 1950 Stein signed for South Wales club, Llanelli, who had just been promoted to the Southern League and were actively signing Scottish players on the strength of that step up.

It was a deeply unsettling time for Jock, his wife Jean and their daughter Ray. Initially he went to South Wales leaving the family in Scotland. As this was unsatisfactory, he then moved them down to Wales.

Before long their house in Hamilton was burgled. As Jean wished to move back to Scotland and there were problems at the Llanelli club, Stein decided to move back north. When asked what he would do he told the Llanelli manager he expected to go back to mining work. But in December 1951 a solution came from an unlikely source.

At the instigation of the Celtic reserve team manager, Jimmy Gribben, he was signed as a reserve team player by Celtic. Before long, due to a series of injuries to first team players, he was promoted. Stein settled well, holding his place and was appointed vice-captain in a prescient move reflecting his influence and leadership qualities.

Once Seán Fallon suffered a broken arm, the captaincy of Celtic passed to Stein. In 1952-53 Celtic were invited to participate in the Coronation Cup along with Hibernian, Arsenal and Manchester United and ended up winning this tournament. The following season Stein led Celtic to a League and Cup double, their first league title in sixteen years. The next season the team finished second in the league and lost the Cup Final to Clyde.

A chronic ankle injury forced his retirement in January 1957 and a few months later he was given his first coaching role with Celtic's reserve team. He was immediately successful, winning the Reserve Cup with a team that included young men with whom he would share much more significant glory ten years later, Billy McNeill, John Clark and Bobby Murdoch. But much was to happen in between.

Stein concluded he could go no further with Celtic and duly left in March 1960 to take up an appointment as manager of Dunfermline Athletic. He guided a team which had not won in four months and which was perilously close to being relegated to six straight wins and safety. The first of these wins was against Celtic and during that winning run to the end of the season, Stein made only one change to the personnel he inherited and that was forced on him by an injury. At the end of the season he took stock and vowed to bring through some younger players but also realised he needed experience if the team was to develop.

Jackie Sinclair and Willie Callaghan were two of the younger ones developed by Stein. Meanwhile he bought Scottish international outside right, Tommy McDonald and Northern Ireland's Willie Cunningham from Leicester City. The latter was regarded as the most important signing by Stein during his time at Dunfermline. Cunningham, a full back who could play on either flank brought experience of six years at Leicester prior to which he had played for St.Mirren and with his international experience he would benefit the team, in particular the younger players.

In Stein's first full season as manager of Dunfermline he took them to victory over Celtic in the Scottish Cup Final after a replay. Thirteen months after his arrival, the club had a Cup win and qualification for European competition with eight of the team which had played in his first game in charge.

Stein's studies of football were extensive and having been hugely impressed with the Hungarians at Wembley in 1953, he attended the 1954 World Cup in Switzerland and eager to learn, was impressed with much of what he saw. His willingness to learn was never more evident than when Cunningham was deployed as a sweeper for Dunfermline against Everton in a Fairs Cup game in late 1962. The 0-1 deficit from Goodison Park was overturned with a 2- 0 home win. It was one of the first times a sweeper was deployed in British football.

The big question was why Stein who had shown immediate ability with Celtic reserves should have felt he could not progress further at the club. Jim Craig posits two possibilities. The first was that he would have been too strong a personality for the board to control.

The second and much less pleasant idea was that Celtic's Chairman and owner, Robert Kelly would not appoint a Protestant manager. Another former Celtic player was adamant that religion influenced Kelly's decision: "I don't have to tell you it was because Jock was not a Catholic, which was quite disgraceful!"

Dunfermline's debut season in Europe, courtesy of their Scottish Cup win, took them as far as the quarter finals of the Cup Winners Cup in 1961-62 while they managed a creditable fourth place in the Scottish First Division. Their league placing then qualified them for the Fairs Cup the following season. Having turned down overtures from both Hibernian and Newcastle United after the Scottish Cup triumph, Jock was again in demand late in the 1963-4 season.

Once Dunfermline lost their Scottish Cup semi-final to Rangers, it was agreed he could leave to take over as manager of Hibernian. Once again, he found himself in a club struggling near the foot of the table. Having avoided relegation, Hibernian then won what was called "The Summer Cup". It might not have been much but it was their first trophy of any sort in ten years.

Stein's greatest ambition was to manage Celtic. This seems quite extraordinary given the background to his departure and the widely held view of why he had to move elsewhere to progress. When Wolves came seeking him before his first season with Hibernian was finished, he contacted Kelly ostensibly seeking his advice on the wisdom of a move to the English midlands. The eventual outcome saw Stein achieve his ambition as Kelly relented and offered him the job he craved.

Ernest Mangnall photographed with his Manchester United team in 1905. Mangnall was one of only three managers to lead the club to League titles. PA IMAGES

Right: Nottingham-born Herbert Kilpin, one of the founders of A.C. Milan and the first Englishman abroad to enjoy success as player and manager.
PA IMAGES

Tom Watson, "The Geordie Messiah" became the first man to manage two clubs to League titles when he succeeded with Liverpool in 1901 having previously won with Sunderland. PA IMAGES

William Garbutt (Back row, 2nd left) with his Genoa team in 1924, the year in which they won the Italian Championship for the third time under his leadership. PA IMAGES

Jimmy Hogan (Back row, extreme left) trainer and coach pictured in 1932 with his Austrian "Wunderteam". PA IMAGES

Herbert Chapman is the only manager to have taken different clubs to success in both Championship and FA Cup. PA IMAGES

Sepp Herberger, manager of West Germany for "The Miracle at Berne" in 1954. The Germans defeated Hungary in the World Cup final having earlier lost 3-8 to the same opposition. PA IMAGES

Matt Busby pictured with Johnny Berry and Duncan Edwards as Manchester United under Busby were heading for another Championship. Less than a year later the 1958 Munich air disaster ended Berry's career. He survived but with almost every major bone broken and amnesia which wiped out any memory of the crash. Duncan Edwards, the greatest player of his generation, died in hospital 15 days after the crash. He was just 21 years old. PA IMAGES

Alex Ferguson and Jock Stein on duty for Scotland. They were the two most successful managers in the history of their clubs: Manchester United and Celtic.
PA IMAGES

Alf Ramsey talks to three debutants in April 1965 – Barry Bridges,
Jack Charlton and Nobby Stiles. Fifteen months later Charlton and
Stiles would play key roles in England's only World Cup win. PA IMAGES

Mission accomplished. Ramsey celebrates with Jimmy
Armfield, Bobby Moore and Nobby Stiles. PA IMAGES

In 1971 Liverpool were beaten in the Cup Final. On the team's return they were greeted by an estimated 500,000 people. Bill Shankly addressed the crowd.

"He promised us this team was going places. He vowed that he would take them back to Wembley and win it for us. And we believed him. (I was)... utterly convinced that the Cup Final defeat had been our darkest hour before the dawn. That Shankly's new side was destined for greatness. That they would win the F.A. Cup next season and that I would be there, finally at Wembley in the middle of it all and my life would be complete. But then if Shankly had told us all we were twelve-foot tall, had four arms and were about to invade Mars, we'd have believed that too. And invaded. It is the nearest I have been to a definition of pure charisma."

BRIAN READE – "44 YEARS WITH THE SAME BIRD" (PAN BOOKS)

The Baseball Ground Derby 1972. The goal that won a Championship. Liverpool's
Ray Clemence is beaten by this shot from John McGovern (out of picture).
It was a first League title for Derby County and for Brian Clough. PA IMAGES

Brian Clough and Peter Taylor celebrate Nottingham Forest's first League title in 1978.
PA IMAGES

He left Hibernian with the club near the top of the league and in the semi-finals of the Scottish Cup, having beaten Rangers in the quarter-final, Stein's last game in charge. He was instrumental in getting Bob Shankly in as his replacement before his own return to Celtic in March 1965.

There can have been few transformations in the history of football like that which he produced at Celtic. Yet again he was walking into a club whose team was struggling. In the remainder of the season league results were patchy but the club had reached the semi-finals of the Scottish Cup in which they beat Motherwell after a replay.

The significant aspect of this tie was the fact that Celtic players actually received tactical advice for the first time in their careers. In the final they met Dunfermline who had just beaten Hibernian and Celtic's win after twice coming from behind brought them their first Scottish Cup in twelve years. Facing into the new season and with a trophy already secured, Stein made just one new signing. He bought Joe McBride from Motherwell. This paid immediate dividends as McBride scored forty three goals in his first season at Celtic.

If there is a counter argument to the one that says managers have little influence, it must include Jock Stein's impact at Celtic. He managed the club from that March day in 1965 until 1978. Prior to his return as manager, the previous victories in league and cup had been in 1954 when he captained the team.

The war had been over for twenty years when Stein was appointed as Celtic manager. In that time, Celtic had won the Cup twice and the League once. The Cup win two months after his arrival in 1965 was just a prelude to the most successful period in the club's history. The League was won in 1966, the first of nine titles in a row through to 1974.

There were two years without the League before it was won again in 1977. After the 1965 Scottish Cup win, that trophy was won again in 1967, 1969, 1971, 1972, 1974, 1975 and 1977. That makes

The Double six times in this spell. Add the Scottish League Cup in 1966, 1967, 1968, 1969, 1970 and 1975 and the crowning glory of Jock Stein's illustrious career, the European Cup in 1967.

In 1970 a semi-final triumph over then mighty Leeds United took Celtic to a second European Cup Final, this time as favourites. While much was made of how Wim Van Hanegem dominated the midfield as Feyenoord shocked Celtic, it has to be said that Celtic played poorly on the night and whether it was overconfidence or just tiredness, they looked a shadow of the majestic side which had dismantled Leeds at Hampden and gone on to beat them again at Elland Road. And of course Feyenoord were led by a manager whose genius had not yet been fully realised, the Austrian, Ernst Happel.

Danny McGrain, that great post-Lisbon full back for Celtic, had been brought along as a young player on the fringes of the squad to that final at Milan's San Siro Stadium on May 6, 1970. He did not feel overconfidence had been a factor: "I don't remember any complacency — if enjoying themselves in training is complacency — but I don't think it is. And they'd all been there before in 1967. And they were using that experience of being in their first European Cup Final, and winning it."

McGrain described how he was in awe of Stein when brought into the club by Sean Fallon and was still in awe when playing for Stein at the 1982 World Cup in Spain. McGrain told a dressing room story which might resonate with students of Alex Ferguson's methods, bearing in mind how Ferguson regarded Stein.

"It was 1971/72. We were playing Hearts here at Celtic Park and Kenny (Dalglish) was playing. I was playing. We came in at half-time winning 2-0. So we come in to the dressing room, sit down, and the door almost breaks as Mr. Stein comes in. He just banged the door shut. I thought 'what the fuck's happening?' He headed for Big Billy (McNeill) and now, Billy was Caesar to us, and tore big Billy to shreds. We were winning 2-0 and he went to wee Jimmy (Johnstone) and gave wee Jimmy dog's abuse. And I'm thinking,

Kenny and I are thinking, 'if he's giving them stick, what's he going to say to us?' Then I think he said something to Harry Hood or Tommy Callaghan and then we had the door tapped, the referee wanted the teams out. So Kenny and I got to the door first and big Billy just came out behind us. I was shit scared. If he'd said what he said to these two players, wee Jimmy and big Billy, two of the greatest players ever, I'd have crumbled."

I asked Danny if the whole thing had been a set-up. He confirmed it had been but said it was not until he had finished playing in 1990 that the truth emerged. So even those who were in on the scheme did not have the temerity to leak the truth until it was truly safe to do so. Of course Stein was having the precise effect he desired on young impressionable players. "If he says this to an established international and club legend, what will he say to me?"

In football, all periods of domination come to an end and by 1978 Celtic's powers were slipping and Stein retired, handing over to Billy McNeill, the legendary European Cup winning captain. It was widely felt that a car crash in 1975 in which Stein was seriously injured, had impaired his powers thereafter.

On retiring, he believed he had an agreement to join the Celtic Board but instead found himself offered an executive role in a subsidiary pools company. Liverpool came to honour Stein with a testimonial game in 1978 and Bob Paisley encouraged Jock not to walk away from a game to which he had so much to offer. Both men were aware of how an ill-timed retirement had damaged Bill Shankly and Stein was now younger than Shankly had been when he retired.

Almost immediately, Jock was appointed manager of Leeds United. It was a posting to which he never really adapted and within weeks of his arrival the Scottish Manager's job became available. So after only forty four days, the identical term spent by Brian Clough, Leeds lost their manager, on this occasion without the bad feelings on either side and Stein became Scotland manager on his fifty sixth birthday, 5 October 1978. Having failed to make it to the

Euro Finals of 1980, he led Scotland to the World Cup Finals of 1982 where the team did not progress beyond the group stages.

By 1985 Scotland were once again on their way to the World Cup Finals in Mexico. On September 10, at Ninian Park Cardiff, Wales hosted Scotland in a World Cup qualifier which ended in a 1-1 draw. This result was sufficient for Scotland to make a play-off which would ultimately take them to Mexico. But the fact that this night will not be forgotten had nothing to do with the result. At the full-time whistle Jock collapsed and was pronounced dead shortly afterwards in the medical room of the stadium.

For all his achievements, and his extraordinary record at Celtic must be judged against their history prior to his appointment, once more the treatment of players, no longer of use, reflects badly on a man who appeared the ultimate all-round manager. John "Yogi" Hughes was scathing of Stein in his autobiography and in subsequent interviews.

Hughes was with Celtic on a month-long tour of Bermuda, Canada and the U.S. in 1966. His pregnant wife was rushed to hospital at home in Glasgow and suffered a miscarriage. A stunned Hughes was offered condolences by a journalist after a training session. The journalist was himself taken aback at the player's stunned response and apologetically said: "I thought Jock would have told you."

Later after Lisbon he was informed that he was no longer in Jock Stein's plans, something which came as a dreadful shock to a twenty-eight -year-old who believed he was entering his peak years. It was made clear to Hughes that if he failed to sign for Crystal Palace he would be left sitting in the stands, with no prospect of appearance money or win bonuses. This type of approach by clubs was common in those years. Players were not on big money. They depended on both appearance money and win bonuses to make a decent living.

Stein's legacy though is the restoration of Celtic in Scotland and making the club a force in Europe. To have won a European Cup with an entire team of local boys was an outstanding achievement, a team which cost next to nothing to assemble. Stein like his compatriot, Bill Shankly, was about the team over the individual and no matter how severe the setback, the team members had the belief that anything was possible. In this case it was.

Bill Shankly

"He wanted to build what he called a bastion of invincibility."

Phil Thompson on Bill Shankly

Bill Shankly, an abrasive and charismatic Scot from the little village of Glenbuck was appointed manager of Liverpool in 1959, a position he held until his ill-timed resignation in 1974. At the time of his arrival Liverpool had won five championship titles, two each in the first decade of the 20th century and in the 1920s and a fifth in 1946-47 just after the war. The club was relegated to the Second Division in 1953-54 and in the 1958-59 season their FA Cup exit was at the hands of non-league Worcester City prompting the decision to seek a manager who could restore the club to past glories.

Shankly, one of a family of five boys and five girls, was born in 1913 and played football at junior level in Scotland for Cronberry Eglinton while working for a living down in the mines. As the local coalmine closed he was unemployed for a very short time before his life turned for the better.

At eighteen he was spotted by a scout for Carlisle United and offered a career above ground. Within a year he had been transferred to Preston North End where he would remain throughout his playing career which was severely disrupted by the war. In all he was a Preston player from 1933 until his retirement in 1949. An FA Cup medal with Preston in 1938 was the highlight of his club career during which he won five Scottish caps.

On quitting as a player Bill quickly returned to Carlisle, now as manager, from 1949 until 1951. This was followed by managerial roles at Grimsby Town for three years, a year at Workington and four years at Huddersfield Town. Finally, the role that destiny had marked for him saw him take over at Liverpool. By the time he was through there were few who would argue with his statement: "Liverpool was made for me and I was made for Liverpool."

In post-war years at Preston he played with Tom Finney, someone for whom he had boundless admiration. Some years later Shankly was asked if a then prominent player was as good as Tom Finney. "Aye he's as good as Tommy," replied Shankly. "But Tommy is nearly sixty now."

His earlier appointment as manager of Grimsby followed a failed interview at Liverpool. In those days Liverpool still held the view that a manager should not have total control over team selection but that the directors should exercise their right to pick the team.

When again approached by Liverpool he was apparently asked by their chairman how would he like to manage the best team in the country, to which Shankly replied: "Why? Is Matt Busby packing up?" Clearly, he was never one to ingratiate himself with boards of directors. One famous quote of his will not have helped him win any boardroom support. "At a football club, there's a holy trinity — the players, the manager and the supporters. Directors don't come into it. They are only there to sign the cheques."

He had a massive belief in the potential of Liverpool and in the summer of 1961 a change occurred which made possible what was to follow. The arrival onto the board of Eric Sawyer from the Littlewoods organisation would prove as significant as Shankly's own installation as manager.

In the Liverpool Echo in 2009, John Prentice quotes the greatly respected former Liverpool F.C. Chief Executive Peter Robinson outlining how he had seen board minutes limiting expenditure on any one player to £12,000 at a time when the going rate for a top player was well above that.

A further minute said that every player should be seen by at least two directors before he was signed and if possible such players should be over six feet tall. Robinson described Sawyer, and his association with Shankly thus: "It was a partnership. Eric was a brilliant businessman. He was the man who built the Littlewoods empire into what it became — and as well as rebuilding the team, they started to rebuild the ground." Clearly, Sawyer grasped how their own guiding rules were making success impossible. He began to free up funds for Shankly's acquisition programme.

Shankly's criteria for success in football management were the ability to speak common sense and to be able to spot a player. And he himself achieved top marks if those were the yardsticks. He had a very clear idea of how he wanted football played. He believed in keeping it simple, give it and go, pass and move.

Training routines were geared to make this approach automatic on the part of players. They would play five-a-sides, sometimes three or even two-a-sides until they were fit to fall down. Intensive work with the ball improved skill levels. His early days at Liverpool were taken up with clearing out players, twenty four in all, and then identifying and signing the right men, as funds were freed up to enable this.

Players like Ian St. John and Ron Yeats were bought. Yeats, a colossus of a centre half was a source of great pride for Shankly who at his unveiling, invited journalists to marvel at this giant and to "take a walk around him." Willie Stevenson was bought from Rangers in 1962 and in 1963 Peter Thompson came from Preston who had previously been raided for Gordon Milne.

Shankly had also forged an immediate and very beneficial alliance with the coaching staff he inherited. This group was headed by Bob Paisley, Joe Fagan and Reuben Bennett. In Shankly's early days an old boot storage room at Anfield was converted into a room where the coaches could meet privately and discuss any and every aspect of their work and their players. Thus was born the legendary "boot room". The vital promotion to the top division was secured in 1961-62 with a team which included such home-grown emerging talent as Gerry Byrne and Roger Hunt, the scorer of forty one goals in that season and a future World Cup winner. Before long Liverpool had become a force, winning the First Division title in 1964, the club's first ever FA Cup in 1965 and the league again in 1966.

Phil Thompson talked about Shankly and his use of the wonderful phrase for what he wanted to achieve at Anfield. "He wanted to build what he called a 'bastion of invincibility,'" Thompson said. And as for the 'boot room' it was not just a meeting room for tactical discussions among the coaches, although that was its primary purpose. Thompson said you could get a call to drop in to the famous room. That usually did not bode well.

If a player had done anything that was considered out of order, he would be summoned to the room and told there was full awareness of whatever misdemeanour he may have been foolish enough to commit. The player would leave there regretting the error of his ways and swearing not to re-offend. And the chastising could be done by Shankly himself or more likely by his lieutenants.

As a personality, Shankly could not have been further removed from Herbert Chapman. Yet he shared the same attention to detail. Upon arrival at Liverpool, he forced the board to spend money on the playing surface. He had major work carried out on the training ground at Melwood which up to then had been a dump that did not even have running water.

Having assembled his squad, his training routines were focussed on making sure players were equipped to play the Liverpool way. He wanted skill, stamina and bravery in his players. Their skills were honed with routines including some he had picked up from watching Tom Finney in his playing days, particularly the famous "sweatbox" a four-sided small area in which balls were thrown from the corners at the player in the box, pressurising him into controlling the ball no matter how it came. Shortsided games were of an intensity that got players controlling and passing the ball at speed and doing so even when they were tired.

He is credited with virtually inventing the warm-down, now a feature of training sessions in all team games. His attention to detail revealed a sharp mind and a man with a clear vision of the type of football he wanted. His reward was to actually realise that vision with teams whose methods were a direct reflection of everything that had been done during the preparation process.

In line with the Chapman approach he wanted every club team playing the same way. Phil Thompson believes he should have got more credit for this approach. "He wanted and he got a like-for-like player in every position. When a first team player was injured or lost form, it was like a jigsaw where one piece got scuffed at the edges. It would be replaced by an identical but smooth piece. This led to seamless changes of personnel."

Thompson described how Shankly had an ability in the way he spoke to you which made you believe you could do anything. His own Liverpool debut in 1972 was a case in point. He was substitute at Old Trafford when only one sub was allowed. John Toshack got injured. Shankly instructed Phil to play behind Kevin Keegan but in front of the midfield so as not to disrupt the team or structure. Despite playing in an unfamiliar role everything went well for player and team as a 2-0 lead eventually became a 3-0 win.

From the off, he was not just interested in psychology, he was one of its leading practitioners. Opposition players were never talked about in the dressing room before games. The only likely Shankly comment on the opposition would be how he had just seen them walk into their dressing room and that they were shaking in fear. Players were constantly told they were at the best club in the world.

He would always turn a setback into something positive. Indeed, his positivity was the leading element which had him branded an obsessive. When he failed to sign Lou Macari, he told his players he only wanted him for the reserves anyway. During a team talk he told Ian St.John: "If you're not sure what to do with the ball, just pop it in the net and we'll discuss your options afterwards."

Hugh McIlvanney described him as a true romantic and it was said that the dip in standards between the league title win in 1966 and the next one in 1973 was due to Shankly's reluctance to move long serving players on. That slump may have been attributable to such a reluctance on Shankly's part but it may simply have been that having too many players of similar age in a side, leads inevitably to a decline until a new team has been built.

Liverpool were not entirely inactive during that period. The young Ray Clemence cost £18,000 in 1967 and spent the next two years being prepared to become the No.1 goalkeeper at the club, a position he would fill with distinction until 1981. Emlyn Hughes was signed from Blackpool also in 1967 for £65,000. Brian Hall came in 1968 straight from University complete with a B.Sc. in Maths. 1969 saw Alec Lindsay arrive from Bury for £67,000 and Shankly had to replace the colossus, Ron Yeats, whose signing brought him such pleasure, with Larry Lloyd, a fairly impressive physical specimen himself, who was bought from Bristol Rovers for £50,000.

The second University graduate was signed from a local junior team in 1970 and Steve Heighway went on to win five league championships and three European Cups. The re-building was still not complete but the acquisition of Cardiff City's John Toshack for £110,000 coupled with Heighway's arrival meant the attack was taking on a fresh and potent look. The addition of Keegan from Scunthorpe for £35,000 would rank as one of Shankly's shrewdest decisions and with the Scot Peter Cormack arriving from Forest for a further £110,000, the squad was as strong as any that had worn the red of Liverpool.

And so in 1973 Liverpool were back as champions of England. This was the club's eighth league title and the third under Shankly. Winning the UEFA Cup in that same year was a tremendous breakthrough. It was Liverpool's first European trophy and the first time any English team had won a European trophy and the league in the same year. Many, including the distinguished journalist Brian Glanville, would say that it perhaps should not have taken that long for European success.

Back in 1965 having reached the semi-final of Europe's premier competition, the European Cup, they were unfortunate enough to encounter Herrera's Inter with the notorious Mr. Solti in the background busily corrupting referees. Some of the decisions of the referee, Ortiz de Mendibil, in the San Siro game were beyond questionable. Having won 3-1 at Anfield, Liverpool lost 0-3. Glanville described one goal as having been scored directly from an indirect free kick with another coming after the ball had been kicked from Tommy Lawrence's hands. Shankly's European consolation was the UEFA Cup of 1973 to go with the league. The FA Cup again was won in 1974.

So what exactly was it that made Shankly different and Liverpool successful? After all, being an obsessive is not necessarily a characteristic which leads inevitably to success. Quite often, the opposite is true. But one of his obsessions was the need to have players who had command of the ball, players whose skill levels would never betray them when the pressure came on. He preached the mantra of football being a simple game, of the basic objective being to pass the ball to someone in a red shirt and move for the return pass.

He was one of the first tracksuit managers and established a better relationship with his players than had he spent those hours in an office. He created a culture of team solidarity, a united dressing room, a climate wherein players enjoyed going to work and enjoyed the mutual trust and confidence that extended from the boot-room through the dressing room and made Liverpool a force in the land and beyond. It was his relationship with the fans that made him unique. The singing of anthems, the adoption of "You'll Never Walk Alone" cannot be underestimated. Anyone who has been inside Anfield on match day, or more particularly on a European football night, can vouch for the extraordinary atmosphere which exists to this day. That all began with the charismatic Bill Shankly.

Sadly, for all his undoubted charisma, the affable and quotable Shankly could treat a once-great player with the same lack of empathy and consideration shown by Matt Busby and Jock Stein in their worst moments. Ian St. John was a true "great" of the Shankly era. He has written of how, late in his career, he arrived for a game at St. James' Park and bumped into Jackie Milburn, then working for a newspaper. It was Milburn who mentioned the fact he was not in the team, thinking the player would have known or may have been injured. St. John's own words explain his feelings: "To this day I cannot shake the belief that, at the end, Shankly let me down."

But by 1974 the 60-year-old Shankly described himself as "tired from all the years." His wife, Nessie, had been anxious that he quit and his daughter, Karen Gill, was quoted some years later as saying: "I think that perhaps it was tiredness, that football had taken its toll on him."

His resignation was confirmed by the club at a press conference in July 1974. It may well be that he believed he would be invited onto the board in a similar fashion to his friend and mentor Matt Busby at Manchester United. Whether it was as some had opined, that he would dominate the board meetings or whether it was a lingering resentment among some members at his earlier views on the usefulness and function of boards, the invitation never came. When he did go, his expressed wish was that his replacement would be Bob Paisley. Having been at Liverpool a lot longer than Shankly he had been a valuable coach and boot-room member during those years of recovery for the club.

It is a desperately sad fact that resentment at various slights seemed to dominate his life after retirement. This was the man who had found Liverpool in a pretty poor condition, on and off the field, stuck almost irretrievably in the Second Division, and had by sheer strength of character made them a world famous club with a world class team. In retirement, he initially went to look at training sessions at Melwood but people began asking what he was doing there. He attended home games but sat well away from directors and club officials. He felt Liverpool should have invited him to attend away games. When this finally happened and he was brought to the 1976 UEFA Cup Final in Brugges, he felt insulted because he was placed in a hotel away from the official Liverpool FC party. He wrote that he was more warmly received at both Manchester United and Everton.

He is yet another example of someone who played in really hard times and who spurned the opportunity to look after his own players when doing so would not have been too difficult. Ian St. John described how his basic weekly pay had risen from £30 when he first joined Liverpool all the way to £35 ten years later. It was the win bonuses and attendance related bonuses that made the difference.

At one point the gap between the players' achievements and rewards became, as St. John put it, 'quite grotesque'. The players formed a deputation to see Shankly and the board of Liverpool F.C. seeking an increase of £10 per week. At a time when the club was at its very peak, generating massive revenues from 50,000 home gates, the players eventually got £5.

Whatever of the club's failure to treat Shankly in the manner he felt appropriate, eventually much was done to redress this but sadly the acts of reparation came after he had succumbed to a second successive heart attack leading to his death on 29 September, 1981 at the age of 68.

In 1982 the Shankly Gates were erected at the entrance to the Anfield Road Stand. In 1997 a bronze statue of Shankly was unveiled outside the stadium. Following his cremation his ashes were scattered at the Kop end of the Anfield ground.

His love for and affinity with Liverpool's supporters made this by far the most appropriate place for such a final gesture. For the record, his success list over fifteen years in charge consists of three league titles, two FA Cups and a UEFA Cup. However, more than any single trophy won, it was his transformation of Liverpool from Second Division also-rans to a powerful winning club, built on proper foundations and with proper values that had Bill Shankly so revered by a support that really would have followed him to Mars.

Harry Catterick

"We don't need a badge. Blue shirts and white socks.
Everyone knows that's Everton."

**Harry Catterick on being told the Everton shirts
would have a crest added for the 1966 Cup Final**

While Bll Shankly was performing a restoration job on Liverpool, a manager with as different a personality as could be imagined was making a decent fist of managing neighbours Everton. Harry Catterick's reign at Everton ran in almost exact parallel to that of Bill Shankly a short distance across Stanley Park. Because of Catterick's closed personality, distrust of and disdain towards the media, his work and achievements went largely unheralded while Shankly's words and witticisms were widely reported.

Shankly managed Liverpool from 1959 to 1974 while Harry Catterick was Everton manager from 1961 until 1973. During the sixties Everton accrued more league points than any other team including Liverpool, Manchester United and Leeds United. Their trophy haul at a time of intense competition was a respectable two Leagues and one F.A. Cup and only once in that decade did Everton finish outside the top six. This antithesis to Shankly was old school. Goodison Park's equivalent of the Anfield boot-room was only partly jokingly called the "bollocking room".

Team sheets at Everton had the players' names in alphabetical order lest any outsider discern how they might line up. Catterick's veiled opinion of his contemporary across the park was that any fellow who seeks popularity has something wrong with him. Shankly reciprocated by referring to the dour Catterick as "Happy Harry." But Catterick was a knowledgeable football man and a shrewd judge of players. One of his best ever signings also provided him with an opportunity to get one across on his neighbour. Having agreed quite a coup to bring Howard Kendall from Preston, he called a journalist and gave him the "exclusive" that Liverpool had signed the brilliant Kendall. "Shankly Swoops for Kendall" made a great headline. Kendall's unveiling as an Everton player would embarrass Shankly and infuriate the unfortunate journalist whose subsequent calls were avoided by Catterick.

While the effusive Shankly died of a heart attack in 1981 at 68, his nemesis died while watching a game at Goodison Park in 1988, also of a heart attack at age 65. And when it came to not treating players well as their careers ended, he was down there with the best. Alex Young had been a star of the Everton teams of the sixties, a top forward for the club and for Scotland in those years. He had an agreement to receive £1,000 when his career would end. When the time came he approached Catterick who laughed in his face telling him he should have got it in writing.

In football, whether the person appointed is loved by the media and adored by the fans or despised and distrusted by the media and tolerated by the fans, makes little difference. The real need is to understand the game, to have a clear idea of what is required in a team and its components and to be able to get the most out of the players at his disposal. In the sixties the city of Liverpool had two practitioners who knew what it took, who were excellent judges of players and who provided not just attractive football but effective, winning football.

Bill Nicholson

"Intelligence doesn't make you a good footballer. Oxford and Cambridge would have the best sides if that were true."

Bill Nicholson

The 1960s was an amazing decade in England. It is remembered for the changes in society, the musical revolution led by The Beatles and the excitement of the fashion scene epitomised in Carnaby Street. It was a time of change, of a country emerging from post-war depression with a new and creative generation with no memories of that war. In football too it was a truly unique decade which brought joy and hope to so many. Eventually it would see the

World Cup won at Wembley Stadium. The European Cup would finally reach British shores through Celtic and Manchester United. But 1961 brought an extraordinary achievement to a team whose manager had served the club as player and trainer before taking the reins in 1958.

Born in Scarborough, Bill Nicholson was a one-club man. At sixteen he was taken on to the ground-staff at the North London club and signed as a professional two years later in 1939. War could not have come at a worse time. Nicholson served in the Durham Light Infantry Regiment, the same regiment in which the famed conductor Sir Malcolm Sargent had served. As a footballer he was chosen for physical education and became a sergeant-instructor training troops. The experience gained in this role provided a foundation for his eventual move into management after his playing career ended.

Despite the disruption, he enjoyed a playing career which lasted until he was thirty five and in which he gained an England cap as well as winning the Second and First Division titles in successive years, 1950 and 1951. That Tottenham team was managed by Arthur Rowe and featured Nicholson's playing colleague Alf Ramsey at full-back. Coaching the Tottenham first team was as far as the Yorkshireman had ever expected to go in football and his appointment as manager surprised him more than it did others.

Throughout Nicholson's time in management he was regarded as a first-class coach. Brian Glanville described his method as "isolating a weakness and concentrating on eliminating it." While assisting at the World Cup in Sweden in 1958, he was credited with devising the plan that enabled England to hold the eventual winners, Brazil, to a goalless draw.

Although he was somewhat lacking in great man-management skills, his vision of the game and judgement of players was sufficient to turn Tottenham into a powerful, winning team. In 1959 Les Allen came from Chelsea for £20,000 while three players were bought north of the border; Dave Mackay from Hearts, John White from Falkirk and goalkeeper Bill Brown from Dundee for a total spend of £66,000. Adding these players to a squad that already included Danny Blanchflower, Maurice Norman, Cliff Jones, Terry Dyson, Peter Baker, Ron Henry and Bobby Smith would soon pay enormous dividends. In 1960-61 Spurs took off at a blistering pace winning their first eleven games in the League.

Only Sheffield Wednesday and to a lesser extent Wolves offered a real challenge. The league was won with a record equalling total of sixty six points and the defeat of Leicester City in the FA Cup final meant the double had been achieved for the first time in the 20th century. The Cup was retained the following season and the team was considered unlucky to lose the European Cup semi-final to Benfica.

Nicholson followed the double win with an immediate swoop for Jimmy Greaves, still only twenty-one and desperately unhappy at AC Milan. In 1962-3 Spurs became the first British team to win a European trophy when they hammered Atletico Madrid 5-1 in Rotterdam in the final of the Cup Winners Cup, Greaves scoring twice on his way to becoming Tottenham's all-time top scorer. Spurs under Nicholson had further success with his third FA Cup win as a manager in 1967, two League Cups in 1971 and 1973 and a second European Trophy, the UEFA Cup in 1972.

His time at the club is frequently referred to as the "glory years" partly because of the successes but also because that word "glory" somehow became synonymous with the team and its manager. "Glory, glory alleluia and the Spurs go marching on", became the anthem of their supporters in the sixties. Writer and inveterate Tottenham fan Hunter Davies wrote a Tottenham story, 'The Glory Game', published while the most famous quote from Nicholson is his brief philosophy on football:

"It is better to fail aiming high than to succeed aiming low. And we of Spurs have set our sights very high, so high in fact that even failure will have in it an echo of glory."

Don Revie

"You get nowt for being second."

Don Revie

In 1961 just two years after Bill Shankly had taken over at Liverpool, a man with whom he would develop a deep rivalry, was appointed manager of Leeds United where he would remain until 1974, the same year as Shankly's Liverpool reign ended.

Don Revie had been a great player, Footballer of The Year in 1955 and an FA Cup winner with Manchester City a year later. Revie's role in that team and for England as a deep lying centre-forward was decades ahead of its time and in an age when players' input to tactics was completely unheard of, City's method known as 'The Revie Plan' was quite exceptional. However, it was as a manager that Donald George Revie would be remembered. As his playing days were nearing an end at Leeds, he was initially appointed player-manager but it soon became clear he should concentrate on the management side which was more than a full-time job.

Leeds were in the Second Division and not particularly well equipped to buy their way out of trouble. The importance of the Chairman-Manager relationship was never more evident at a club. From Chapman at Arsenal, Clough at Derby, Sacchi at Milan to Ferguson at Manchester United, they all proved the rule that simply being good at the job is not enough. In every case they needed time and that meant a fully committed and supportive chairman.

Leeds Chairman was Harry Reynolds and he gave the inexperienced manager what has been described as 'unfaltering loyalty.' Revie sought and got better conditions for the players. He decided on a youth policy and set about attracting the best young players. A tribute to his persuasiveness is the tale of how Eddie Gray signed for Leeds. It was calculated that no fewer than thirty five of the top clubs north and south of the border wanted to sign Scotland's best schoolboy player in a generation.

"A scout for Leeds one day came up to me and asked if I'd go down to Leeds and to be perfectly honest with you, I'd never heard of Leeds United. Because when I was growing up in the fifties and early sixties, the big teams in England were Wolverhampton Wanderers in the Stan Cullis era and the Busby Babes of Manchester United.

Anyway, I decided to go down to Leeds, basically just for a weekend. And that's when I first met Don Revie. Now the club had no tradition but Don impressed me so much and I was only here for two or three days, it was the winter of 1962. I got back to my mum and dad and I says 'I'm going to Leeds.' Mum and dad could not believe it, especially my dad. Of course he wanted me to go and play for Celtic and he more or less said 'why?'

"I said because of the manager...Don never sent me training with the trialists. He took me training with the first team, which right away impressed me. He had the attitude that if you want to sign a boy you better look after him. (Because of the lack of major funds) Don formulated an idea. He was going to try and sign the best schoolboy players in the country. He already had Billy (Bremner) at the club so now he started to get the likes of Jimmy Greenhof, Peter Lorimer, myself — as many good schoolboys as he could get."

Revie's signing of Peter Lorimer, another superstar in the making was more dramatic as it involved arriving at the young player's home at 2.00 a.m. to get his signature before a rival came knocking next morning. While waiting for youth to develop, Revie had to keep the club from sinking even further as they struggled in the Second Division. He signed Scottish goalkeeper, Tommy Younger and Sheffield United full back Cliff Mason but it was his third signing of a mature player that was the turning point for Leeds.

Bobby Collins, the diminutive firebrand arrived from Everton to take over in midfield from the player-manager. Jack Charlton described Collins influence: "He was only a little guy, about five feet six inches tall, but he was a very, very strong, skilful little player. But what marked him out, and what made the difference to the Leeds sides he played in was his commitment to winning. He was so combative; he was like a flyweight boxer. He would kill his mother for a result. He introduced a sort of 'win at any cost' attitude into the team. Probably because we had a young side at the time, the other players were very much influenced by his approach to the game."

With a team consisting of Bremner and Charlton whom Revie had inherited, the veteran Collins, FA Cup winner, John Giles, who had come in from Manchester United and a group of the young players he had been developing, the Second Division title was won in 1964. By then the manager had changed the club colours to all white a la Real Madrid. He had also prevailed upon the chairman to foot the bill for the best hotels when Leeds played away on the basis that there was little point telling players they were good and valued and going somewhere as a team if that somewhere turned out to be a dingy boarding house.

Revie and Leeds were famed for producing dossiers on opposing players and teams. The origin of this was a request by Revie to his coach Syd Owen to assess a particular player and report back to the manager. Owen produced a detailed account of the player's strengths and weaknesses that so impressed Don Revie he was inspired to develop the idea and to have such reports done on all opposing teams as a matter of course from there on.

Having made it to the First Division, Leeds United went on to become a force in the land, competing every season for most competitions. But the culture of the dossier was to be Revie's greatest weakness. In contrast to his fellow Middlesbrough native, and sometime nemesis, Brian Clough, the obsession with the opposition was what prevented Leeds achieving as much as their talent deserved. At their best they were a fantastic football team, strong in every department. Both John Giles and Eddie Gray expressed the view that had they been let off the leash, much more could have been won.

What Revie's team did win was two League Championships but finishing second on five occasions indicates missed opportunities.

One FA Cup win and three times runners-up reflects further consistency but also tells of further missed opportunities. That Leeds team won one League Cup and two Inter-Cities Fairs Cups, also losing two finals in that European competition and they lost the European Cup Winners Cup Final in 1973 before losing the European Cup Final to Bayern Munich in Paris in 1975, even though they had dominated the Germans for most of the game.

Their consistency was such that in ten years their lowest finishing position in the First Division was fourth on one occasion. One unappreciated aspect of Revie's ability was the manner in which he changed player's playing positions with dramatic effect. John Giles had been an outside right at Manchester United but was switched to midfield in a highly successful move. Terry Cooper was an outside left, turned into a brilliant left full back. Eddie Gray had come to the attention of all those scouts as an inside left or more usually a left half or No.6. Revie moved him to the left wing. In the words of Gray himself: "When Don came to the club, Norman Hunter was a failed inside forward and was on his way out the door. Don made him into a centre back alongside Big Jack." Hunter would later win the inaugural PFA Players' Player of the Year award in the 1973-74 season as well as becoming a mainstay in the England team and a consistently brilliant performer for Leeds United.

Revie went on to manage England. After several managers had failed to maintain the standards of the Revie years the club flourished briefly before entering a decline that sees them out of the Premier League and showing little sign of returning. There had been allegations that Revie had tried to fix games, most famously from Bob Stokoe then at Bury who insisted Revie tried to buy a game to ensure safety in the Second Division.

He departed the England job in haste having found his dossiers were poorly received and his efforts at creating a bond between players a failure. He was slated in the press for negotiating his next contract to manage the United Arab Emirates while still in the England job. After three years in the Emirates he had spells with clubs in Dubai and Egypt before retiring to Scotland. He was then diagnosed with Motor Neurone Disease and died at just 61 years of age in 1989.

Bob Paisley

"The sort of lad I'm looking for is a kid who will nutmeg Kevin Keegan in training and then step aside him in the corridor."
Bob Paisley

While Leeds United under Don Revie underachieved and then failed to manage continuity when replacing Revie, quite the opposite was the case at one of their greatest rivals, Liverpool. If the Shankly years saw recovery of a once great club, the next manager of Liverpool was set to take them to unprecedented success.

Promoted from within, Bob Paisley, in his nine years managing Liverpool, took the club to new heights. He had spent thirty five years at the club before being appointed manager in 1974. The man from County Durham won an Amateur Cup Final playing for Bishop Auckland in 1939 following which he immediately joined Liverpool F.C. War interruption notwithstanding, Paisley played until 1954 and was part of the Championship winning team of 1947. He was in the 73rd Regiment of the Royal Artillery and served with Montgomery's Eighth Army. At one stage he was based in Naples and cited the eruption of Vesuvius as the most thrilling spectacle he had ever seen. When Liverpool won their first European Cup under his guidance, beating Borussia Monchengladbach in Rome, he said: "This is the second time I've beaten the Germans here. The first time was in 1944. I drove into Rome on a tank when the city was liberated. If anyone had told me I'd be back here to see us win the European Cup thirty three years later I'd have told them they were mad!"

Like Shankly, Paisley had a keen interest in physiotherapy and excelled in that practice after his playing career ended. His thirty five years of service before being appointed manager were as a player, captain, physiotherapist and coach. No one knew or understood Liverpool, the club or its supporters, better than the naturalised Liverpudlian Bob Paisley. And as coach to Shankly he had already played a significant part in the restoration of Liverpool F.C.

One of the strangest aspects of Paisley's ascent to the managerial throne at Liverpool is not that it took so long but that clearly, he did not have the desire or ambition to manage the club. Thoughts of becoming manager in Paisley's earlier days may have been stifled by the prospect of dealing with committees and boards of directors and the lack of authority to do the job as one saw fit without frequent and mostly unwelcome interference.

Brian Glanville described the managerial transition and contrasts in character rather well: "Paisley had none of the idiosyncrasies, the sublime intransigence, of Shankly. He was a quiet man who wore baggy suits and took any criticism of Liverpool to heart. He didn't want the job, he said, at first, but was finally persuaded to take it. He did it uncommonly well, a natural heir to Shankly in all but temperament."

Phil Thompson had a simpler explanation for Paisley's reluctant ascent to power. "Bob was introverted and particularly disliked the thought of having to deal with the press. He was so shy and uncomfortable speaking in public, he could not even do a team talk. As a motivator he did not function at all. But he had others like Joe Fagan and Ronnie Moran to do that and it never caused any problem."

Much of what he had contributed to Liverpool under his predecessor was on their tactical approach and he had been a key figure and a much respected one within the club. During Shankly's final year as manager there had been internal discussion about Europe and specifically why Liverpool could dominate in England yet find difficulty in Europe against teams which did not appear to be of the highest level. The conclusion was that a more patient approach was needed. Liverpool, whose style was already regarded as the nearest to a European game would have to become more European. One of the consequences was the replacement of Larry Lloyd with the young tall midfielder Thompson, the replacement of a stopper centre half with a more skilful ball player, in this case a converted midfielder.

Liverpool already played the pass-and-go style so common among the better European teams. They just decided they had to start the process from the back rather than after the ball had first been cleared. In Bob Paisley's first year Liverpool finished second in the League. In the next year, 1976, they recovered their title and in his nine years in charge they finished outside the top two only once, with six Championships and two second place finishes.

Under Paisley, success became domination. And that extended to Europe where the club won a first European Cup in 1977 in Rome, having already taken the league title. The other two European Cup wins under Paisley were in 1978 and 1981, two of the three years in which league titles were not won, demonstrating the difficulty of competing for the top prizes on two fronts.

Paisley was a genial man and a superb judge of footballers. One of his initial reservations was a concern that he did not have the same charisma as Shankly and that he would have difficulty dealing with the media. He was hardly in the job when two journalists gave him the hardest time with constant criticism of his every action. Also, he found the administrative side of the job a real struggle, as he had feared it would be. Club secretary, Peter Robinson, then stepped in and arranged that he would deal with the press while the administrative work would be carried by other staff members, thereby freeing Bob to concentrate on what he wanted and liked doing, dealing with the playing side of things.

Having been appointed after Shankly's resignation in July 1974, he was barely in the hot seat when the Charity Shield game came around. It would turn out to be one of the most remembered Charity Shield games ever, featuring a punch-up between Kevin Keegan and Billy Bremner of Leeds. Bremner and Keegan were both sent off and as they left the pitch they both threw off their shirts. This latter gesture was considered a crime more serious than what had gone before. Keegan was given a three match ban for fighting and a further eight games for removing his shirt. As the website LFCHistory so brilliantly put it: "It's a bit like a man on trial getting 15 years for murder and an additional 37 years for contempt of court."

All of this meant the new manager would be deprived of his star player for the first eleven games in a forty two game campaign. It was no wonder they could "only" finish second. But by the following season, 1976, Paisley had Liverpool back at the top as League Champions with the UEFA Cup won for good measure. 1977 brought another League title, this one twinned with the club's first European Cup. The European Super Cup was then added making it the most successful year in Liverpool's long history.

Kevin Keegan's departure to Hamburg that summer was seen as a massive setback for the club. At Hamburg, he would twice win European Footballer of the Year in addition to a Bundesliga title but that Hamburg team's European Cup Final appearance ended in failure at the hands of another great rival of Liverpools — Nottingham Forest. The question for Paisley was how to replace Keegan.

In one of the smartest pieces of business ever conducted, the twenty six year old Kenny Dalglish, just eighteen days younger than Keegan, arrived from Celtic in time for the new season, having cost less than the proceeds from Keegan's sale. In his first year, he confounded the sceptics who had doubted Paisley's judgement and the player's ability. Thirty one goals in sixty two games was an impressive return. The following year, his second in England, saw Dalglish voted Footballer of the Year, having scored the winning goal as Liverpool retained the European Cup against Club Brugges at Wembley Stadium. He went on to become a greater Anfield legend than his illustrious predecessor.

For the man whose decision it was to plump for Dalglish, his success was no surprise. There have been few managers with Bob Paisley's eye for a player. In his time he either bought or brought through Phil Neal, Terry McDermott, Alan Hansen, Graeme Souness, Alan Kennedy, Ronnie Whelan, Ian Rush, Steve Nicol, Joey Jones and Craig Johnston. His decision to convert the former Arsenal striker, Ray Kennedy, to a midfield player proved a masterstroke reminiscent of Herbert Chapman, and lauded by Brian Clough.

As Phil Thompson put it: "He bought Ray Kennedy and changed him from a striker to a left sided midfielder and in doing so added to the team a stream of goals from midfield." Thompson said Paisley was tactically brilliant but that it was in his judgement of players that his genius was most evident. Furthermore, he learned a lesson from the experience with Bill Shankly, where a winning team was kept together a bit too long leading to a decline before the next team was built. Paisley never let the decline happen through constant renewal.

Once again, a manager noted for his very pleasant demeanour was well capable of ruthlessness when it mattered to Liverpool FC. Graeme Souness told a tale of how he had been injured and then dropped a glass on his knee, leaving a wound which required several stitches. Liverpool were to play next day and although his replacement had done an adequate job and believed he should hold his place, Bob Paisley wanted Souness back despite his additional cut knee problem. He said Paisley only saw what was best for the team and acted accordingly, dropping the other player without the slightest hesitation.

Despite having to take the tough decisions, and showing no reluctance to do so, the dressing room remained a united and happy one during Paisley's nine-year tenure. He retired at the end of the 1982-83 season in which the League and League Cup had both been won and in which he would be awarded an incredible sixth Manager of the Year award. Bob Paisley went on to serve Liverpool as a director up to his retirement through ill health in 1992. He died on February 14, 1996 (coincidentally Kevin Keegan's birthday) aged 77. The Paisley Gates at Anfield were named after him, complementing the Shankly Gates. Fittingly, the two men who had done most to make Liverpool FC a world famous club are now remembered by the supporters with whom they each had an extraordinary bond and with whom they shared unprecedented success and joy.

Bobby Robson

"Good morning Bobby."

"You're Bobby. I'm Bryan."

**Exchange between England Manager,
Sir Bobby Robson and team captain, Bryan Robson**

That Sir Bobby Robson is best remembered for his extraordinary capacity to get names wrong is not necessarily an entirely bad thing. He provided unquestioned entertainment in that regard as well as in a general ability to mix up words rendering many utterances meaningless, and usually in a quite hilarious manner. The most oft repeated story was how he would mix up people, in this instance two black players from his Newcastle United team. Shola Ameobi, unable to answer a question as to what his nickname might have been is eventually asked, "Well what does Bobby Robson call you," to which came the reply: "Carl Cort."

And it was not something which reflected any decline in his faculties because Bobby, famously, back in his Ipswich management days, apparently could never remember Eric Gates name.

That this idiosyncrasy of Robson's is treated with deep affection by all who encountered the man is a tribute to someone who stood for everything that was good about the game and the business of football. He was honest, friendly, gentlemanly, decent and phenomenally hard-working. He was devoid of pomposity and hubris and was never given to bullshit in all his years in the game. And those years included what must have been some personally difficult challenging times. When he died in 2009 it was as a result of his fifth battle with cancer in just under twenty years. His battles included surgeries, including one operation for the removal of a brain tumour.

Born in 1933 in County Durham, a fruitful region for the production of footballers, he grew up a fan of Newcastle United. When it became clear that the young man had what it took to make it in football, he was disappointed that Newcastle showed no interest as he signed for Fulham in distant London. The son of a coal miner, Bobby Robson knew the meaning of hard work and made himself a better player to the extent that he represented England on twenty occasions. His playing career in England lasted from 1950 to 1967, starting and ending at Fulham with a six-year hiatus from 1956-1962 when he played for his only other club, West Bromwich Albion.

His move to West Bromwich represented a record fee paid by the midlands club. The man making the decision to spend heavily on wing-half, Robson, was Vic Buckingham, no bad judge of footballers as he proved again when discovering the young Johan Cruyff.

While Bobby Robson's playing days yielded nothing in the way of trophies, over six hundred appearances at the highest level represents a seventeen year career of real consistency. It was as a manager that Robson would make his mark. His last appointment as a player was at Vancouver where he was engaged as player/manager immediately his playing days at Fulham had ended. Soon the London club summoned him back in a late and vain effort to avoid relegation

Only in football does someone learn of their sacking from a newspaper vendor's billboard. Having had the publicly declared decision confirmed in private, Bobby Robson moved on and was soon appointed manager of Ipswich Town. The rural club was owned by the brewing Cobbold family who achieved legendary status for the integrity they applied to the running of their club. Their decision to appoint the young and unproven Robson was one of their best. He would not bring them world domination but showing a clear understanding of the circumstances in which he would operate, he was a perfect fit for the Suffolk club. Showing mutual loyalty, the manager and board worked together for thirteen years. At the end of this period, Robson's standing was such that he was an obvious choice for the England job. During his Ipswich years he steadily crafted a team which played open attractive attacking football. Fittingly for a club outside the heavily populated regions with their large fan bases, a youth policy was followed with astonishing success. Correct recruitment and coaching methods would have to produce what other bigger clubs produced by way of writing large cheques.

In this respect Bobby Robson's accomplishments were quite remarkable. A production line of young players was established. The club consolidated its position in the top division and in time began to challenge for silverware. Expenditure in the transfer market was limited – very limited, amounting to the acquisition of an average of one player every year of Robson's time in charge. But the carefully selected players were, to a man, an addition to the home-grown boys.

Among those signed from elsewhere were Allan Hunter, Paul Mariner, Arnold Muhren and Frans Thyssen. Home-grown talent included, Kevin Beattie, Alan Brazil, George Burley, Terry Butcher, Eric Gates, Mick Mills, Brian Talbot, Colin Viljoen and Trevor Whymark.

The result of Robson's team-building was consistency in league performance as the team rarely dropped below the top six once the first four years of spadework and been undergone. An FA Cup win over Arsenal in 1978 and a UEFA Cup success in 1981 brought trophies and glory to a club which had known nothing of either since Alf Ramsey's ascent some twenty years before.

His career trajectory would soon replicate that of the previous successful Ipswich manager. In 1982 Bobby Robson was appointed manager of the England team. Failure to qualify for the 1984 European Championships in France, was a severe setback. It was felt that the only thing which kept Robson in his job at that point was that Brian Clough was the obvious replacement. The FA had no stomach for appointing their greatest critic. So Bobby survived.

England qualified comfortably for the 1986 World Cup in Mexico. It is a tournament remembered as much for the manner of England's quarter-final defeat to eventual winners Argentina, as for anything that happened afterwards. Diego Maradona's second goal was unquestionably a work of prodigious skill as he slalomed through an England team leaving a trail of fallen opponents in his wake and slotting the ball past Peter Shilton. However, his earlier "Hand of God" goal is one of the key moments in World Cup history. Bobby Robson was quick to give his honest and entirely understandable appraisal of that particular act. "It wasn't the hand of God. It was the hand of a rascal. God had nothing to do with it. That day Maradona was diminished in my eyes forever."

A very poor 1988 European Championship appearance in which England lost all three games in Germany led to further pressure on Robson. Again he survived and then, in 1990, he led his country to their best ever performance at a World Cup on foreign soil. Two draws and a win over Egypt was enough for England to top their group and advance with fellow qualifiers, The Republic of Ireland and Netherlands. A 1-0 win over Belgium and a 3-2 extra time defeat of Cameroon, saw England reach the semi-final to be played in Turin. The game against West Germany ended in a 1-1 draw before England's old failings cost them a final place as they went out 3-4 on penalties.

Identical score-lines in the other semi-final meant Argentina qualified for a repeat final against West Germany, with the Germans avenging their Mexico defeat thanks to a late penalty in a foul-ridden entirely forgettable game of football.

Undoubtedly England were unlucky not to have won their semi-final and to lose through poorly taken penalty kicks was a most unsatisfactory end to a tournament which had given Bobby Robson hope that history could be made by his team. Prior to the tournament the manager knew his contract would not be renewed and immediately afterwards he made the somewhat surprising move to PSV Eindhoven. At this time PSV had been very successful, the high point being their European Cup success in 1988. They were also reigning league champions and the Englishman continued this pattern, leading the club to two further league titles during his two years at the helm.

Continuing to show a sense of adventure, Robson moved to Sporting Lisbon. Some eighteen months later, the club which he had quickly discovered to be completely dysfunctional, sacked him while his team were top of the league. Maybe he should have applied the Bela Guttman principle that a manager's contract should include a stipulation that this could not occur. However, with the chairman of Sporting it seemed virtually anything was possible and Robson's time there saw repeated player arrivals about which he had known nothing in advance.

Porto saw an opportunity and hired the former England boss. This was a happier move, made with his Sporting Lisbon interpreter, a young man called Jose Mourinho, in tow. Two League titles and a Portuguese Cup were won in Bobby Robson's two seasons at Porto before he was recruited by Barcelona. The interpreter had been upgraded to assistant manager at Porto where Robson also gave a coaching role to another young man called Andre Villas-Boas.

In his one and only year at Barcelona, he took the club to a Copa Del Rey win over Real Betis and a European Cup Winners Cup victory over PSG. While Robson's tactics were not always understood by Barcelona fans, fresh from living on Johan Cruyff-led triumphs, his personality and inherent decency, good humour and honesty had endeared him to all of Catalonia as a result of which he was offered an upstairs role at Barcelona. Despite this, his relative success in filing the giant hole left by the sacking of Cruyff brought him the award as European Manager of the Year for 1997

Within a year he answered a call from PSV and returned to drag the club to Champions league qualification on the final day of the season. In September 1999 Bobby Robson was appointed manager of the club he had supported as a boy, the club which disappointed him greatly by ignoring him as a young up-and-coming local lad. His final job as manager of a football team would last five years until 2004. He found a Newcastle United club which must have had echoes of Sporting Lisbon, with its Chairman Freddy Shepherd and Deputy Chairman, Douglas Hall, providing anything but convincing leadership to a club with a uniquely passionate fan base.

Robson brought some stability to the club. They qualified for the Champions League in 2002 and 2003 but were unable to progress to the lucrative latter stages of that competition. After a poor league start Sir Bobby Robson was dismissed in August 2004. While he may not have been held in such high regard by the people who dismissed him, he was made a Freeman of the City of Newcastle just five months later in March 2005, reflecting the respect in which he was held by everyone else within and outside football in the city.

He briefly acted as a consultant to the Football Association of Ireland in 2006-7 in that body's effort to provide support to a young and inexperienced team manager. His declining health and final battle with unrelenting cancer was reason enough to finally retire from the game he loved and the game he served with impeccable character over his lifetime.

4

Brian Clough

"Brian Clough's advice to me on my debut for Forest, away to Liverpool was; 'Get it – pass it to one of your teammates and move – can you do that?' And I went, 'Yeah, of course I can do it.'"
Roy Keane – The Second Half

BRIAN CLOUGH keeping it simple when and where it mattered most.

"Idiosyncratic, eccentric, wholly unpredictable from one blink of an eye to the next...capable of being unforgivably rude, unnecessarily cruel, appallingly bombastic and arrogant...he could be extravagantly generous, emollient and warm, ridiculously kind, and loyal to whoever he thought warranted it." This was a description of Brian Clough from Duncan Hamilton, someone who knew him well.

There was never before or since anyone quite like Brian Clough. There are other words which could be applied to Clough such as charismatic, counterintuitive, mischievous, impatient, cantankerous as well as brilliant, successful and unique.

What made him different from any other manager was his complexity. He was all of those things and a lot more besides. He frightened the living daylights out of the FA who to their eternal discredit, would not give him the England job. His reaction to that was: "I'm sure the England selectors thought if they took me on and gave me the job, I'd want to run the show. They were shrewd because that's exactly what I would have done."

While at Derby, Clough called Blackburn trainer Jimmy Gordon who when they had both been at Middlesbrough had been Clough's greatest critic. Gordon assumed the only possible reason for this call was an approach for full-back Keith Newton. Instead he was offered the trainer's job at Derby County. His immediate response was to remind Clough that all they had ever done was argue. Clough replied that this was precisely why he wanted him. The story shows that behind a lot of the superficial stuff around Clough he understood one of the fundamental truths of excellent management, a truth contained in a piece of advice from John Wooden the legendary basketball coach — "surround yourself with people strong enough to change your mind."

Much has been made of the Leeds United days, few but lucrative as they were. It was known that before Leeds, to everyone's astonishment, appointed Brian Clough, Don Revie had canvassed hard for John Giles to succeed him. Giles would later prove his ability as a manager at West Bromwich Albion and the Republic of Ireland. So if any Leeds player had a right to feel resentment at this appointment Giles was the one. However, he has always acknowledged that Clough had a persona, an indefinable quality that as he put it "made you want to impress him."

Clough and his long-time sidekick Peter Taylor claimed never to concern themselves with anything as mundane as tactics. The evidence is that while they never filled their players' heads with statistics about the opposition, they could spot a threat and ensure that someone was allocated to deal with it. You don't win what they won without an acute awareness of what you are up against. But it was typical of Clough and of Taylor for that matter. Create an air of mystique wherever possible. Pre-match team meetings were not filled with debate about the opposition. Players have been known to talk about Taylor regaling them with tales from his past that had them rolling with laughter. No doubt Taylor's ability as a stand-up comedian was put to good use to distract nervous players in the run-up to a big game.

Clough, famously on the eve of a Wembley League Cup Final noted that his players looked tense and drawn and fearing several of them would have difficulty sleeping that night, had a solution. The players were taken to a meeting room in their hotel, given several magnums of Champagne and told no one leaves until this lot has been finished. Result: relaxed team and victory.

Martin O'Neill had this to say regarding Clough and coaching: "One of the great myths was that he was a manager, not a coach. The fact is every day was a coaching lesson from Brian Clough. When he came down to the training ground you would pick up enough in a 25 minute spell to last you a lifetime."

Clough's frequent media assignments made him a household name. While establishing himself as a manager he was a regular TV pundit and had deals with newspapers for columns to appear under his name. Such quotes as: "I wouldn't say I was the best manager in the business .....but I'm in the top one" drove the legend of his arrogance. But he said so much more that made sense he is always worth quoting. There was a practical common-sense and an ability to inspire that is so rare as to be almost unique to the man. He could be cutting. There is the story of the former Wolves manager Sammy Chung expressing criticism of the Forest players' level of fitness and claiming to Clough that he would have them all throwing up if he got them for fifteen minutes on the training ground. Clough replied that when the League started awarding points for that he would give Chung a job.

It is one of the great tales of football that a young Scot called John McGovern would win a league title with Derby, play at Leeds during that notoriously ill-fated sojourn and finally captain Nottingham Forest to League Cups, the First Division championship and two European Cups. Unappreciated by many in the football world, here was a player whose career was a model and who ultimately performed a critical role on the field. Clough and Taylor saw qualities in the young Scot that had them put him in a Hartlepool first team at sixteen. His glorious career is as much a tribute to Clough and Taylor and their judgement as it is to John McGovern himself. McGovern described Clough: "Unique, he saw things differently, he acted differently, handled players differently to anyone else."

When Clough and Taylor arrived at Derby they were in the old second division and struggling. They had to quickly identify the players they would keep and those who had nothing to offer. They then had to identify their replacements and go about securing the new players. There was nothing simple about doing that and getting it as right as it could be. Clough himself described what it was that had brought himself and Taylor together and how the partnership worked. "We were mates."

An example of how brilliantly it worked was in those early days at Derby where Taylor would identify the player they needed and Clough would go and persuade the target to help them turn Derby County into something great. Roy McFarland was a youngster at Tranmere Rovers when Taylor told Clough they had to sign him. Clough went to Tranmere to an evening game. Realising other clubs had become aware of the teenager he insisted on striking a deal with Tranmere immediately after the game. That deal became famous for the pretend phone conversation conducted by Clough with an imaginary Derby Chairman as he used the fake call to confirm the maximum figure Derby could agree for McFarland.

He then persuaded the Tranmere manager to guide him to where McFarland lived with his parents. By then it was around midnight. The player was roused from his bed and having grasped what was going on wisely said he would sleep on the offer and let his visitor know the following day. Clough told him that was no problem, that he would stay in the spare room that night and get his signature at breakfast. That did it. McFarland signed and went on to become one of the best centre halves ever to play for England. And Brian Clough went back to his Derby home.

Archie Gemmill, another player selected by Taylor was more stubborn. In this case Clough slept the night in the spare bedroom of Gemmill's Preston home and got his man next morning. Gemmill himself had already decided he would go to Everton who had held discussions with the player and his Preston North End employers. The promise by Clough to Mrs. Gemmill of new carpets in their next home was the clincher. They then went back to Hartlepool for John McGovern.

Their greatest coup was the signing of Dave Mackay from Tottenham. The double winner was on his way to take up the role of assistant manager at Hearts when Clough arrived. Despite being told by Bill Nicholson, one of the managers he most admired, that he had absolutely no chance of changing Mackay's mind, Clough persisted and talked Mackay into coming to Second Division Derby County as a player. Even more outrageously he and Taylor then informed Mackay that he would now have a completely new role. He would play as sweeper. They always maintained that this was the most important signing they made. Derby won the old Second Division in 1969, their second season in charge and became league champions for the first time within three years.

In terms of pure management skills and vision the identification of Mackay was the first step. Persuading him to join a club about which he knew very little was the second. Getting a man who was ending a career in London for a new one in Edinburgh to scrap all of that and relocate to Derby was plain evidence of Clough's powers of persuasion. Clough himself declared that while he had previously said he had never seen anything that was perfect "Dave Mackay playing in that Derby defence was as near to perfection as makes no difference."

Following their initial League success Derby embarked on a first ever European Cup campaign. This took them to the semi-final where Juventus were their opponents. The first leg in Turin was lost amid controversy. It was noteworthy that the only two Derby players booked, Roy McFarland and Archie Gemmill, were the only two Derby players carrying yellow cards into the game. These further cards meant they would now miss the return leg. Juventus though were the better team on the night and finished 3-1 winners.

Clough was apoplectic after the defeat in Turin refusing to speak to Italian journalists claiming: "I will not talk to any cheating bastards." The return leg ended predictably in a scoreless draw but before the game the appointed Portuguese referee declared he had been offered a significant inducement to see that Juventus won. Subsequent investigations showed that Dezso Solti the notorious Hungarian fixer had been behind the offer.

A lengthy investigation by The Sunday Times and Brian Glanville uncovered some hair-raising evidence regarding Solti and his actions over the years on behalf of Inter and Juventus. But he always managed to be one step away from the club, providing them with deniability. As to his endeavours around the Derby/Juve semi-final, UEFA investigated and found that Juventus did not have a case to answer as Solti had acted independently.

When in 1973 just a year after that first League Championship win Clough and Taylor walked out of Derby County, Mackay was appointed manager. It was the first step in a pretty undistinguished managerial career which peaked fairly rapidly with a second ever league title for Derby in 1975 under Mackay's stewardship but with a team largely put together by Clough and Taylor.

For a man who achieved so much Clough had some serious misgivings and regrets. The joint resignation by Taylor and himself from Derby County was one of his three great regrets. He remained convinced that had they stayed there they could have turned Derby into what Manchester United became under Alex Ferguson.

When Clough and Taylor resigned from Derby County in October 1973 they never expected their resignations would be accepted. Eighteen months earlier they had resigned but within hours matters had been resolved when Derby Chairman, Sam Longson, gave them a wage increase.

This time they were furious at the interference of a newly arrived Director who wanted to know why the club needed them both and asked to meet Peter Taylor so he could have Taylor explain to him what exactly he did at the club. While joint management teams were almost unheard of at the time this was a club, a founder member of the Football League in 1888, over whose ground the League Champions pennant flew for the first time. Here was a busybody who knew nothing about the game sticking his nose into an area where it was unwelcome. Clough and Taylor were right to be peeved. Unfortunately, their solution, resignation, was the wrong call.

There was no denying who had brought the success to Derby. The inspirational and clinical assembly of a winning team, the transformation of a club and indeed a town could never be over-stated. The brilliance with which this was done was quite extraordinary. One would have said it was a once-off, something so difficult to do that it would never again happen in English football. Except that within a few years they went down the road and did it all over again. Only this time they did it even better. Derby was going through a pretty rough time with massive layoffs at Rolls Royce and miners strikes having an extraordinarily damaging effect on the local economy and on local morale. The football club was an oasis of success and of promise of a brighter future in what was otherwise a very dark bleak time for the town.

In his final years Clough saw in Alex Ferguson what might have been for him. It is hard to argue that given what was achieved later at Forest, that the initial success at Derby could not have been turned into something long-lasting. That untimely and ill-judged resignation became one of those tragic regrets as the man who had led a fabulously successful career in football management looked back at the road not taken and the parallel life not lived and yearned for what might have been.

His other great regrets were centred on the irrevocable break-up with Peter Taylor and the failure of the FA to appoint him England Manager. One can only wonder what might have been had someone at the FA got the nerve or the imagination to have made Brian Clough England Manager. Clough had also resented the fact that he received only two full England caps while banging in goals at a higher rate than anyone else. As he said in another context, looking back at such events: "Here I come with another chip on my shoulder to go with the rest."

Brian Clough was born in Middlesbrough on March 21, 1935 the sixth of nine children. His parents were hard-working and his mother in particular was a great influence. Upon leaving school at fifteen he was taken on at the local ICI plant. He played football for more than one junior team and was apparently willing to turn out several times a week, often leaving him exhausted when it came to the working day. He was soon recruited by Middlesbrough, his prodigious scoring achievements bringing him to their attention, ten goals scored in a 16-0 win being an example of his precociousness. At Middlesbrough he turned professional on his seventeenth birthday but was soon in Scotland briefly before being stationed in Somerset on his two years of National Service. Others had been able to obtain a posting nearer to home but Clough was left frustrated that a senior officer wanted him playing for the regiment and so kept him in the south, a long way from home and too far away to facilitate his career at Middlesbrough Football Club.

Eventually his national service complete, he resumed life at Middlesbrough but soon realised he was a long way from first choice with manager Bob Dennison. This led to further frustration but it also led to what was to become a long-term and extraordinarily successful friendship with Taylor. During his post army days at Middlesbrough Clough was third choice centre forward and bursting with frustration. Taylor came to him and said the right thing. "I can't work out what's going on at this place. You're the best player in the club."

It was the re-assurance that he desperately needed. Taylor was a few years older than Clough but they shared an interest in football bordering on the obsessional with how the game should be played, with how things could be done better. Their visits to a coffee shop on the way from training resulted in condiments being used to illustrate how a team might be set up or how a manoeuvre might be carried out. Their coffee shop of choice in Middlesbrough was Rea's, owned by the family of another man who would achieve success in a different field — Chris Rea.

Clough eventually made it into the Middlesbrough first team and proceeded to score goals as he knew he could. At the time Middlesbrough were in the Second Division but no matter how many goals Clough scored the defence contrived to concede in sufficient numbers to ensure promotion would not be achieved. A 6-6 draw at Charlton Athletic with Clough scoring a hat-trick was, for him, evidence that something untoward was going on at the club.

He raised the matter with Bob Dennison and separately with a director who was also a solicitor but nothing came of those efforts to cast a spotlight on possible wrong-doing. Some years later, one of the two defenders whom Clough suspected of betting against their team was jailed as part of a bribery scandal within football. Having made 296 appearances for Middlesbrough in which he scored 267 goals, Clough was glad to accept a transfer offer from Sunderland where he would go on to score thirty four goals in forty three games in his first season. In his second and fatal season, by Christmas he had twenty four goals scored in the same number of league games before his career was cut short at twenty nine years of age by a knee injury which turned out to be to a ruptured cruciate ligament, something which in those days was irreparable.

Alan Brown had brought Clough to Sunderland and he credited the manager with teaching him discipline. His other influence was a man who had managed Peter Taylor and who had also previously managed Derby County and whose common-sense and words of wisdom greatly impressed both Clough and Taylor. That man was Harry Storer.

The Jonathan Wilson biography of Clough takes its title from Storer's words in relation to what a manager should expect from certain quarters most notably from directors: "Nobody Ever Says Thank You." Clough rejoiced in passing on one great piece of advice from Storer which centred around getting on the bus for a difficult away game. Storer's approach was: "Count the hearts".

Having tried to return to fitness Clough had to acknowledge the futility of the task. Sunderland got their insurance payment and he got £1,000. His immediate concern as reality dawned was that he needed to earn a living. He was a young married man with two small children and a footballer's income in those days provided little opportunity to save for what in Clough's case had become about as rainy a day as one could imagine. A benefit game yielded around £10,000, an exceptional sum in those days demonstrating how popular he was with the Sunderland supporters. Alan Brown had moved to Sheffield Wednesday but his replacement George Hardwick gave Clough an opportunity not only to continue earning but to do something he really believed in — to work with the youth players at Sunderland. It was the start he needed, the first step on a managerial career.

In 1965 Clough was offered the position of manager at Hartlepools United (later to change their name to Hartlepool, dropping the s). At thirty he was the youngest manager in the entire league. The club was a sad joke, perennially seeking re-election to the league, a fate which in those days awaited the bottom clubs in the Fourth Division. So bad were things at Hartlepools that a former manager and the by now available George Hardwick both turned down the opportunity to breathe life into the moribund club. However, Hardwick recommended Brian Clough and with the legendary former Sunderland player Len Shackleton also pushing his case, he was given the job.

With Taylor on board as assistant manager, so began the first step for a duo who would conquer Europe. In echoes of Herbert Chapman's acceptance of the manager's job at Northampton, indisputably they were at the worst club in England. Financially it was a mess. Off the field Clough began to stir up interest in the area doing whatever it took to get publicity for the club and already making claims that they would soon rise from the depths. He and Taylor were not above painting the dressing rooms and stand. Clough got a licence to drive the team bus, something which had practical benefits for an impoverished club and enormous publicity benefits as the media lapped up this type of story.

The chairman who brought Clough in was erratic. Clough's own description of his appointment went as follows: "Their chairman, a little bloke called Ernie Ord who turned out to be an absolute shit, offered me the job." At one point Ord tried to have Clough sacked. This was during an unseemly row between Ord and the board over money which Ord had put into the club and which he was now demanding be re-paid. It is not clear how he dragged Clough into the argument but he was shown the door by the other board members who by then appeared to have come around to Clough's opinion of Mr. Ord.

Clough and Taylor signed players on free transfers or because they were free agents. They signed one player on the basis that Hartlepools would visit his existing club for a friendly from which the home team could retain all gate receipts. Against this background they managed to avoid relegation while wheeling and dealing to shift deadwood and get in some players who would bring about improvement.

Having avoided the re-election process, the team finished in a very respectable eighth place the following year. By now Taylor was becoming tired of the battle against the odds. Undoubtedly they were making progress but money was still a huge issue both in terms of getting in better players but also in terms of their own earnings. He had a word with Len Shackleton asking him to keep an eye out for a better club, a better opportunity.

That was how an approach from Derby County came about. The period between Derby and Nottingham Forest is probably the most bizarre in their managerial and coaching careers. During their final year at Derby, the Clough-Taylor relationship began to disintegrate. Clough was concerned that Taylor was not delivering the new players, especially young players. Taylor was showing signs of increasing insecurity and concern that Clough was not only earning more than him but was receiving wage increases while he was not.

Taylor ended up spending several weeks in hospital with chest pains while seeing little of Clough who it must be said, had a deep pathological aversion to injuries and illness, but the experience could only have further fed Taylor's paranoia. The protests after the dual resignations had been accepted dragged on for weeks, with the possibility of a players' strike at one point.

Clough and Taylor bizarrely agreed to take over at Brighton & Hove Albion in the Third Division. Albion were not just in the wrong division they were in the wrong part of the country. Clough himself admitted as much when he later said it had been crazy to try to manage on the south coast while continuing to live in Derby.

He appeared to want to rule by fear, something which had a negative effect on most of the players who were in awe of him any-way. They saw less of the manager than they had expected. His bullying approach seems to have been at its worst. On one occa-sion he flew to New York to attend a world heavyweight boxing bout missing a Brighton league fixture. Players were brought in and some better performances happened but there was a discon-nect between the south coast club and a man who still harboured the idea that Derby would have him back, long after that door had closed forever.

Meanwhile Brighton was not a particularly big club to begin with. Like many Third Division sides they were operating on very limited resources with the usual debts and concerns about their viability. It was the kind of club that was at home in the Third Division with players who were at home in the Third Division and who would have regarded being there as their appropriate station in life while Clough would have regarded this as a complete lack of ambition. His personal demons prevented him ever taking to the task like he had at Hartlepool and his success at Derby County made him intolerant of the calibre of club and players to which he had mistakenly hitched his star. After one season Clough was on his way to the team he had openly criticised more than any other in his role as TV pundit and newspaper columnist, Leeds United.

Initially Brian Clough had a regard for Don Revie but his apparent turning point came during a trip to Leeds when he visited Revie in his Elland Road office after a game. The referee who had just officiated came to the doorway and thinking Revie was alone, enquired if his own performance had been to Revie's liking. According to Clough, the Leeds manager made an effort to shush the referee and have him move quickly along.

There were other unsubstantiated allegations against Revie but we can only go on Clough's version of this particular incident to try to explain why Leeds became the subject of so many Clough tirades. As to what possessed Leeds United to hire Clough, he himself said Leeds chairman Manny Cussins told him that the Derby County players' willingness to go on strike for their manager meant he must be a really good manager. Clough's reasons for accepting were more complex.

Peter Taylor stayed on at Brighton having agreed with their chairman that he would continue alone once Clough went north. On Clough's arrival at Leeds he encountered a mature team which had won a lot but a lot less than most neutrals would have felt they should have won. There was a feeling abroad that Revie, with his obsession with the opposition and dossiers on their players, over-complicated matters and created inhibitions in his own players.

These were accusations that certainly could never be levelled at Clough whose whole approach was to keep it simple, talk about your own team and not the opponents. To start by telling this group of players to chuck their medals in the dustbin because they had won them by cheating could never be a prelude to a decent relationship.

In his autobiography Clough appears to allude to the fact that by not trying to work with John Giles he missed a chance to turn Giles into the successor to Peter Taylor as his right hand man. This makes sense and it might have been the only way to go if Clough were to get any level of co-operation from the players at Leeds. His distrust of Giles was misplaced and he himself acknowledged that in later years. Clough lasted forty four days at Leeds before being sacked. It had been a disastrous experience for Leeds. They had won just one game of the six for which Clough had been in charge and now had to pay up on a contract they should never have put in place.

For Clough the financial compensation eclipsed the footballing failure. Duncan Hamilton wrote that the compensation of £92,000 was the making of Clough. It gave him financial independence for the first time in his life and removed pressures and distractions, something which later helped him concentrate on the task he took on at Nottingham Forest. Clough himself made no bones about it: "The feeling of independence and security that Leeds gave me together with the sack was a big factor in winning so much during my eighteen years as manager of Nottingham Forest, not least the league championship and two European Cups. It meant I could approach the job without a financial care in the world."

Sacked in September 1974 by Leeds, Clough was back in football as Forest manager by January 1975, replacing Allan Brown (not to be confused with the former Sunderland manager Alan Brown). The team was in 13th place in the Second Division when he arrived. His first full season in charge saw Forest finish in eighth place after which in July 1976, he was again joined by Peter Taylor, some of those previous doubts notwithstanding.

A season later the pair had taken Forest to third place and promotion to the First Division. Replicating what had been done at Derby, they radically changed the team with players not deemed good enough quickly shipped out. Their golden touch in player selection was back. Clough's priority of getting a balanced team was once again to the fore. The emphasis, as always, was on skill, technique and team balance.

Martin O'Neill and John Robertson were transfer listed and

on their way out of the club when Clough arrived. With hindsight, given what those players achieved under Clough, their position on his arrival probably tells everything about how badly that club had been run. Nottingham Forest were languishing in the lower reaches of the Second Division and willing to dump players of this calibre who could have, and eventually did, help get them out of there.

The other players retained were Viv Anderson, Ian Bowyer, Tony Woodcock and goalkeeper John Middleton. Clough returned to Leeds to re-sign two players he had bought during his short time there. The two, John O'Hare and John McGovern were not valued by Leeds and both were sold to Forest at a loss. Archie Gemmill was once more united with the Clough-Taylor management team at a cost of £20,000. Peter Withe was cheap at twice that price while Frank Clarke came on a free transfer.

In a typical piece of Clough and Taylor magic, Kenny Burns, the Birmingham striker and proven goal scorer was bought for £150,000 and immediately placed alongside Larry Lloyd in a central defensive partnership. Lloyd cost £60,000 from Coventry two years after he had joined the Sky Blues from Liverpool for £240,000. At Liverpool he had won a championship as well as a UEFA Cup.

Clough's principles included having a strong spine to the team. Goalkeeper, centre half and centre forward were seen as critical. Beyond that the team had to have a balance. The structure of the team was deemed highly important but next came behaviour. Dissent of any sort was not tolerated. Players did not question a referee any more than they could question the manager. Kicking a ball away or doing anything which could be considered other than exemplary was unacceptable. Any failures were dealt with through fines and the behaviour changed or the player was out. That approach had been consistent throughout Clough's time in management.

The final piece in the Forest rebuilding process was a goalkeeper. Clough had long admired Peter Shilton who had a year earlier been bought by Stoke from Leicester City. Once Stoke were relegated Clough was convinced Shilton would soon begin asking himself what he was doing at some of the really unattractive and sparsely populated grounds in the old Second Division.

Clough knew where the crucial ground was and with the fixture list in front of him he knew it would happen sooner rather than later. So after a handful of games in the league campaign, the Second Division programme had Stoke away at a bleak Mansfield Town ground. Immediately after that game, Clough was in for and succeeded in securing a player who had twice previously eluded him when in charge of Derby County and later at Leeds United.

This transfer became the cause of severe criticism from all quarters at what was deemed an astronomical fee of £270,000 for a mere goalkeeper. But for a management team which constantly preached clean sheets, which obsessed about not giving goals away, the purchase of the best goalkeeper in the country was a logical step.

Clough believed Shilton was so important that he would have offered value at twice what he cost. With Shilton in goal from game six, the team conceded only eighteen goals in those remaining thirty seven league games, keeping twenty three clean sheets and setting a record for the lowest number of goals conceded in a season.

The handling of Shilton's signing showed Clough at his most idiosyncratic. Shilton explained that he had a couple of businessmen, friends of his acting as as advisors. This was before agents had come into the game. A meeting was arranged at The City Ground. Shilton and his two pinstripe-suited advisors arrived, were ushered into a waiting area by Clough, decked out in his squash gear and his green sweatshirt and told he would be with them in five minutes.

About an hour later Clough's secretary returned and asked them to follow her to the Manager's Office. The first advisor walked in the door only to go sprawling, his folders and files spilling in all directions. At this point Shilton realised Clough was sitting on the floor and using his squash racquet to trip the man. He thought, quite rightly: "These negotiations are not going to go well."

Shilton was distraught. He wanted to sign for Forest but the negotiations quickly broke down. Clough did not want to engage with the advisors. Next morning Shilton's home phone rang at 8.30. It was Clough saying he wanted to meet him in a hotel in Derby at 11.30. When the goalkeeper arrived he was met by Clough and Peter Taylor who had an open bottle of champagne on ice. Terms were agreed and as Shilton put it, he went on to the most successful time of his life in club football.

To complement all the on-field changes Jimmy Gordon was appointed trainer. Gordon had been brought to Leeds by Clough and left Leeds with Clough, finding himself unemployed before taking a job outside football in Derby. Despite his continued inability to like Clough the person, he did not hesitate to return to football in Nottingham working for Clough, the manager. It is a strange fact that many of those who showed extraordinary loyalty to Clough, among them players who would have gone on strike at Derby, had one view of him as a person and an entirely different view of him as a manager.

Stuart Webb who had come from a similar role at Preston to become Secretary at Derby, appointed by Clough, to the chagrin of Chairman Sam Longson, became someone with whom Clough had a mutual view which bordered on hatred. Webb once said Clough had at least five personalities. Archie Gemmill said: "I hate the bastard but I'd give him my last half-crown."

As well as the league title, Forest won the League Cup, defeating Liverpool 1-0 in the final replay at Old Trafford. And that league title was won by a margin of seven points by a team playing disciplined counter-attacking football, this at a time when a win was worth two points with one for a draw.

A game which many regard as the defining one in that glorious season was the meeting with Manchester United at Old Trafford in December 1977. But before Forest ever reached Old Trafford, a brilliant piece of management provided evidence of an ability to think under pressure and to move quickly finding not just a solution but a perfect solution.

At Forest, Larry Lloyd had formed a formidable defence barrier with Kenny Burns. Before the Manchester United game Lloyd was injured and worse news was that he would be out possibly for a couple of months. Centre back Dave Needham had moved from Notts County to QPR at the start of the campaign but Taylor had heard that, although playing well, he had not settled in London. Before anyone realised what was happening, Needham was a Forest player making his debut in that memorable Old Trafford game.

It was a game which illustrated, better than any other, Forest as a counter-attacking team without equal. On a not particularly great winter surface, defence was turned into attack with devastating pace, power and accuracy, to the extent that the 0-4 final result did not flatter Forest.

After the game, the Manchester United Manager, Dave Sexton said: "They don't play with eleven men. They seem to have sixteen or seventeen. When they attack, about seven of them come at you and when they are defending, there are about nine of them." It would appear the Arrigo Sacchi 'multiplier' theory that with proper movement and organisation a team could appear to have more than eleven players, the basis of his tactical beliefs, had already been tried and proven.

Following the title, Forest's first, Trevor Francis was acquired, becoming Britain's first million pound man. Rather surprisingly Peter Withe was sold to Newcastle United early the following season. Clough would have another crack at the European Cup, a trophy he always believed rightfully should have been won by Derby County were it not for the "cheating bastards." In the first round Forest were faced with the European Champions, a side aiming for a third consecutive European title. But Liverpool held no fears for the team from the City Ground. A 2-0 win there was followed by a 0-0 draw at Anfield in what was widely seen as a tactical master class from a management which professed not to bother too much about tactics. Gemmill man-marked Ray Kennedy and McGovern did likewise to Souness while Ian Bowyer took care of Terry

McDermott. Robertson was far deeper than usual. The clean sheet was on this occasion the only objective. Forest got their match-ups right and Liverpool's European domination was over.

A comfortable 7-2 aggregate win over AEK of Athens was followed by a similarly comfortable passage with a 5-2 aggregate victory over Grasshoppers of Zurich. The sale of Peter Withe meant promotion for Steve Elliott. Once it became clear he was unable to deliver, third choice centre forward, Garry Birtles, found himself playing European Cup football. Birtles scored in each of the rounds against Liverpool, AEK and Grasshoppers and was again on target in the first leg of the semi-final against Koln at the City Ground, pulling a goal back after Forest had gone two down within twenty minutes. The final score-line of 3-3 left Forest with an enormous task in the away leg. Once again, tactical smartness and counter attacking skills took them through thanks to an Ian Bowyer goal in what turned out to be a gruelling and difficult game.

And so it was that on 30th May 1979 at the Olympic Stadium in Munich, Nottingham Forest became champions of Europe. Their opponents that night were Malmo of Sweden and Forest could hardly have anticipated meeting so dull a team in so dull a game. The only spark was the goal created by John Robertson who fired over a cross which Trevor Francis, having sprinted in from the right, stooped to head home from close range.

Clough and Taylor had now taken Nottingham Forest from the depths of Division Two to the league title and on to be crowned Champions of Europe. Just as that display at Old Trafford before Christmas 1977 was probably the defining performance for this team, the first European Cup was the pinnacle. There would be more success but from now on Forest's journey was away from rather than towards perfection.

Retaining the League title proved a step too far. Forest's committee had agreed to proceed with a new stand which was budgeted to cost £2.5m. This was entirely driven by Clough just as the same issues and demands for a stand had been played out in his

Derby County days. But Forest were not supported as well as they should have been or as well as they deserved. Clough never hesitated to let the locals know what he thought of their lack of commitment to a club of which any population ought to have been proud. There were hooligan issues over the years at Nottingham which he tackled in his inimitable way, once clouting young fans that had run onto the pitch. There was the famous banner calling on the Trent end to stop swearing. This from a man who could eff and blind with the best of them demonstrated hypocrisy and ambivalence which were part and parcel of his complex character.

Gemmill had been sold after the European Cup win, ostensibly because he was in decline but possibly because he had reacted very badly to not playing in the Munich final. As a new season approached, Asa Hartford was brought in as a replacement for Gemmill. Two months later, after mixed performances, he was suddenly sold to Everton. Frank Clarke accepted that time had caught up with him and left to coach at Sunderland. Frank Gray was bought from Leeds as a replacement. Stan Bowles arrived from QPR but never settled. Charlie George came on a one-month loan and scored the winning goal in the European Super Cup win over Barcelona. The young reserve goalkeeper Chris Woods who had been brilliant when replacing the cup-tied Shilton, was sold to QPR, with an ageing Jim Montgomery coming in from Sunderland to understudy Shilton.

In their championship-winning season of 1977-78 Forest had amassed sixty four points, seven more than runners-up Liverpool with Everton third on fifty five. As Forest chased their first European Cup, Clough estimated sixty points would suffice to retain the League title. They duly finished with that precise total. However, Bob Paisley's Liverpool delivered him his third league title with sixty eight. By any standards, European Cup success, retention of the League Cup and second place in the league made 1978-79 a very successful season for the club. And so in 1979-80, England again would have two representatives in the European Cup, the same two as the previous season, with reversed routes to qualification this time; Forest as holders and Liverpool as league champions.

Forest started in Europe where they had finished so gloriously the previous season, playing the Swedish champions. A 2-0 home win courtesy of two Ian Bowyer goals and a 1-1 draw in the return leg against Oster saw them comfortably through to the next round. They would be England's only representatives as Liverpool took a 2-1 lead to the away leg with Dinamo Tbilisi only to lose 3-0 before a crowd of 90,000. The second round was wrapped up by early November with holders, Forest, progressing comfortably on an aggregate 4-1 margin over Arges Pitesti of Romania. Meanwhile Tbilisi were surprisingly exiting at the hands of Hamburg, who like Forest won both home and away legs in that second round.

The quarter finals would not come round until March. By then Tony Woodcock had been sold to Cologne. Meanwhile, Forest seeking a third consecutive win, lost the League Cup final to Wolves by a single goal from an untypical defensive mix-up involving Shilton and Dave Needham. Nor was there any joy in the league. It was won this time by a team with sixty points. Sadly for Clough, the team was Liverpool with Forest finishing fifth, which was an accurate reflection of how they had played throughout the campaign.

But Europe still held promise. In an amazing quarter final tie, they were the only team to lose their home tie with a first leg 0-1 defeat to Dynamo Berlin. But this was Nottingham Forest with Clough and Taylor at the helm. Where other teams may have faced the second leg psychologically damaged by the home loss, Forest seemed to be in quite a different frame of mind. Taylor maintained he watched the Dynamo players walk the long path from dressing rooms to pitch and their drawn faces convinced him they were filled with fear.

How much of it was true and how much psychology is hard to tell but he certainly convinced his players. They were fearless and whatever concerns the Dynamo boys took into the game they soon knew they had reason to be afraid. By the twenty fifth minute Trevor Francis had put Forest two goals ahead and a Robertson penalty four minutes later made it 3-0. A penalty conceded shortly after half time reduced the margin but Forest were in the driving seat that took them into the semi-finals again.

Next up was a club which had done it all before, a club which had rebuilt its team with only one remaining star from the side that won three European Cups in the early seventies. The team was Ajax of Amsterdam and the man the elegant Ruud Krol. On April, 9, 1980 Nottingham Forest beat Ajax in their semi-final first leg while Real Madrid were similarly dealing with Hamburg, both games won by 2-0.

The second legs, two weeks later told a different tale. Forest were given a roasting by a side which included Danes Soren Lerby and Frank Arnesen and which had been racking up huge scores during this campaign. But chalking up big scores against teams from Finland and Cyprus is a different task from facing Peter Shilton in his prime with Kenny Burns and Larry Llyoyd in front of him. Those three players took most of the credit for a defensive performance in Amsterdam, which although edgy at times was sufficient to restrict Ajax to just one Soren Lerby goal.

Forest were back in the final where they might have expected to encounter the home team at the Bernabau. After all, Real Madrid took the same lead to Hamburg as Forest had taken to Amsterdam. But Madrid were shocked as two goals each from Manny Kaltz and Horst Hrubesch and one from Memering gave Hamburg the most unexpectedly easy 5-1 result.

By the time the final was played on May 28th, Trevor Francis had suffered an horrific Achilles tendon injury in a league game so Forest would now field eight rather than nine of the previous year's winning team. Frank Gray was in for Frank Clark. Martin O'Neill who had come perilously close to being transferred earlier that season, was this time in the team and a young 100 metres sprinter, Gary Mills replaced the million pound Trevor Francis.

Once again it was 1-0 to Forest. Once again it was a dismal game for the neutral observer. But this time there was the spectacle of Nottingham Forest defending resolutely against a more attack minded team. Within twenty minutes, Robertson had scored after a typical Forest passing move started by Frank Gray and ended when Birtles played Robertson into a scoring position.

The management that had no truck with tactics got it tactically right as their five-man midfield cut out the supply lines to Kevin Keegan and to the giant Hrubisch when he eventually came on, having failed to start because of injury concerns.

The win meant that this relatively small football club became the only ones ever to win the European Cup more often than they had won their own Championship. No sooner was that second final success complete than the decline that had been hinted at became a sad fact.

Clough had an ability, among the many he possessed, to completely spoil a great occasion. After the Malmo game he demanded all winners' medals be handed over in the dressing room. He wished to have replicas made for several people around the team who would not have received medals. The basic sentiment was admirable but the method appalled.

Several players such as Larry Lloyd refused point blank, fearing they would end up with replicas rather than the real thing. Archie Gemmill virtually threw his medal at Clough, disgusted at not having played. In reality, it would have been so simple to have arranged to borrow one medal for the purpose of having the replicas made after which the original could have been returned to its owner.

Now, a year later, after the second great victory he demanded players return to a hotel an hour outside Madrid rather than link up with their wives who were based in the city. Again, through a streak of perversity, he spoiled a moment of great joy.

This was to be as good as it got for Forest. Taylor continued to exhibit paranoia because of the attention and credit Clough got for the successes. By winter 1980 Taylor's book, "With Clough by Taylor" was published. Clough claimed not to have known about this project but it later emerged that he had been aware of it for some time, though not via Taylor. He was annoyed about not being told and rather than confront Taylor, had chosen to await the publication and then make it an issue between them.

Birtles wanted out as his relationship with the manager declined and he was eventually sold to Manchester United. Ian Bowyer was sold to Sunderland, Martin O'Neill to Norwich. Larry Lloyd went to Wigan as player-manager. Trevor Francis, fully recovered from his Achilles injury was back, his form matching his reputation but his relationship with Clough, never great, was now such that his departure from Nottingham appeared inevitable.

And the cost of building the stand had increased. Any prospect of a third European Cup and the money such a run would generate was soon dashed. In the first round Forest were drawn against CSKA Sofia. A 0-1 away defeat was not considered a disaster but the return game at the City Ground could hardly be described otherwise. Forest never competed as they had done during the great days and ended losing by the only goal. CSKA progressed to the quarter finals where they were emphatically beaten, 1-6 on aggregate by Liverpool, on their way to keeping the title in England.

The new stand, the European elimination, the drop in attendances, were all critical factors in the demise but the transfer expenditure and what it brought was what expedited the decline. Young players such as Bryn Gunn a substitute in Madrid, Colin Walsh and Gary Mills represented the new-look Forest. They were supplemented by Mark Proctor costing over £400,000 from Middlesbrough. July 1980 saw Clough spend £1.25m on Coventry striker, Ian Wallace and the following month Justin Fashanu arrived from Norwich at a cost of £1.0m. But these were misjudgements, a sign that the Midas touch with which Taylor identified the players and Clough signed them, was suddenly absent.

Sadly, this was best illustrated in the case of Fashanu. The signing was an unmitigated disaster. It was to all intents and purposes a million pounds up in smoke. Fashanu had scored a spectacular goal for Norwich against Liverpool, which was selected as BBC Goal Of The Season but it proved an illusion as he failed to score many goals, spectacular or mundane, managing just three in thirty two games in a Forest shirt. In Clough's autobiography he expressed real regret at how he dealt with Fashanu and at his complete lack of sympathy and incomprehension at the player's homosexuality.

The player's suicide at thirty seven was something which affected Clough as he reflected on how brutally cruel he had been to a very young player, who did not ask to be bought for £1m. He was sent out briefly on loan to Southampton before the next step in a personally exhaustive journey through a multitude of clubs of various standards in several countries.

Having exited the European Cup in the first round, Forest could only look on as Liverpool recovered that trophy with a win over Real Madrid in the final. Aston Villa won their first league title in more than seventy years while ironically, the league's top scorer with twenty goals was Villa centre forward Peter Withe. Having endured the disappointment of being surprisingly transferred before Forest won their European Cups, Withe played a key role as Aston Villa became the latest English Club to win that great competition in 1982. Despite a couple of impressive 5-0 home wins Forest could do no better than seventh place in the final league table, ten points behind Villa whose total, ironically, was sixty points.

With three points for a win the following season, Liverpool were again Champions with Ipswich second as they had been to Aston Villa the year before. Forest were in a distant 12th place, not quite managing sixty points even under the new system. By summer of 1982 Taylor resigned saying he was tired and wanted to retire from football. Clough accepted this at face value and they parted on good terms despite some of the stresses and strains which had first emerged in their Derby days and which had impacted their relationship periodically at Nottingham Forest.

Six months later Taylor was announced as the new manager of Derby County. Clough was less than happy but soon that unhappiness would descend to something worse as Taylor signed John Robertson without consulting Clough. It caused bitterness beyond belief. Clough claimed he would sooner drive over Taylor than give him a lift if he found him on the Derby-Nottingham road.

The two men, friends from their Middlesbrough days and partners in astonishing success at Derby and Forest would never again exchange a single word. As tends to happen, coincidence brought their respective sides together in an F.A. Cup tie which Derby won and during which they completely ignored each other. Taylor soon grew tired and suffered ill-health causing his retirement. He died in the Canary Islands in October 1990. Clough was deeply upset at the death and dedicated a 1994 autobiography to Taylor. A statue of the two of them side-by-side has since been unveiled in Derby.

Brian Clough continued to manage Forest through the eighties. By 1982 they had sunk to finishing twelfth in the First Division. The remainder of the 1980s heralded stability and even a slight resurgence as once more Forest became a top three club, however fleetingly. They finished fifth, third, ninth, eighth, eighth again in 1988, third in 1989 and ninth in 1990. The League Cup which Forest had won in 1978 and 1979 was again won in 1989 and 1990. By now Clough was showing real signs of the effects of his alcoholism and in 1993 the unthinkable happened and Forest were relegated leading to his final departure from the club.

English clubs were banned from European competition from 1985 to 1990 following the Heysel Stadium disaster. As a consequence, a third place finish by Nottingham Forest was to no avail in respect of European competition. Because of this it transpired that his final assault on a European competition was the 1984 UEFA Cup. It was both ironic and desperately unjust that this campaign should end as it did. The man who refused to talk to "cheating bastards" after what looked like dodgy refereeing when his Derby County team was eliminated by Juventus at the semi-final stage of the European Cup was about to experience a repeat of history.

In the 1983-4 UEFA Cup, Forest were drawn against Anderlecht of Belgium in the semi-final. The first leg at the City Ground was won 2-0. The away leg saw Anderlecht win by three goals to nil. Forest had a perfectly good goal disallowed, a goal which would have been sufficient to take them through. The second Anderlecht goal was a penalty awarded when a Belgian forward went to ground inside the penalty area. The quality of the video available is not great but it does appear that the player was not touched. It is the disallowed goal however which provoked protests and demands for an investigation. Eventually, some thirteen years later, Guruceta Muro, the Spanish referee having died in a car accident in 1987, UEFA reported that he had been given a "loan" of £20,000 by Anderlecht before the game. That club was then banned from European competition.

Of all the cases of probable corruption to the disadvantage of English clubs, this is still the only one where a definitive verdict has issued. So, Brian Clough, still yearning to show he had not lost it, to show he could still set up a team to succeed in Europe, all those years after his first fatal foray with Derby County, was once again robbed, this time by confirmed cheating bastards. He was inconsolable.

The relegation in 1993 which brought an end to his career left him in anguish as he pondered what he might have done that would have avoided such an awful outcome. Later, as he reflected on that year he seemed more sanguine about what happened but was convinced that the alcoholism had played a huge part in impairing his judgement and affecting his performance.

His retirement years were spent reflecting on his regrets, struggling with the bottle and defending accusations of financial wrong-doing. The court case in which Terry Venables and Alan Sugar were in confrontation led to the Sugar quote about Venables, when he managed Tottenham, allegedly telling his Chairman, "Cloughie likes a bung." This was to explain where some additional money had to go during the transfer of Teddy Sheringham from Forest to Spurs. Clough always vehemently denied getting such money. Venables denied having said it. Sugar never repeated the accusation outside the courtroom.

In 1993 the FA set up an inquiry to investigate bungs but there was insufficient evidence against Brian Clough. However, his assistant Ron Fenton was found to have received sums for which there was no other explanation and was banned from working in England. Although those responsible for pursuing the matter felt Clough had been in receipt of bungs, a lack of solid evidence and the man's declining health put an end to that particular chase.

There were so many conflicting accounts of precisely how much was paid for Sheringham and how it was divided between player, club and player's agent, it was very difficult indeed to know who or what to believe. Clough's own appeal that he be judged on what he had achieved in the game and what he had to say about the game, however big headed it may have been, rather than for accusations which were never substantiated, shows the concern he had that his reputation had been irretrievably damaged by the widespread talk of what was undoubtedly an acknowledged and unsavoury practice within the game over many years.

As for his reputation in football, taking a team from the lower reaches of the country's second division to promotion and a first ever League Championship is not unique. Alf Ramsey, for one, did that. But repeating the exercise with a second team is quite extraordinary. And these were not two fallen giants. These were modest clubs in the British Midlands, neither of whom were seen as powers within the game. To take the first of those so close to European success and to follow up by taking the second to two European Cup wins, would not be accepted as a credible plot in a work of fiction.

Brian Clough, ably supported by Peter Taylor, was a man who brought success and hope to Derby when it was most needed. He was a man who put Nottingham on the map and who took Forest to unimaginable success. For these things he should be remembered.

5

Good & Evil
& Catenaccio

THIS chapter looks at the extraordinary Hungarian, Bela Guttman, intelligent, dynamic and charismatic, the first manager to supplant Real Madrid as European Champions.

It also looks at the contrasting personalities who brought the first European Cups to Italy, with the two Milan clubs. Helenio Herrera was credited with changing the perception of the manager. He had considerable success and a large ego, which made much of that success about him rather than about some of the great players he had at Inter in the 1960s. Nereo Rocco was the cross-city counter to Herrera and he too had historic victories with a club which today shares the honours for most international competitions won, A.C. Milan.

It was now the age of the manager as a personality. Just as the trend was towards descriptions such as "Matt Busby's Manchester United", it became "Herrera's Inter." Clubs were beginning to be defined by their managers.

Bela Guttman

"The third season is fatal."
Bela Guttman's advice to football managers

He has been described as the original Jose Mourinho, but upon closer inspection, he was a far more interesting character than the Portuguese. Mourinho could hardly be described as boring, but while there are some notable parallels in their careers, Bela Guttmann got around so much, it could be argued that parts of his career had parallels with those of many great and successful managers. Taking a Portuguese team to European Cup (Champions League) victory and managing in several countries including Italy are just two of the obvious similar experiences. A propensity to offend the right people and to make bold statements are a couple of other aspects of their personalities which help justify the original description.

Guttmann's biography, is as appropriately titled as any book on football. "A World History of Football in One Person."

Born in 1899 in Budapest, he died in what was his spiritual home, Vienna, in 1981. His parents were dance instructors and he too was a certified classical dance instructor by the age of sixteen. His background in dance brought him an elegance which assisted on the field, as football became his preferred choice of activity, taken as he was with the style of football in Hungary and Austria at that time. But what an amazing career he had.

As a player his success began in Budapest with the Jewish owned MTK as a twenty year old, winning two Hungarian League titles in only three years at the club, before moving to SC Hakoah Vienna. His next two titles were won under the management of Jimmy Hogan and given Hogan's reputation for having a lasting impact on those who played under him, no doubt the receptive Bela was the beneficiary of Hogan's great coaching skills. He was capped by Hungary on six occasions, this at a time when Hungary was one of the leading teams in world football.

Of Guttmann's six caps, two were at the Olympic Games in Paris in 1924. Bela took exception to the fact that there were more officials than players in the Hungary squad. He was further disgusted that the chosen hotel was far more suitable for socialising than for match preparation. As international career-ending moves go, his decision to nail dead rats to the doors of travelling Hungarian officials was probably among the more effective.

His management career got underway, at SC Hakoah Wien, where he served from 1933 to 1935 and again from 1937 to 1938 with a two-year spell in Netherlands at Enschede in between. His time in the Netherlands was not without its drama. He arrived to a team in a desperate relegation battle and was appointed by a chairman who readily agreed a huge bonus should Guttmann lead them to improbable championship success. By the following year, the chairman was, like the youth who sowed his wild oats, praying for crop failure. His prayers were answered as SC Enschede just missed out on a championship win which would have created a bonus liability big enough to bankrupt the club.

In 1939, back in Hungary, he took Ujpest to the double of both a Hungarian championship and outright victory in the Mitropa Cup. The war years and how he spent them became part of the mystery of Bela Guttmann. His brother died in a concentration camp and while it is believed he stayed in Switzerland, his answer to all such questions was always the same: "God helped me."

He also helped himself while in Vienna taking a degree in psychology, which would stand him in good stead during his many years in football management which he likened to animal training saying the same principles apply: lose your nerve, let fear show in your eyes and you are lost. But his football beliefs were pure. Guttmann wanted and got skilful attacking teams with the emphasis on positivity. After the war he managed Vasas SC of Budapest, Ciocanul of Bucharest, Ujpest FC and Kispest A.C., each for no more than a single year. Of these experiences by far the best story comes from his departure from Bucharest. Guttmann informed an interfering Ciocanul director that the best option was for him to take over the running of the team, as "you appear to have all the basics" while Bela would immediately depart for pastures new.

By 1949 the now fifty-year-old Guttmann took up his first Italian coaching position. Including this appointment at Calcio Padova, he would hold seventeen managerial roles over the following twenty three years. He would manage some of the greatest players in the history of association football and would carve a reputation as a truly great and gloriously eccentric manager. The Padova job came after he travelled to Italy, believing he had been appointed to AS Roma. Unfortunately, when he arrived at Roma, they professed to know nothing about any such arrangements. So Padova was a fortunate fall-back. The Padova directors, however, had this notion that Bela Guttmann may not have survived the war so included in his contract was a clause stating that were it to emerge that he was not the "real" Bela Guttmann they could immediately terminate the appointment.

After a single-season stay at Padova, Bela moved to U.S. Triestina Calcio, in the North East corner of Italy. The club had greatly over-achieved in the previous seasons under Nereo Rocco but Guttmann found little joy and little success as he and the team struggled through a difficult year. This may well be explained by studying the basis of Rocco's unexpected success — the deployment of 'cattenacio' — while Guttman's philosophy was infinitely more positive but not necessarily easy to implement when following a coach like Rocco.

Guttmann had always enjoyed a loyalty and friendship with the colleagues from his Hakoah Wien days. It was through these friends that, following the dismal days at Trieste, he found work managing first Quilmes of Buenos Aires and then APOEL of Nicosia. But these were short stopovers before the next call came from a big club and a return to Italy.

In 1953 he took over at AC Milan and managed a team which included the Swedish legends, Gunnar Nordahl and Nils Lidholm. In his second season at Milan, with nineteen league games played, the team was at the top of the table but a succession of disputes between manager and board resulted in the manager being fired. The subsequent press conference was marked by one of the most unforgettable departure lines ever uttered when Guttmann announced to a stunned audience: "I have been sacked even though I am neither a criminal nor a homosexual. Goodbye." Following his dismissal he joked to Brian Glanville that future contracts would include a stipulation that he could not be sacked while his team topped their league table.

Honved of the mid 1950s is one of the iconic names in the history of football. Having been taken over by the state and turned into the Hungarian Army team in 1949, they were close to being the national team. In the 1956 European Cup they were drawn against Athletic Bilbao. With such a fantastic line-up of Hungarian greats, everything most have looked positive to their manager, Bela Guttmann. But between losing the first leg 2-3 in Bilbao and the return leg, their world turned upside down. The Hungarian Revolution collapsed and the Soviet Union invaded. The second leg was scheduled for Brussels as the players were reluctant to return to Hungary. Their goalkeeper was then injured in that game and could not be replaced by a substitute. With the great Zoltan Czibor in goal, Honved drew 3-3 and were eliminated on a 5-6 aggregate.

The Honved players then declined to return home. Guttmann quickly arranged a fund-raising tour of Italy, Portugal and Spain during which Honved drew 5-5 with a Madrid XI and beat CF Barcelona 4-3. The European tour was followed by participation in a tournament in Brazil involving Botafogo and Flamengo. Honved, incidentally, declined an offer from the Mexican F.A. to move en masse to that country and join their league.

FIFA, prompted by the Soviets who by now controlled Hungary and Hungarian football, had quite disgracefully declared the team illegal. On their return to Europe, the players dispersed with Puskas famously signing for Real Madrid while Czibor and Kocsis went to Barcelona. Meanwhile, Bela Guttmann stayed in Brazil leading Sao Paulo to the National Championship in 1958 before departing for Portugal just six games into the 1958/59 season. This Guttmann-led Sao Paulo team deployed the new 4-2-4 system which was to bring Brazil such success in Sweden at the 1958 World Cup.

When Guttmann arrived at Sao Paulo, the coach Vicente Feola

stepped down to remain with the club as assistant to Bela. The same Feola managed Brazil to World Cup success in 1958 by which time Bela was back in Europe.

When he joined Porto they were five points behind league leaders Benfica but by the end of that campaign Porto were league champions. In keeping with his history of moving on and Benfica's stature and superior resources, Bela decamped to Lisbon on a hugely lucrative contract. He proceeded to dismantle the ageing Benfica team, replacing several of them with youngsters. A second successive Portuguese league title with a second club soon followed. The retention of that title in 1961 made it three-in-a-row for the manager.

Meanwhile, there came that success for which Guttmann will always be most famous. Real Madrid, having won the initial five European Cups were finally halted by Barcelona who then lost 2-3 to Benfica in the final played at Bern. On the way to that final, Guttmann made the most important signing in the history of Benfica when a young boy called Eusebio was brought from Mozambique, from under the noses of Sporting Clube de Portugal. Eusebio played for a feeder club of Sporting but when Guttmann was made aware of his potential he moved quickly.

Sporting were offering the young man an opportunity to play, effectively on a trial basis, without a contract. But Jose Carlos Bauer, a scout who had himself played under Guttmann, and a man in whose opinion Guttman had faith, recommended that heaven and earth be moved to sign this player. Eusebio made his senior debut on the day after Benfica's first famous European Cup win, as the club surprisingly was forced to fulfil a domestic cup fixture.

A year later he would play a starring role, scoring the last two decisive goals in one of the greatest finals ever, the thrilling 5-3 win over Real Madrid, as the Portuguese champions, having trailed 2-3 to a Puskas hat-trick, retained their European Cup at the Olympic Stadium in Amsterdam.

Almost inevitably, Bela and the board had an unseemly row just as the club seemed to be set for a long spell of domination. Guttmann demanded a bonus for the great achievement of winning the second European Cup. The board refused pointing out that it had not been part of his contract. Claiming that he had received more for winning a domestic league than the ultimate trophy, the European Cup, he walked. Legend has it that in walking he cursed Benfica, saying: "Not in a 100 years will they win another European Cup." If he did utter such words it is difficult to understand why he would have gone back there, albeit briefly, in 1965.

Guttmann had a keen sense of his own worth but Benfica may have been better served to have taken care of someone who had led them to a place they had never before been and to which they have never been since. If the curse rumours are right, and to date they have lost five European finals since that 1962 win, the good news is they may have fewer than fifty more years to wait for redemption.

An insight into the type of game Guttmann espoused can be had from his time in Brazil. Jonathan Wilson describes the Sao Paulo training sessions as being entirely about rapid passing, not dwelling on the ball and getting players so familiar with what was wanted that they eventually would play by instinct. He says Guttmann's calls for "tat-tat-tat" and "ping-pang-pong" became catchphrases, so frequently did he make those calls.

Guttmann's own instincts were never better illustrated than in the signing of Zizinho for Sao Paulo and in giving him, at thirty four, a creative midfield role which was completely new to him. The signing was key to Sao Paulo's emergence from a period of struggle to take the 1957 State Championship.

The transformation of Zizinho in this way was later replicated by Guttmann at Benfica where with even greater success he converted Mario Coluna from a striking role to that of a central midfielder.

After Benfica Guttmann continued on his incredible travels, to Penarol of Uruguay, back to Europe and the Austrian national side for five games, to that brief return to Lisbon in 1965, followed by postings at Servette of Switzerland and Panathinaikos of Greece. A break of six years was followed by two final short stays at Austria Wien and lastly back at Porto in 1973.

In all that time and in all those jobs, Guttmann espoused open intelligent attacking football. Fittingly, he spent his final years in Vienna until his death in 1981. His wife lived until 1997 and as they had no family, souvenirs of his football career ended up in Viennese antique shops before an eventual auction in Germany which disposed of many of his possessions. The catalogue for that auction declared — "Many years later he would sit in Sao Paolo, New York and Lisbon and dream about the days he spent in Viennese cafes and discussed soccer with his good friends."

Guttmann was a man who lived life to the full and saw the world. He saw it all and did it all. He was his own man, unique among football legends. The ultimate demonstration of his great leadership abilities was in winning those European Cups with Benfica.

Helenio Herrera

"We won without getting off the bus."
Helenio Herrera

There's a tale from the Wild West about the death of Abe, the most reviled man in town. Now that he has to officiate at Abe's funeral, the Reverend James is obliged to comply with custom and say something nice about Abe. Eventually, he steps up to say the final farewell over the grave and utters the words: "I'll say one thing for old Abe. He wasn't as mean all the time as he was most of the time."

The more one learns about Helenio Herrera, the more that story resonates. Herrera was extremely successful. Of that there is no doubt. He was also a coach who was hugely respected by many who played for him. He coached the national teams of three top nations as well as taking some of the major names in International Club Football to success. So what is the problem? Let's start at the usual place and time.

Helenio Herrera was born in Buenos Aires in 1910 to Spanish parents, his father a well-known anarchist forced to flee his native country. Having moved, with his parents, from Argentina to Morocco as a child, his playing career commenced at RC Casablanca in 1931 and ended with Puteaux in France in 1945. His coaching/managing career began seamlessly at Puteaux as his playing days ended. After a short stay in his first coaching job he moved to Stade Francais, where after three years with no success, the owner sold the club and Herrera went to Real Valladolid. Within a year he was again on the move, this time to Athletico Madrid and success in the form of two Spanish Championships in 1951 and 1952.

Still moving, he arrived at Malaga in 1952, from there briefly joining Deportivo de La Coruna in 1953, before taking the reins at Sevilla from 1953 to 1957. Next it was Bellenenses in Lisbon for a year while success would only come again once Herrera went to a big club, this time Barcelona, where in 1959 he led the Catalans to a notable treble of League Championship, Spanish Cup and Inter Cities Fairs Cup. 1960 saw the retention of both the Championship and Fairs Cup. Then came the period that would define the career of Helenio Herrera, the years 1960 to 1968 at Inter Milan.

Herrera's achievements at Barcelona must be judged in the context of conditions at the club at this time as well as the players at his disposal. Assessments should be based on all the circumstances surrounding a manager's time at any club. And Herrera's time at Barcelona was unusual in several respects. It has been said, his arrival "marked the beginning of one of the most dynamic if fleetingly successful periods in the club's history."

Herrera applied his so-called powers of psychology to a team riven with inhibitions and complexes. At least that was one interpretation of how success came about after his arrival. While some players were undoubtedly taken with the urgings from Herrera, the slogans on the dressing-room walls, the positivity, others thought it a load of claptrap. But the response was so positive it raised questions about the speed of the transformation. Herrera's arrogant, bombastic manner had not endeared him to many. The local media dubbed him — among other things — "the pharmacy cup coach." They alleged that the team's medical staff had their bags stuffed with every conceivable performance-enhancing substance during a time when there was no dope-testing in football.

Author Jimmy Burns says officials and players with whom he spoke deny this but he questions whether they were being truthful or simply showing loyalty to Herrera, or perhaps to the club and its history. Fuste, a Spanish International, is quoted as flatly denying any such wrong-doing — "All that stuff about him giving us drugs is all lies." And of course one problem in such scenarios is that it is difficult to find a player who will say, "yes of course we were taking drugs when we won all those cups."

Ladislao Kubala had arrived at Barca in 1950 via Italy, having fled his native Hungary a year earlier as it became a communist state. During his brief time in Italy, Kubala turned out for Pro Patria but had agreed to guest for the all-conquering league champions Torino in a benefit game in Lisbon. But Kubala had to withdraw at the last minute as his little boy became ill. The child recovered but his illness saved his father's life as he avoided the most tragic event in the history of football in Turin — the Superga mountain crash of 4th May 1949 in which the entire team perished with no survivors among the thirty one passengers and crew.

Apart from his own massive contribution on the field for Barcelona, Kubala, later proved influential in attracting two other famed Hungarians to join him at Barcelona in 1958, greatly strengthening the team. Sandor Kocsis still holds the record for the highest ratio of goals/games in international football for those winning more than 40 caps. His ratio of 1.10 is ahead of Gerd Muller's 1.09 with Ferenc Puskas a close third on a ratio marginally below 1.00.

The other 1958 recruit was Zoltan Czibor. A measure of Czibor's greatness was that he was top scorer in the Honved Championship winning team of 1955 which also contained not just Kocsis but Ferenc Puskas and Jozsef Bozsik. With such players in Herrera's line-up and Luis Suarez pulling the strings is it any wonder Barcelona could win championships despite the greatness of multiple European Cup Winners, Real Madrid who were themselves powered by Puskas and Di Stefano?

If Herrera was dealt a good hand here, it has to be said he blew it catastrophically when it came to the European Cup. The rivalry between Barcelona and Real Madrid has never been an easy one and Madrid's annexation of the European Cup from its inception in 1956 was a source of anguish for the Catalans. When Barcelona met Real Madrid in the European Cup semi-final of 1960, Herrera had had a long-running feud with Kubala. The player was known to like the good life but unquestionably he was the star of that Barcelona team. It was widely felt that Herrera could only have one star in any set-up — Kubala's biographer wrote — "It was not that he didn't appreciate Kubala or that he didn't recognise his qualities, but that he saw him as a rival and Herera always wanted to be the boss."

He then showed who was boss at the semi-final against Real by dropping both Kubala and Czibor enabling Barcelona to lose both home and away, 1-3 on each occasion. The outcome signalled the end of Herrera's time at Barcelona. With regard to his achievement in managing three top national sides, he took Spain to the 1962 World Cup but without Di Stefano who refused to play for him, the team failed dismally. Tellingly, Di Stefano was never considered a difficult player.

In a poll among members in 1999, the club's centenary year, Kubala was voted the best player ever to have played for F.C.Barcelona. He seems to have been liked by everyone with whom he had contact except Herrera. Brian Glanville mentions how both Kubala at Barca and Gerry Hitchins at Inter found all Herrera's "cod psychology" really insulting.

Herrera's Inter is famed for the catenaccio defence system. There are misconceptions regarding Herrera and catenaccio. Firstly, he did not create the system. Credit for this is given to an

Austrian, Karl Rappan, who coached Switzerland in the 1930s and 1940s. Then the idea was known as the verrou with the sweeper known as the verroulliere, playing behind the back four. The system was introduced into Italian Football in 1947 by Nereo Rocco who used it to lead tiny Triestina to the runner-up position in the championship of that year. The terms verrou in French and catenaccio in Italian simply mean the door-bolt.

At Inter, Herrera was teamed with a man described at the time as "the up-and-coming Sporting Director," Italo Allodi. The club had been acquired five years earlier by petroleum magnate Angelo Moratti and at the time of his arrival in 1960, Herrera was the 11th managerial change at the club since 1955. Herrera's previous teams had been much more adventurous and it appears that it was his belief that the system suited Italian players and the Italian mentality which led to its introduction at Inter.

But it was to Barcelona that he returned to make what was then the most significant signing in Inter's history. Luis Suarez had just won the Ballon d'Or as European Footballer of the Year when Herrera brought him to Milan. This Inter team included some of the greatest players of the era and some of Italy's greatest ever footballers including Giacinto Facchetti, probably the world's first real attacking full back, the esteemed libero Armando Picchi and the much revered Sandro Mazzola who scored 116 goals in 417 games for Inter, including two of their three goals in the 1964 European Cup Final victory. These players were supplemented by the Brazilian, Jair, and by the full back Tarcisio Burgnich, signed from Palermo, who would go on to win five championship medals.

Moratti's club was to enjoy unprecedented success under Herrera, winning a glittering collection of trophies between 1963 and 1966. First came the 1963 championship followed by Inter's first European Cup in 1964 to which was added the World Club Championship (Intercontinental Cup). Another league title arrived in 1965 as well as the retention of the European Cup. To crown an incredible year they also won the Intercontinental Cup again. Inter added another Championship in 1966.

That level of success puts Herrera up there with the legends of football. He is credited with being the first coach to enforce a complete ban on smoking and drinking as well as controlling players' lives to an unprecedented degree with mid-week "bed-checks" and the introduction of mandatory diet regimes for team members. Some of these elements are commonplace today or have been superseded by more enlightened ideas but Herrera was certainly ahead in his belief that psychological preparation was hugely important, a view not widely shared in the 1950s and 1960s.

To create a greater bond within the team he would assemble his squad on Thursday and take them away to a hotel until Sunday's game. This idea had its detractors especially among players, some of whom complained of boredom, but it had an impact and when a team is getting the right results, anything different they are doing is seen as a contributory factor. Something of Herrera's character may be gleaned from one incident at Inter. The father of Inter player, Aristide Guarneri died before a game and Herrera was made aware of this. However, he declined to inform the player until after the game. Bad as that action, or inaction was, it is nothing compared to some of the other allegations about Inter, Herrera and especially the up-and-coming Italo Allodi.

Stories of attempts to suborn referees by Allodi and his fixer, Hungarian Deszo Solti and of the administration of "pills" by Herrera make for fascinating reflection on the wonderful "achievements "of Grand Inter as they became known.

Writing in "The Guardian" upon the death of Allodi in 1999, in reference to the period Allodi and Herrera were running Inter, Brian Glanville described how Solti had no official position within the club, "but was responsible for seducing referees — and he answered directly to Allodi."

When Allodi was later appointed to head up the national training centre at Coverciano, near Florence, it was former Italian international manager, Fulvio Bernardini, who expressed his astonishment with the words; "All Allodi knows how to do is give gold watches to referees."

In 1964 a Yugoslavian referee, Branko Tesanic, presided over a European Cup game at the San Siro where Inter played Borussia Dortmund. A key moment in this return leg was the unpunished elimination of a Dortmund player, clearly kicked by Suarez in full view of the referee. Mr. Testanic later admitted his subsequent Adriatic holiday was paid for by Inter.

In 1965 when Inter defeated Liverpool, the referee was a Spaniard, Ortiz de Mendibil. Some years later, The Sunday Times conducted an investigation into match-fixing and bribery of referees during this period when Solti was at Inter and later when he was at Juventus. Mr Ortiz de Mendibil was implicated while an honest Portuguese referee, Francisco Lobo, stated that he was offered $5,000 plus a car to assist Juventus through a difficult European Cup semi-final against Derby County in 1973. Jonathan Wilson succinctly sums up the investigation by Brian Glanville for the Sunday Times: "He showed that the games of Italian clubs in Europe tended to be overseen by a small pool of officials, and that when they were, those Italian clubs were disproportionately successful."

In 2003, The Times reported that Angelo Moratti had attempted to fix a European Cup tie with Malaga in 1965 by offering inducements to the referee, Hungarian, Gyorgy Vadas. It was also suggested that Inter had attempted to fix matches during the previous two seasons. Again, Glanville wrote as follows describing Il Grand Inter's success as: "The fruit of bribery and corruption in which Angelo Moratti played a crucial part in a process implemented by two men also now dead: Deszo Solti, the Hungarian fixer and the serpentine Italo Allodi."

Herrera was not implicated in attempts to fix games during his tenure at Inter but all around him appear to have been well capable of doing everything within their power to make sure the right result would be achieved.

Valentino Mazzola was captain of Torino and Italy. On 4th May 1949 as Torino were on the brink of their fourth consecutive championship their plane crashed in bad weather at Superga, a mountain outside the city, as they returned from a game in Portugal. All on board were killed. His son, Sandro went on to win European Cups with Inter and a European Championship with Italy. Ferruccio Mazzola was the younger son of Valentino and the younger brother of Sandro. The least known of the Mazzola men was a player with Inter during the time of the legendary manager, HH.

Giacinto Facchetti was captain of Inter at that time. Facchetti was revered as a player and as a person. His entire career was at Inter spanning the years 1960 to 1978 during which he played almost 500 times for the club while also amassing ninety four caps. At the time of his death aged sixty four he held the honorary position as President of Inter. But it was the death of Facchetti that prompted an extraordinary interview by Ferrucio Mazzola. Facchetti died following a long battle with pancreatic cancer. Mazzola said: "To speak ill of Facchetti at the moment is like blaspheming in church. Not even I will do that. But to talk of his death is a duty."

Ferrucio spoke about how Herrera had given Inter players pills to be placed under the tongue. His brother Sandro, aware of his concern and that of other players told Ferruccio that if they did not like to take them they could simply go to the toilet and spit the pills out. This is what happened but when Herrera found out he changed the routine so that the pills were dissolved in coffee. What became known as "Herrera's Coffee" had to be consumed in front of the coach.

Elaborating on his belief that these pills and whatever they contained were a source of the terrible illness that took down Facchetti, Mazzola went on: "From then on my companions got sick and perhaps have died. Lots. The first was Armando Picchi, the team captain. He died of a tumour to the spinal column at 36 years old. Then it was Marcello Giusti's turn. He played in reserve and was killed by cancer of the brain at the end of the 1990's. Carlo

Tagnin, (was) one who never refused pills, because he wasn't outstanding and he wanted to extend his career running like a young lad. He died of osteosarcoma (a cancerous malignant bone tumour) in 2000. Mauro Bicicli went in 2001. He had a tumour in his liver. Ferdinando Miniussi, the reserve goalkeeper, died in 2002 from cirrhosis that evolved from hepatitis C. Enea Masiero, with Inter from 1955 to 1964 is having chemotherapy. Pino Longoni, who was in Inter's youth team before going to Fiorentina has a vasculopathia and is in a wheelchair with no hope of recovery."

One is reminded of the Barcelona based journalists' dscription of Herrera as "the pharmacy cup coach" and of the tragic death of the great Sandor Kocsis, widely believed to have been unable to cope with the dual diagnosis of leukemia and stomach cancer, as he fell to his death in July 1979 from the fourth floor of a Barcelona hospital, aged just forty nine.

The postscript to the interview containing these allegations is that Inter via Chairman Massimo Moratti immediately sued — and lost — and then declined to appeal the verdict.

After his time at Inter, the man known universally as HH moved to A.S. Roma where he managed from 1968 to 1970. Roma won the Italian Cup in 1969 but Herrera's time at Roma is best remembered for what happened to a forward named Giuliano Taccola. The player had been ill for some time. His tonsils were removed in the hope that they had been the cause. Eventually it was established that he had a heart murmur.

Herrera decided against telling the player this important detail about his medical condition. He took Taccola to an away game against Cagliari in March 1969. Despite the fact that he would not be playing he was instructed to train in bitterly cold conditions. Later that day, Giuliano Taccola collapsed in the Roma changing rooms and died on his way to hospital by ambulance. The official cause of death was heart failure due to pneumonia. The president of Roma, on hearing the news and in a state of shock, called Herrera who was still in Cagliari, and was further shocked to find his coach more interested in reporting on how well the game had gone than on the death of the player.

Herrera went on to manage on three more occasions, each time for only a short spell, a year at Inter, a year at Rimini after a three-year break and for two years at Barcelona before exiting the game. Later he featured regularly as a pundit on Italian television. However, the role did nothing for his reputation and in some quarters HH was derisively described as representing "habla habla" or talk talk.

His utterances were frequently seen as ridiculous and self-serving. His long-time nickname, "Il Mago" lost much of its sheen as he rambled on semi-coherently, turning himself into a figure of fun. He died in Venice in 1997 and is interred in the beautiful cemetery there, with an urn in the shape of the European Cup marking his grave. Sadly, the Reverand James was not available to preside at this funeral.

Nereo Rocco

"In Milan I may be the Master, but back in Trieste I'm still the f***ing butcher."

Nereo Rocco expounds on the theory of the prophet not being recognised in his own land.

The sixties were certainly great years to be a fan of club football in Milan. While Inter were racking up three Serie A championships, two European Cups and two Intercontinental Cups, their neighbours AC Milan were not exactly inactive when it came to picking up trophies. During the decade they won two Serie A Championships, two European Cups, two Cup Winners' Cups, an Italian Cup and an Intercontinental Cup. With the exception of the 1967 Italian Cup win, all of the victories came while Nereo Rocco was in charge. He departed Milan to manage Torino between 1963 and 1967 before returning to win a further three Italian Cups in the 1970's.

Rocco was born in Trieste in 1912. The city was then part of the Austro-Hungarian Empire but with the demise of that empire, it became a part of Italy in 1918 at the end of World War I. Nereo Rocco's grandfather had originally come from Vienna and the family name was Rock, a most famous name in that city. Nereo's cousin, Joseph Rock, was a botanist of world renown, acclaimed for his discoveries in China and featured in the writings of Bruce Chatwin and Ezra Pound. Nereo's father had a meat business in Trieste but his acute awareness of the rise of fascism and the potential bureaucratic implications for non-Italians was what saved him and his family. He quickly and successfully changed the family name to the Italian sounding Rocco.

So five-year old Nereo Rock soon became six-year old Nereo Rocco. As he progressed through school, he was a first class-pupil in every respect, academically as well as in subjects as diverse as gymnastics and music. It was a boy two years his senior who paved the way for the teenage Rocco to join the local football club, Unione Triestina Calcio. The boy in question was Piero Pasinati who would go on not just to play for Triestina but to win a World Cup medal in Paris in 1938. Pasinati was a teammate of Rocco's for eight years at Trieste and would succed him as manager in 1954 when Rocco moved to Padova. It was to his parents' consternation that Nereo wanted to commit to a career in football when, in his mother's mind so many other options existed. His father had only one thought, that his son should enter the family meat business.

At Triestina in 1930 he was the youngest player in the squad, regarded as a mascot by some of the older players who included Guglielmo Cudicini, the father of the future Milan goalkeeper and grandfather of a future Chelsea goalkeeper. Unione Triestina is a small club which has spent far more time outside rather than in the top division. In Rocco's eight years there as a player, the highest finish achieved was a sixth place in Serie A. He spent the years from 1937 to 1942 first at Napoli and then Padova.

The remainder of his playing days were disrupted by war. A single international cap in 1934 did not bring inclusion in what was to be a World Cup winning squad but it did Rocco an enormous service. At that time in Italy in order to become a manager it was necessary to have played international football. His playing career having petered out during the war, the thirty-five-year-old Rocco was appointed manager of his hometown club Unione Triestina Calcio in 1947. It was exactly at this time that a man whose path would cross that of Rocco was making a name for himself at another small club, Salernitana.

Giuseppe (Gipo) Viani, another native of a north eastern town, in this case Treviso, had won a championship as a player with Ambrosiana/Inter. Viani managed Salernitana from 1946 to 1948 winning the Serie B title in 1948. It wasn't so much the winning as the method that drew attention to Gipo Viani. He had reasoned that most games in Italy involved individual confrontations and battles for supremacy.

In such games the smaller teams had no chance, so instead of adopting what was still seen as the English game, he concluded that a "system" was what was required if a smaller club was to have any chance. While Karl Rappan is acknowledged as the creator of the "verrou" or catenacio, it would appear that Viani, quite independently, was arriving at conclusions which led to a similar approach.

He himself was happy to seek credit as the creator of the system which in Italy at that time became known as "vianema". It was a system based on setting the team up in a more defensive formation, deploying a sweeper and aiming to hit opposition on the counter attack. Viani claimed to have conceived the idea while watching fishermen using a net with a second back-up net to catch any fish that escaped the first one.

In 1947 Salernitana blitzed their way to promotion with the best defensive record of any team in the three parallel Serie B divisions to make it into the top flight for the first time in their history.

Despite their immediate return to Serie B after one season, Viani's reputation was made.

Meanwhile Rocco, having taken over at Triestina, had similar thoughts. In his first season he took little Triestina closer than they had ever been or ever would be to a championship when they finished runners-up to the all-powerful Torino team. After three years Rocco had a disagreement with the club owners, as a result of which he moved to another relatively small team, Padova. There, he brought promotion to Serie A and a third place finish in the top league. His time at Padova is recalled as that club's best ever period. His method was still based on the same principle as Viani's; that the smaller teams needed something different to be able to compete with the big powers. Rocco's name was now synonymous with catenaccio which in the 1950s became fashionable and popular with the bigger clubs.

Italian football which had been similar to English football suddenly developed this reputation for defensiveness and negativity. In 1961 Rocco finally, arrived at the helm of a big club. AC Milan had already been to a European Cup Final, becoming one of the victims of Real Madrid as they dominated the continent, winning the first five European Cups. Gipo Viani had been Milan manager but because of a heart attack, he now moved upstairs to become Technical Director with Rocco coming in to a role which was effectively head coach. Rocco led Milan to the 1961-62 championship with a surprisingly positive record, heading Inter by five points and scoring eighty three goals compared with fifty nine by Inter with Roma in fifth place the second highest scorers on sixty one.

While Milan defended well, they certainly knew how to turn defence into attack. With a team captained by Cesare Maldini and containing the Brazilian born of Italian parents, Jose Altafini, the side was certainly equipped to attack. Also they had a young man who would go on to become the most highly rated Italian footballer of all time, still topping such polls in 2015 — Gianni Rivera.

Given what this team would achieve it was a great pity that

Jimmy Greaves who could have been part of the success failed to settle and was shipped back to England after just six months in Milan. Greaves scored nine goals in fourteen games but had a disastrous relationship with Rocco. He was replaced by Dino Sani the Brazilian who went on to share in the glory at Milan. The question for Italian football in 1963 was whether their champions, Milan, could succeed in Europe using Rocco's system of playing.

At this point, Real Madrid's run of five successes in the European Cup had been ended and Benfica led by Bela Guttman were their successors with wins in 1961 and 1962. With Rivera and Dino Sani running midfield, increasingly supported by Giovanni Trapattoni, Milan were formidable. The defence was marshalled by Maldini and Altafini could be relied upon to provide goals. A 14-0 aggregate win over the Luxembourg Champions in the preliminary round set the tone. Surprise package, Ipswich Town managed by Alf Ramsey were beaten 4-2 on aggregate before Galatasaray were despatched 8-1 in the quarter finals. The semi-final again had Milan play a British team and 5-2 was the final outcome as Dundee, despite the best efforts of Alan Gilzean, were clearly not quite at this level. In the final, Benfica were deprived of a third successive title when two Altafini goals gave Milan a 2-1 win, making them the first Italian side to lift the European Cup.

Rocco or El Paron (The Master) as he was known, jumped ship to Torino, a club desperately seeking to restore their glory days. A cup final defeat to Roma and a third place in Serie A were the highlights of the four seasons Rocco spent in Turin prior to returning to A.C. Milan in 1967. For Torino, there was improvement but not quite the breakthrough they had been seeking. Ironically, as Nereo Rocco settled back in at Milan for a further seven years in charge, Torino won only their third ever Coppa Italia.

Rocco, back in familiar surroundings was quick to get a grip, his team running away with the league title in 1968 as well as winning the European Cup Winners Cup before adding a second European Cup in 1969.

That winning team had only two survivors from Rocco's 1963 side, Giovanni Trapattoni and Gianni Rivera. But there was no lack of star quality with Fabio Cudicini in goal, Karl-Heinz Schnellinger at left back, the Swede, Kurt Hamrin on the right wing and the young local sensation Pierino Prati on the left flank. In the final in Madrid, Milan eclipsed an inexperienced Ajax team 4-1 in front of what must have been a truly disappointing crowd of fewer than 32,000 at the Santiago Bernabeu.

By the time Nereo Rocco finished at Milan in 1973, he had added the club's first Intercontinental Cup in 1969, two Italian Cups, and a further UEFA Cup Winners Cup.

Rocco was a tough man and a tough manager. He was an extremely strong character with firm ideas about the game. He was known to like a glass or two of wine and to base himself at a local restaurant which would effectively become his second office. He had a strong friendship with Gianni Brera, the very famous football journalist. But Rocco was his own man. Brera could never quite "get" Gianni Rivera regarding him as a luxury in any team. But Rocco never wavered or bowed to Brera's opinion and Rivera and Rocco enjoyed success together to an extent that might not have occurred had their careers not coincided.

Possessed of a sharp sense of humour, Rocco referred to Ivano Blason, who has been described as clumsy, but who became a sweeper of note under Rocco at Triestina, later achieving great things at Inter, as "il mio manzo" (my bullock). He was almost as intolerant of Altafini's reluctance to track back as he had been of this trait in Jimmy Greaves and christened Altafini "coniglio" (the rabbit).

When Viani as his Technical Director introduced Dino Sani, Rocco took one look at the Brazilian and said: "He looks exactly like my grandfather". During the successful years at Milan, he once said to Viani: "In Milan I may be the Master — but back in Trieste I'm still the fucking butcher."

6

World Cups and a European Breakthrough

THE World Cup has been responsible for some of the greatest stories in football. After Vittorio Pozzo had led Italy to two successes in 1934 and 1938 war intervened and the competition went on hold until 1950. Brazil hosted this tournament. England, having given football to the world, finally deigned to take part in the world event but left South America having been embarrassed by the U.S.A. at Belo Horizonte.

The hosts built the Maracana stadium as a fitting venue for their anticipated inaugural World Cup victory. Sadly, they too were to experience humiliation when tiny neighbouring Uruguay defeated Brazil in the final, played before an estimated 200,000 spectators in a stadium built to hold 150,000. 1954 brought a breakthrough for West Germany, engineered by a brave and clever manager.

1966 saw England finally win the coveted trophy. Guided by a man who took the job in 1963 insisting that for the first time, an England manager would select his own squad and team, something Pozzo had done for Italy in 1934. Helmut Schön took the long road and showed extraordinary patience to bring the trophy back to West Germany. Enzo Bearzot brought Italy their first win since 1938 with unexpected success in 1982.

Spain had long been regarded as under-achievers. Their European victory in 2008 under the guidance of Luis Aragones, opened the door for further glory in South Africa two years later by which time Aragones had handed the country's finest ever team to his successor.

Sepp Herberger

"The ball is round. The game lasts 90 minutes.
This much is fact. Everything else is theory."

Sepp Herberger

The greatest achievement by a European manager at international level in the fifties was that of Sepp Herberger. Legend has it that on the big occasions German teams are hard to beat. This German reputation for not yielding easily and for frequently defying the odds goes back to events of 1954 which will never be forgotten, either in Germany or for that matter in Hungary.

Herberger's career is a demonstration of how managerial stability and succession might be achieved. Born in Mannheim in 1897, he first played for Waldhof Mannheim from 1914 to 1921 before moving to deadly rivals VfR Mannheim with whom he stayed until 1926. This move was not without difficulties as it sparked accusations of illegal payments and a year's suspension for Herberger.

As a young man he had been described as a gifted, hard-running striker who would battle to the end. Capped three times by Germany, he concluded his playing career with Tennis Borussia Berlin where he spent the years 1926 to 1930.

While in Berlin he studied at the University of Physical Education, graduating top of his class with a coaching diploma. Initially he managed Tennis Borussia for two years before taking on a role as assistant to National Team Coach, Otto Nerz in 1932. He replaced Nerz after a poor showing by the team at the infamous Berlin Olympics of 1936. His career was soon interrupted by war and one of Herberger's great services to German football was to maintain contact with players during the war years.

The country's eight year absence from international football was formally ended in 1950 when he was re-appointed national team manager, in time to plan for 1954. His most famed attribute was an uncanny ability to get the most out of the players in his charge. This was best illustrated when he summoned Helmut Rahn from a club tour of South America, at the very last moment. Rahn was included not only for his ability but for his personality. He was the character of the squad, keeping the more intense members such as Fritz Walter relaxed with his infectious good humour. Rahn went on to operate a motor dealership after his career ended. His famously honest answer to how that business worked was: "I buy a car for one thousand marks and I sell it for four thousand marks. And I live off the three per cent profit."

Herberger's teams were well drilled and he was tactically astute. Having prepared his players for their clashes with Hungary by letting them watch a fairly grainy film of the Wembley destruction of England, he got them to overcome any feelings of awe about the supposedly indestructible Magyars. Apparently there were some gasps of admiration and nervous laughter at the first viewing. By the second session, the manager and his players were beginning to see weaknesses that might be exploited. Herberger saw that there was a solution to the deep lying role played by the hugely influential Nandor Hidegkuti and by having Horst Eckel follow and mark the Hungarian star, he greatly reduced his influence. It was video analysis which predated video.

When it was all over West Germany had won their first World Cup and their manager, Sepp Herberger, was a hero for masterminding the most improbable of victories. Hungary's preparation included their 6-3 Wembley win in late 1953 and the 7-1 annihilation of England in the Budapest return game. Unbeaten in four years and over thirty games, they were the strongest of favourites to win their first World Cup in Switzerland. Herberger had been slated for losing to Hungary in the initial round, a crushing 3-8 defeat. But realising they would both qualify he had deliberately played a weakened team.

The final appeared to be going the long-expected route, as Hungary went into a 2-0 lead within eight minutes. They were the better team throughout the game, bombarding the German goal for long periods. Goalkeeper Turek had the game of his life, making several miraculous saves. Hungary could have had a hatful of goals but a powerful Hidegkuti shot hit the post and the same player, usually so reliable, missed the easiest of chances, shooting wide of an empty goal.

This day would forever go down in German annals as the most significant in the history of their football but also as a day of huge significance for a nation trying to emerge from a long cold winter of war and shame and guilt. Their 3-2 win was achieved and while no World Cup winning team before or since has done so without truly great players, it was the manager, Sepp Herberger, who was recognised as the architect of "The Miracle of Berne."

The Germans had a technical advantage available to no other team, and quite an important one in such awful weather conditions. Adi Dassler, the founder of Adidas, sat on the bench with Herberger during this World Cup campaign. His company was supporting and sponsoring the West German team. And that company had just achieved a new product breakthrough, the invention of removable screw-in studs. So, uniquely, the West German players could adapt their footwear, better to cope with difficult underfoot conditions.

Reading the different reports of this win, the German view and the alternative view, is like reading about two different unrelated games. The reports in the British Press went with the story of how Ferenc Puskas had been deliberately kicked in the first round game, resulting in the injury which kept him out until the final by which time he was still unfit and really should not have played. The German counter view was that the tackle by Werner Liebrich in the first game had been fair, that Puskas had taken a knock but was fully recovered in time for the final. Furthermore, he scored within six minutes of the kick-off and was still going at full speed when his second goal, after eighty six minutes, which would have brought the sides level at 3-3 was disallowed for offside.

The British press saw this offside decision as a grave injustice while the German view was that it was a correct decision confirmed by the fact that the legendary commentator, Zimmermann, had called Puskas offside well before he put the ball in the net.

The facts are that Mr. Ling, the English referee, was awarding the goal until his Welsh linesman, Mr.Griffiths, raised his flag and insisted Puskas was offside. Film footage at the time was inconclusive as the cameras were not well positioned for this particular incident. Some years later film footage emerged indicating that Puskas may not have been offside. It was one of those difficult decisions but as the linesman seemed certain, the decision stood. West Germany confounded everyone except their own inner circle of players and manager by winning their mould-breaking World Cup.

Herberger continued to manage the West German team until 1964 by which time he handed over to his assistant, Helmut Schön who would go on to lead his team to the Wembley final in 1966, to third place in Mexico four years later before finally winning out on home soil in 1974.

The big controversy that followed the World Cup Final was the doping allegation against the Germans. Among several claims made was the charge by Puskas that he saw several German players vomiting when he went in their dressing room after the game. Fritz Walter responded saying this was ridiculous and that Ferenc Puskas had not been near their dressing room. The team doctor acknowledged and several players admitted they had received injections but claimed they contained only vitamin C. A subsequent outbreak of jaundice among the players was said to have been the direct result. Meanwhile, a German viewpoint was that Helmut Rahn was among those who contracted jaundice as was his club goalkeeper, who was not a part of the national team at the finals, providing the basis for the theory that a virus could have been picked up in South America and spread via Rahn to his international teammates.

In 2004 Walter Bronnimann the former groundsman at the Berne stadium claimed he found syringes in the German dressing rooms after the game. The New York Times in August 2013 reported on a study which had been taking place in Germany for some time. A sports historian who participated in this study at the Humboldt University in Berlin alleges: "There are several strong indications that point to the injection of (methamphetamine) pervitin in some Germany players and not vitamin C as it was claimed." Pervitin was a known stimulant at the time and had certainly been given to German soldiers during the war.

The German Olympic Sports Union, the country's umbrella sports organisation which launched the "Doping in Germany from 1950 to Today" project with other sports authorities, advised caution before rushing to judgement on this one. The objective of their study is to try to establish the facts about the use of drugs in sport in Germany, East and West, over the years. Their comment on the Humboldt study was "Keep in mind these are indications, not proof."

And unlike the case of Herrera where a former player has given evidence and the doubts about his integrity went with him from Barcelona to Milan, there is no record of anyone questioning Herberger's integrity.

George Raynor

"The Greatest Coach England Never had"
(Title of Biography by Ashley Hyne)

In 1939 George Raynor was reaching the final days of his ten-year career in professional football. As war broke out and the season was curtailed he bid farewell to Aldershot, his sixth club in what had been a remarkably undistinguished career spent in the lower leagues.

In a route taken by many footballers, he immediately signed up as a physical training instuctor and found himself training British Army soldiers in Iraq. While in Baghdad, he trained a team of locals, taking them to play representative sides in other Middle Eastern states.

On his return to Aldershot he was given charge of their reserve team. He was known to Sir Stanley Rous through his work in Iraq and Rous provided a reference for Raynor to coach in Sweden. A six-month trial period there in 1946 resulted in his appointment to manage the national team.

In 1947 he led a Sweden team to play England at Highbury and while England won 4-2, Raynor's charges gave a good account of themselves. The following year he and Sweden were back in London taking gold at the Olympics. The 1950 World Cup was his next challenge and having qualified for the finals in Brazil, Sweden went on to emerge from their group and finish a highly creditable third in a tournament remembered in England for the national team's elimination by USA at Belo Horizonte.

The 1952 Olympics saw Sweden take bronze medals in a competition which heralded the arrival of the great multi-talented Hungarian team that won Olympic gold without difficulty. Sweden were a purely amateur side and had already lost the services of their great attacking players who had moved to Serie 'A' after the 1948 triumph at London's Olympics. Gunnar Gren, Gunnar Nordahl and Nils Liedholm had been snapped up by Milan and Lennart Skoglund was at Inter.

Famously Raynor took Sweden to play Hungary in Budapest in 1953 and achieved a 2-2 draw against a team in the middle of the lengthy unbeaten run which made them hot favourites for the 1954 World Cup. The key to Sweden's result was George Raynor's plan for dealing with Hungary's brilliant deep-lying centre forward, Nandor Hidegkuti. Following that game he met and advised England coach, Walter Winterbottom, on how to deal with the swash-buckling Hidegkuti. Hungary's 6-3 win at Wembley reflected the arrogant rejection of George Raynor's advice as Hidegkuti was given the freedom of Wembley, tearing the English defence apart.

By 1954 Raynor had moved to Italy where he had short spells in charge of Juventus and Lazio before returning to England two years later to join Coventry along with Jesse Carver who himself had led Juventus to a Serie 'A' title. Carver quit within six months, lured back to Italy by big money and Raynor remained a further year before being demoted to coach, by which time Sweden were seeking his return.

Despite having only a year to prepare, Raynor had his team in shape, physically and tactically as Sweden hosted the 1958 finals. Having progressed through the group stage, the hosts proceeded to beat both the Soviet Union and the World Cup holders, West Germany.

Their final opponents, Brazil, had a star studded team which included Djalma and Nilton Santos, Didi, Vava, Zagallo, Garrincha and a seventeen-year-old called Pele. Brazil were unstoppable, winning 5-2 but Sweden's achievement in reaching a World Cup Final was remarkable. George Raynor was knighted by the King of Sweden for his work.

After the 1958 tournament Sweden were ranked No.2 in world football while England were nine places lower. Raynor was a very patriotic individual and desperately wanted to manage England, not out of vanity but in the belief he could actually achieve success. Such was his desire that he eventually published an autobiography in an effort to make his case. Not only did this ambition prove impossible but astonishingly on his return to his native land the only job he could get was managing Skegness Town in the Midland League.

In 1959 he took a short break from that post to prepare Sweden for their 3-2 win over England at Wembley. His almost tragic appeal after that game was: "I want to work in England, for England. They want me in Ghana, in Israel, in Mexico and in Sweden. I am a knight in Sweden and have a huge gold medal of thanks from King Gustav. I have a letter of thanks and commendation from the Prime Minister of Iraq. My record as a coach is the best in the world. I don't smoke. I don't drink. I live for football."

His book presciently included arguments for three points for a win in a slimmed-down premier league. It argued for youth development programmes. All to no avail. Within a short few years of competing with Brazil in a World Cup Final, he was working in Yorkshire as a storeman. When he passed away in 1985, the news escaped the English papers. His story has to be one of the saddest in the history of English football — a tale of inexplicable rejection, of injustice and of a glorious possibility wantonly spurned.

Alf Ramsey
"We will win the World Cup."

Alf Ramsey giving hostages to fortune upon his appointment as England Manager in 1963

When Alf Ramsey was offered the job of managing England, he insisted that he would accept on one condition — that he and he alone had complete control over the selection of the squad and team. His predecessor, Walter Winterbottom, had held the post from 1946 until 1962. During those years, the committee which picked the team allowed Winterbottom participate in the process. He had one vote, just like every other committee member. So more than thirty years after Vittorio Pozzo had demanded and received similar autonomy, England finally had a manager who would be his own man, who would be a leader succeeding or failing on his own decisions.

Born in Dagenham in 1920, Alf Ramsey was nineteen when war broke out and having enlisted he played for army teams and then for Southampton before moving to Tottenham. Despite the long interruption to his playing career, he made more than 250 appearances for Tottenham. He played in the Spurs team which won the Second Division championship in 1950 immediately following up by taking the First Division title in 1951. Ramsey earned thirty two England caps at right back, captaining the team on three occasions when Billy Wright was absent.

On retiring in 1955 he immediately joined Ipswich Town of the Third Division South as manager. In his second season he led Ipswich to the league title. It took a little while to achieve stability in the Second Division but in 1960-61 Ipswich were crowned Second Division Champions and on their way to the top tier in English soccer for the first time.

With a collection of ordinary players, albeit hardworking and committed ordinary players and a modest budget, the critics felt they stood no chance of surviving in the top flight. But Ramsey was about to pull off the most amazing achievement of his short managerial career. With a counter-attacking system which relied on a withdrawn winger, the veteran Scot, Jimmy Leadbetter, and getting early ball to his two central strikers, Ted Phillips and Ray Crawford, Ipswich confounded everyone and ended the season as champions.

For his biography of Ramsey, "Sir Alf," Leo McKinstry interviewed several players from Ramsey's Ipswich team. The over-riding impression is of players who were astounded by the manager's grasp of football, by his ability to brief them with astonishing accuracy on the strengths and weaknesses of every opponent. The other aspect of his man management ability, echoing Busby, was his reluctance to criticise. Ray Crawford described Ramsey's team meeting: "At Portsmouth, I was never told anything. But Alf would come out and talk to you. And if you wanted to be successful, you listened. Because of Alf, moving to Ipswich was the best thing I ever did. On Fridays he would give a talk to us about the previous Saturday's game...the man's memory was amazing. It was like he was replaying a film of the entire match in his head. Every incident, every mistake would be analysed. Then he'd move on to the game coming up. He'd tell us the mannerisms of the opposition and made you aware of what your opponent would be up to...when things went wrong he did not slag us off. All he would say was: 'You did not do well today boys and you did not deserve anything.' Just the look on his face would cut right into you. If he came in and said: 'Well done lads, it was like being given £100...Alf never got into confrontations. You didn't argue with him, you just listened."

After only eight years in senior management it was unsurprising that he was named England manager designate in late 1962, taking up the role in May of 1963. As a person Ramsey was not given to bombast so his promise that England would win the World Cup was out of character. Much of what is written about Ramsey tends to be slightly condescending and frequently reference is made to his attempts to "improve" his speech, moving as far as possible from his Dagenham accent and background in an attempt to sound "posh". He may have had some issues in that regard but judging him as a football man, there were few reasons to doubt his ability as a leader. Having established an incredible legacy at Ipswich his success with England did not come easily or happen accidentally.

Ramsey did not assume the England job in the belief that he already knew it all. He was prepared to learn, to deconstruct and to re-construct. He was prepared to try as many players as he thought might offer something and ultimately he was prepared to be ruthless in following the courage of his convictions.

His approach to the task was a model for managers inside and outside football. With intelligence and bravery he achieved what he said he would and no one could ever take that from the only English manager to win the World Cup. He needed enormous strength of character to withstand the kind of scepticism and criticism which his selection decisions invited.

When he first took charge of England the team played a 4-2-4 system. While he had toyed with 4-3-3 sporadically, a 1-0 defeat to Argentina during a tour of South America in 1964 was the catalyst for a permanent move to what became known as the wingless wonders. England had dominated that game but Argentina caught them on the counter attack. Ramsey concluded that 4-2-4 was all very well when your team was on top but against a counter-attacking team it was not so effective defensively.

Having experimented further with the 4-3-3 system he was satisfied it was a better method to deploy at the World Cup in 1966. By the time that World Cup was won it had been further modified to something more like 4-1-3-2. Despite his belief that he had a clearly preferred method he still used the 4-2-4 system in some of the warm-up games on the run-in to the tournament. It seems he did not want to give his opponents too clear an idea of how England would set up. Also, he still needed a Plan B so it was sensible to ensure his players were familiar with more than one tactical option.

What is instructive about Ramsey's development of a world beating team is to see how the eleven evolved over the two years leading to Wembley 1966. In 1964 England played fifteen international matches. At this stage it was clear that the manager favoured Banks in goal, Cohen and Wilson as full backs, plus Bobby Moore and Bobby Charlton. These players were deployed in most of those games while quite a variety of others were chosen during that year. Some who appeared to be leading members of the core group were Peter Thompson and Gordon Milne of Liverpool as well as George Eastham and Johnny Byrne.

From around the middle of 1964 Jimmy Greaves was also a more regular team member. In 1965 nine games were played. The core players, Banks, Cohen, Wilson and the two Bobbys remained in place, but now Jack Charlton and Nobby Stiles had joined them as fixtures on the team with the former playing all nine games and Stiles missing only one. Terry Paine featured in six of those games and must have been close to nailing down a permanent place. A young Alan Ball of Blackpool began to appear in the team as did Roger Hunt of Liverpool. Jimmy Greaves played in five of the 1965 games while George Eastham was also well in contention, earning four caps that year. A further eight games were arranged in 1966 before the opening of the World Cup at Wembley.

By this time Ramsey's idea of his strongest team was becoming clearer. His emphasis was on the system. Despite the fact that many of the positions on the England team were secured well ahead of the finals, it is worth noting that both Geoff Hurst and Martin Peters were playing in only their eighth international game when they shared all four goals for England in the World Cup final.

An illness affecting Jimmy Greaves let Geoff Hurst in and once in the team he stayed there. This proved quite controversial at the time as there was a clamour in the media for Greaves' restoration once he had recovered from his illness. When Hurst was initially called up with a view to having him play against Poland, he performed so badly in training that his debut was postponed. On his own admission, he was a bag of nerves and felt unworthy of being on the same team as some of the great names around him. Ramsey, realising the problem, had a quiet word with the player and put him in the side for the next outing, against West Germany at Wembley just over five months before his historic performance against the same opposition. There can be few examples of a manager reaping such a reward from his patient and considerate treatment of a player.

Ramsey earned complete respect and loyalty from those who played under him. Norman Hunter described a time in the lead up to the 1966 campaign when he was a squad member. "I was never going to play because of the great Bobby Moore but Alf had a special way of treating you. He made you feel so important. He used to come up to me — he didn't have to — but after a game he used to come up — 'thank you for coming Norman, I know you haven't played this time but don't worry I may play you next time'." And to illustrate both how strict and correct he could be and how Ramsey saw the game, Hunter told of one experience he had with the England manager. "He was at a game once and I did something — Hunter bangs his hand indicating the "something" may have hurt someone else more than it did Norman — I had a go at somebody because they kicked one of my own players, and he got me at the international team and he says: 'Don't you ever do that again — you're a better footballer than that.' I said, 'yes but he kicked my teammate.' He said: 'Don't you ever do that — you're better than that.' "

There was a strong view that the team was functional but unattractive to watch. Ramsey took the view that he was there to win games. The players bought in to what the manager was preaching. In that February game against West Germany, England were booed off the pitch after winning by the only goal, finished unspectacularly by Nobby Stiles. Ramsey reminded his players that the same result to win a World Cup would bring about a different response.

To Ramsey, the football manager, the players were the most important thing. He shared a trait with other greats before and since, of never ever criticising a player in public. Those who played under him, speak of his immense loyalty but also of his fierce determination to have things done according to his vision. His apparent lack of emotion, especially evident as he sat still after the final whistle had sounded the end of extra time in the World Cup Final was merely an example of how he choose to behave in public. In the relative privacy of the changing rooms, his emotions were very evident as he went to each and every player to thank them and compliment them on what had been achieved.

An incident earlier in the finals created deep controversy when late in the game against France, Nobby Stiles ploughed into Jacques Simon, leaving him writhing in agony before being carried off in an age when substitutes were not permitted and injury had to be real for a player to leave the field. The tackle, if it could be called such, was hideously late and under the nose of the Japanese referee who took no action.

Not only were foreign journalists quick to criticise, so were many English reporters, some of whom openly wrote that Stiles immediately should be removed from the team. The FA put pres-

Ernst Happel was the first of 5 managers to win European Cups with different clubs. He managed teams to win league titles in 4 countries. PA IMAGES

Mario Zagallo won 4 World Cup medals, 2 as player, 1 as Manager/Coach and 1 as Technical Director. Here he appears in a team photo from the 1958 team that won in Sweden. The 5-man forward line in the front row here says it all: L to R. Garrincha, Didi, Pele, Vava and Zagallo. PA IMAGES

Carlos Bianchi reacts to the full-time whistle signalling another Copa Libertadores final win for Boca Juniors. The most successful coach in the history of South American football, Bianchi was named South American Coach of The Year 5 times.

PA IMAGES

The Ernst Happel Stadion, Vienna, 2008. Luis Aragones encourages his Spain players as Joachim Loew of Germany looks on. Aragones team ended Spain's long drought, winning this game to become European Champions. PA IMAGES

Guy Roux watches as his Auxerre team defeats Arsenal. Roux managed the club for an astonishing 44 years. PA IMAGES

Nereo Rocco in discussion with his A.C. Milan player Luciano Chiarugi.
Rocco led the club to its first great International successes. PA IMAGES

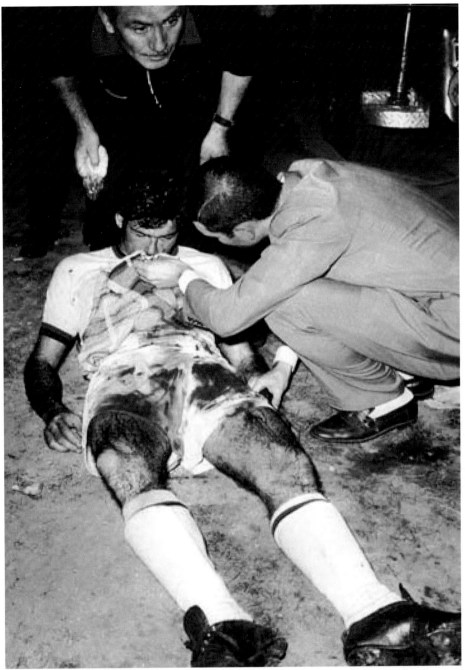

The Intercontinental Cup (World Club) Final second leg on 22nd October 1969 featured the notorious Estudiantes de la Plata, a team that had wreaked havoc in the previous final against Manchester United. Here A.C. Milan's Nestor Combin is helped from the La Bombanera pitch with a smashed nose and cheekbone. The photo brought worldwide attention to one of the most violent teams of all time and their manager, Oscar Zubeldia, the father of anti-football.

Left: A well established and not always friendly rivalry in Spain was resumed in Manchester with the appointments of Pep Guardiola and Jose Mourinho to City and United. PA IMAGES

Above: Jurgen Klopp, Liverpool, and Antonio Conte, Chelsea, compete at Anfield in January 2017. They have each won League titles in their home countries, Klopp with Borussia Dortmund, Conte with Juventus. PA IMAGES

A Dream realised! Barcelona Coach, Johan Cruyff looks on at Wembley Stadium as the club finally wins the European Cup on 20th May, 1992. Cruyff's Barca "Dream Team" also won four-in-a-row Spanish Leagues. PA IMAGES

Arrigo Sacchi coaching his star forward Marco Van Basten, a key figure in Milan's extraordinary success under Sacchi. PA IMAGES

sure on Ramsey to get rid of Stiles but the manager refused. Some reports claimed he threatened to resign rather than bow to such interference while others claimed he threatened a one-out all-out response if there was any attempt to remove the player from his team or squad. Either way, one man's stubborn obstinacy is another man's total loyalty to his players and the situation could only have bolstered the players' loyalty to the manager.

While England did not necessarily need to become a brutal team, they certainly needed toughness and a level of resilience which had been fostered during an intensive and sometimes difficult eighteen day lockdown at Lilleshall where they trained on seventeen of those days. Their quarter-final against Argentina was a dogfight of the worst type. Antonio Rattin, the Argentina captain, was sent off and having first refused to leave, eventually departed the field. Scores were hard to come by and only a great headed effort by Geoff Hurst in the seventy seventh minute saw England through. A 2-1 win over Portugal in a far better game, courtesy of two Bobby Charlton goals, had England in their first final and one game away from fulfilling Ramsey's prophecy.

The final was then won by 4-2 after extra time with Hurst becoming, and to this day remaining, the only player to score three goals in a World Cup Final. Those wishing to quibble with the achievement talk about home advantage, about a controversial decision by a Russian linesman or about the devotion to a system to the exclusion of individual brilliance. Home advantage helps but it is no guarantee of success. Controversial decisions happen all the time and even after watching, in slow motion, the ball come off the crossbar, it is difficult to say categorically whether or not it crossed the line. The officials decided — the world has accepted it so if anyone out there still harbours doubts — that's football. Managers and coaches work with the resources available to them. No one understood that better than Alf Ramsey. He made the most out of what he had. His squad building was a model. His planning and preparation were outstanding. His tactics were suited to the players and vice versa. His decision-making in terms of which players to trust was perfect. That is why England won the World Cup.

As for his uncharacteristic prediction, upon taking the job, that England would win, Norman Hunter again had an insight. "I remember going down to Lilleshall when there was twenty eight before the twenty two had been picked and he stood there and talked in that posh voice of his, and he said: 'We will win this World Cup — we will win it.' I personally don't think we thought we could win it initially. In my opinion the game that turned that around was I think after we had played against Uruguay in that first game and it was 0-0 and the press slaughtered us. 'Win the World Cup?' — all this type of stuff. And then I can remember — we played France — and I remember Bobby Charlton picking one up, and he was about thirty yards out and only Bobby could do it the way he did, you know he swayed and he just went forward and he hit this ball, he smacked it right in the top corner of the net. And after that Alf kept saying 'we will win it'. And then I think we started to believe."

Winning the World Cup was difficult but retaining it would always be infinitely harder. Being dismissive of journalists, home grown as well as foreign ones and being devoid of any diplomatic qualities ultimately would become a terminally damaging problem for the England manager. While the England results between 1966 and 1970 were not bad, losing only four of thirty three games, the performances did nothing to endear the team to a media and supporters who rightly or wrongly wanted a more expansive style of play from World Champions.

The lack of any effort to be diplomatic, particularly on a 1969 tour of Central and South America was cited in comparison to how the Brazilians cultivated the Mexican people and authorities. Ramsey's attitude was interpreted as contempt for the press and contempt for the authorities and peoples of the countries in which England played. As if heat and altitude would not be problematic enough, the non-diplomatic approach would create other problems.

England started the 1970 tournament by beating Romania via a single Geoff Hurst goal. England players got a taste of how they were perceived by the locals as Romania proceeded to kick everything that moved once it was English and the Mexicans cheered every foul as if it were a goal. Five days later they met Brazil. The choice of hotel, The Hilton, in downtown Guadalajara, was disastrous. Fans had easy access and came and went as they pleased. Players had no privacy. Requests to officialdom to help protect the players were ignored.

On the night before the first major game of the tournament, the game between the holders and the winners of the previous two World Cups, England's players were subjected to a non-stop barrage of noise from outside their hotel. Players could not sleep, while the Brazilians had no such difficulties in their secluded hotel. Despite all of this, England lost by a solitary goal in a game which would always be remembered for the incredible Gordon Banks' save from a Pele header. A 1-0 win over Czechoslovakia in the final group game was enough to see England through to the quarter finals to face West Germany in Leon.

The German's desire for revenge for Wembley looked beyond them as with fifty minutes gone England sat comfortably on a two-goal lead. Peter Bonetti had been a last-minute replacement for Banks. Then Ramsey made the most famous and disastrous double substitution in the history of English football. He replaced both Bobby Charlton and Martin Peters to rest them for the semi-final. Bonetti was badly at fault as Beckenbauer scored from distance. Uwe Seeler levelled matters leaving England struggling desperately in a game in which they had been in complete control at 2-0. Almost inevitably now, worse was to follow as Muller struck for the winning goal in extra time. Whatever about the substitutions, there was little doubt that had Banks played, the German recovery would not have happened.

Ramsey, true to form, refused to criticise Bonetti amid recriminations and widespread dissatisfaction at a defeat that should never have happened. Hunter's view of proceedings was thus: "He was very unlucky in that game against the Germans because Gordon Banks was the best goalkeeper in the world at that time, but unfortunately Gordon went down with some trouble in his tummy and then Peter played. But Peter wasn't right — mentally he wasn't right and we were two up and they beat us."

Following the end of England's reign as world champions, Ramsey remained in charge as the team went into decline. Failure to qualify for the 1972 European Championships was followed by another failure. Losing to Poland in Katowice in June 1973 was damaging but not fatal. It was the failure to beat the same opposition at Wembley in October of that year which heralded the beginning of the end for Ramsey as England missed another major tournament.

It took the FA until May 1974 to summon their manager to the fatal meeting at which he was dismissed. Ramsey had made enemies within the F.A. some of whom never forgave him for bringing about the abolition of their beloved selection committee. Ultimately, only the players retained total loyalty to their manager. But the players don't decide when a manager's time is up — and this time it was no different as the career of England's most successful manager ended in horrible anti-climax.

In 1977-78 he was appointed director of Birmingham City and acted as caretaker manager for a short spell. He then went to Panathinaikos of Greece as technical director for the following year. In his retirement in June 1998 he suffered a stroke and died in April of the following year from a heart attack. He is buried in Old Ipswich Cemetery. The saddest aspect of Sir Alf's life was the manner in which a vengeful FA shamed themselves by treating him so badly with a derisory pay-off and miserly pension. He may have had his faults but those charged with running English football should have been bigger than that.

Helmut Schön

"My biggest fear is that the road to football as total showbusiness will lead to the Harlem Globetrotters. I hope the young players are not being brought up that way."

Helmut Schön expressing pessimism as he departed the international scene in 1978

In seeking an example of a formula for stability and continuity it is hard to find a better one than West Germany's management of their national team over the decades. Sepp Herberger was appointed assistant coach in 1932, stepping up to take complete control in 1936. He continued in charge until 1942 when war stopped play, returning in 1950 and remaining in position until 1964. In 1956 Helmut Schön was placed alongside him as assistant coach. He then took over from the retiring Herberger in 1964. Schön went on to lead his team to a World Cup Final in England in 1966 and in Mexico 1970 his team took third place before Schön eventually emulated his predecessor by bringing the country its second World Cup victory in Munich in 1974.

Between those two World Cups, West Germany reached the finals of the 1972 UEFA European Football Championships. It was only the fourth ever such championship and structures and qualifying arrangements tended to vary quite a bit for both Euro and World Cups over the years. On this occasion the initial eight groups of four produced eight winners, the quarter finalists. These then played on a home and away basis before the final four emerged. The four competing semi-finalists were Hungary, Soviet Union, West Germany as well as the hosts Belgium, who nevertheless had to qualify. West Germany's win over England in the quarter final was regarded as one of their greatest ever performances. Although they had avenged Wembley 1966 four years later in Mexico there were enough doubts about the merits of that win to leave a degree of dissatisfaction that any case for West German supremacy over England was far from proven.

When Schön brought his team to Wembley for the first leg quarter final on April 29, 1972 the general expectation was that England would win. The previous league season in West Germany had ended in chaos and scandal arising from which fifty two players were suspended, some for life. Among those ruled out were three Schalke 04 internationals, Klaus Fichtel, Reinhard Fischer and Reinhard Libuda. Injuries which ruled out the ever-present right back, Bertie Vogts, key midfield playmaker, Wofgang Overath and Wolfgang Weber were seen as a further blow to any chances the Germans may have had. As a result of so many regulars being unavailable, Schön was forced to turn to youth.

He arrived at Wembley with a team whose average age was just twenty-three, four years younger than their hosts who were on a run of ten games without defeat. What followed was a master class in free flowing football. The enigmatic midfielder Gunter Netzer, when he wasn't running midfield, was interchanging with his sweeper, Beckenbauer. The movement of attacking players, Grabowski, Siggi Held and Hoeness was fluid, their interchanging mesmerising. Meanwhile Gerd Muller threatened as he always did and finally scored the third and decisive goal which ensured a West Germany win and made the return leg irrelevant. Hoeness had scored to put the Germans ahead at half time. Francis Lee equalised against the flow. A penalty by Netzer, conceded by Bobby Moore, restored the lead before Muller struck late. L'Equipe led the accolades with the phrase, 'Football from the year 2000'.

It was West Germany's first ever win in England and Schön described it as the best performance ever by a German team. While several of Schön's top players were still emerging talents, it was no small task keeping every ego happy in a team that included Beckenbauer, Netzer, Sepp Maier and Gerd Muller. Hoeness reflecting on that European win said: "That squad was Germany's finest and I believe that was all down to Schön, a great character. He managed to bring all these people together, so many strong personalities." Gerd Muller commented that, it is a rare thing to meet someone like him. His caring approach and strength as a coach were appreciated by his players. A less authoritarian style than that of his predecessor, Herberger, seems to have been more appropriate to the changing times and consequently more effective.

The victory was regarded in Germany as their most important since the 1954 World Cup Final. But Schön's young team was not done with flamboyant exhibitions of football. The second leg a fortnight later in Berlin was scoreless. A semi-final against the hosts and conquerors of Italy was won 2-1 with both goals coming from Muller for whom the Belgians had no answer.

The Final was played at the Heysel Stadium and West Germany's performance was considered better than at Wembley. The Soviet Union were taken apart as the team captained by Franz Beckenbauer, won 3-0 with two goals from Gerd Muller and a third from Netzer's Borussia Monchengladbach colleague, the Belgian born Herbert Wimmer. The team that beat the Soviets was made up of nine players from just two clubs, six from Bayern Munich, while Netzer and Wimmer were joined by their Borussia Monchengladbach club-mate Jupp Heynckes.

The World Cup win on home soil in 1974 made it the first time a team had held both the European and World Cups. And just as that World Cup is remembered by many as the one that got away from Netherlands, it stands as a truly great achievement for Schon, a man who calmly and systematically went about re-building the revered 1972 team so much so that by the time West Germany took the field in the World Cup Final on July 7th 1974 there were five changes to the line-up that had overwhelmed the Soviet Union two short years earlier. A shock defeat by East Germany in the group stages actually afforded West Germany a slightly easier path to the final as they then went into a pool with Yugoslavia, Sweden and Poland while the other pool contained East Germany, Brazil, Argentina and Netherlands. Their form then improved and three clear wins took them to the final. If the Dutch got the respect and sympathy of many football lovers across the globe, the Germans got the cup, something few could begrudge a manager at his third World Cup Finals.

Helmut Schön grew up in Dresden in East Germany where his earliest coaching influence was Jimmy Hogan. An inside left, he played for Dresdner SC and SG Dresden-Friedrichstadt between 1937 and 1944. He won two National Cups and two league titles and was an elegant and formidable scorer of goals as his international haul of seventeen goals in sixteen games testifies.

In 1950 he escaped to the West and played briefly for Hertha BSC before pursuing his interest in coaching. His international apprenticeship with Herberger proved the key to his subsequent success. Schön continued to manage the German team at the 1978 World Cup in Argentina. As so often happens it was a competition too far and the team bowed out early. West Germany's most successful manager ever, Helmut Schön, passed away in Wiesbaden, Germany in 1996 aged 80.

Enzo Bearzot

"Coaching Italy was a vocation which has become a profession. Football has become a science, but for me it is first and foremost a game."
Enzo Bearzot

After double World Cup success in the thirties, Italy had to wait forty four years before they could again be called World Champions. Their victory came in a tournament held in Europe, this time in Spain. This Italian team was managed by Enzo Bearzot, a native of the Friuli region in the north east of the country, a region which produced more than its share of top football managers including Nereo Rocco, Dino Zoff, Fabio Capello and Capello's lifelong friend, Edy Reja.

Bearzot had an eighteen year playing career as a centre-half which could be described as solid rather than spectacular, a Serie B win with Catania in 1954 proving the only incursion into trophy territory. His career took him from his local club, Pro Gorizia, to Inter, on to Catania, then Torino, a return to Inter and finally a return to Torino. He also gained a single cap in 1955 in a game against Hungary.

Torino was the club with which he spent most of his career and where his playing days ended and which at that time was managed by Nereo Rocco who immediately gave Bearzot a coaching role with the under-age teams at the club, a role he held for four years until 1967.

A brief attempt at managing Prato led to an appointment to the Italy Under-23 team in 1969. This became a stepping stone to the senior post where first he assisted Feruccio Valcareggi at the 1970 and 1974 World Cups. He continued as assistant when the veteran Fulvio Bernardini succeeded Valcareggi in 1974. Within a year Bearzot had assumed the top job as Bernardini stepped down. Most of his coaching/managing career was therefore spent with national teams.

It was very much in the manner of how West Germany had groomed its managers over the decades. Italy has since adopted the policy of appointing experienced club managers, such as Sacchi, Trapattoni, Lippi, Prandelli and more recently, Conte. But Bearzot's appointment was not greeted with universal acceptance for the very reason that he came to the job without significant managerial experience at club level. A fourth place finish at the Argentina World Cup in 1978 was considered acceptable but a similar placing at the 1980 European Championships held in Italy was not as warmly received. Outside of Italy the team was noted for the new attacking approach which made it the most attractive Italian national side in decades.

Bearzot was very much the elder statesman, calm and polite at all times. Even when the press were savaging him he always kept his composure, in the belief that he knew more than they did, a belief that was proven conclusively when Italy won the World Cup. It was a tournament in which, characteristically, they took quite a while to warm up before finding their feet in a most dramatic encounter with favourites Brazil.

In that fateful 1982 campaign, Italy had come through the qualification series a point behind Yugoslavia and four ahead of Denmark, a typical Italian campaign, doing enough to qualify but hardly tearing up any trees in the process. In Spain, they resumed activity in an even less impressive manner, drawing with Poland, Peru and Cameroon, leaving them tied in second place with Cameroon. Only their higher number of goals scored allowed them rather than Cameroon to advance with group winners Poland. A score total 2–2 for Italy compared with Cameroon's 1-1 was the difference. By now the Italian media were frantic and Bearzot applied a media ban to try to protect his charges from the onslaught. The second round meant groups of three and Italy had Argentina and Brazil for company. The top team from each group would qualify for a semi-final. Argentina were despatched by 2-1. Then Brazil finished their South American rivals' involvement in the tournament by going one better with a 3-1 win. For the final game, a draw would suffice for Brazil but Italy had to win because the Brazilians had scored that extra goal.

This was the Brazil team that knew only one way to play. Unfortunately for them their commitment to exuberant attack while neglecting some defensive basics was to prove fatal. Italy won 3-2 in an extraordinary game in which Brazil played, well, like Brazil. Italy were a goal up in five minutes and Brazil were level in twelve. Italy led 2-1 at half-time but Brazil equalised on sixty eight minutes. All Brazil now needed to do was hold on for a draw. But nothing would do them but to press on for the win. It was their undoing and for the third time that afternoon, Paolo Rossi scored taking Italy into a semi-final meeting with Poland.

The semi-final and final proved less taxing than the exhausting classic against Brazil. Italy had burst into life and suddenly achieved an awareness of what was possible. Their 2-0 win in the semi-final did not flatter Bearzot's team nor did the 3-1 victory over

West Germany in which three second half goals made the Italians safe before a late German consolation score from Paul Breitner. Rossi, the scorer of both goals against Poland, had again opened the scoring and finished top scorer at the finals with six goals in all.

The irony of Rossi's outstanding achievement was that, arguably, he should not have been playing in this tournament. His performance in Argentina four years earlier had been exceptional and Bearzot was grateful to have such an outstanding striker. Meanwhile Rossi was implicated in one of those regularly occurring Italian scandals involving match-fixing. He received a three-year ban, which had it not been commuted to two years would have kept him out of Spain 1982. When he was recalled to the team he showed all the signs of someone who had not played competitively in quite a long time. This was partly to blame for the sluggish start in Spain. It was also the cause of much of the grief being inflicted on Bearzot for sticking with a clearly out-of-sorts player.

Bearzot was not forgetting how well Rossi had played at the 1978 tournament in Argentina when Italy were beaten semi-finalists and the striker was voted second best player in the tournament. So despite three non-performances by Rossi he remained in the team against Argentina and was viewed as a complete passenger. But Bearzot, against all the odds, was proven right.

The explosive awakening against Brazil was the first step. The goals against Poland and West Germany concluded the argument in favour of the coach who defied virtually all the experts in selecting the player. Astonishingly, from such a dreadful start, Rossi won not just the Golden Boot as top scorer but the Golden Ball as top player and later the Ballon d'Or as European Player of the Year.

The Brazilian players had made a huge impression on world football and nowhere was this more evident than in Italy. The midfield player, Falcao, had signed for Roma in 1980 but within two years of the 1982 World Cup as many as eight members of that Brazil squad were playing their football in the home of the World Champions.

There were echoes of Alf Ramsey's experience when Bearzot's team lost to France at the 1986 World Cup finals in the last sixteen. The most pointed criticism was that he had been too faithful to the players who had brought glory in 1982 and that failure to re-build had been the cause of the Italian demise.

His belief in a positive type of approach on the field met with heavy criticism especially when results did not go well. His selection decisions were the subject of not just criticism but derision. But Bearzot was steadfast and despite the flack he picked the players he believed in and omitted some darlings of the press. In this respect his finest hour was his ability to hold his nerve until the badly malfunctioning Paolo Rossi came good and effectively won Italy the World Cup.

After the failure in 1986 he resigned to spend a long time away from football. He was appointed President of FIGC Settore Tecnico in 2002 for a three year period until 2005. By an extraordinary coincidence his death took place on December 21st 2010 aged 83. His predecessor as Italian World Cup winning manager, Vitorio Pozzo, had died on December 21st 1968 aged 82.

Luis Aragones

"Pirlo, I agree, is an important player.
But if Gattuso is critical then I'm a priest."
Luis Aragones responds to claims that Italy would be without two key players in their game against Spain

When Carlos Bianchi was hired in 2005 for his short-lived stay at Atletico Madrid he became the 10th Argentinian to manage the club, and a couple of those had more than one stint in charge. Since then they have appointed Diego Simeone, with somewhat more success. The list of nationalities to have managed this club runs to eleven including five Englishmen. Across the city at Real Madrid the story is similar. They have had thirteen different nationalities in charge including three Argentinians and three Englishmen. Barcelona have had no fewer than eight English bosses, four Argentinians, four Dutch and eight other nationalities in their hot seat. Atletico Bilbao has had eight English managers and Sevilla, in their time, even went so far as to twice employ Irish managers. Without a doubt there has been in Spain an underlying feeling that foreign is best.

Against such a background it has been difficult for native coaches or managers to get a break with a top club once some big name is available overseas. And there is always a big name available. This may go some way to explaining the relative lack of success by Spanish managers at club and national level. But now in the 21st century the country has enjoyed unprecedented success, winning successive European titles and a World Cup, while achieving universal popularity because of the style of football played. The breakthrough in 2008 took place under the guidance of native veteran coach, Luis Aragones.

July 1938 was a decidedly difficult time in Spain, between a savage civil war and the commencement of the Second World War. In that month Luis Aragones was born on the outskirts of Madrid. Educated by the Jesuits he was seen to be a talented footballer. Losing his father when he was only fifteen put enormous pressure on the young man as he had to divide his time between studies and helping on the family farm.

His first club was Getafe. He was then on the books of Real Madrid but all of his two years was spent on loan to different clubs. It was not an easy time for a young forward to make a breakthrough at Real with a first team containing world class stars such as Puskas, Di Sefano, Francisco Gento and Raymond Kopa. Moving about to Oviedo and then Betis he was not much more than another journeyman player until he found the club he needed. And it was right back in his home city.

At twenty six he arrived at Atletico Madrid, a club with which he went on to enjoy a long relationship and success both as player and manager. Ten years as a player ran in to a further fourteen as manager, interrupted by a brief one-year hiatus when he went to manage his former club Betis in 1981. In his ten years as a player, the team won three La Liga titles and was twice runner-up. Two Copa del Rey wins made it an exceptional period. To this day, he is the club's all-time top scorer. As manager he led the club to a league and three cup wins. One of those Copa del Rey final wins, in 1992, was famous for his team talk, which inspired his team to a 2-0 win over Real Madrid. Having gone through the routine tactical directions, he became emotional. It was genuine emotion coming from a man who had given so much of his life to this club.

"Is that clear? I'm asking you is that clear? Yes? Well, this and this (thumping the tactical whiteboard with his fist) means nothing. What matters is that you're better than them and I'm fed up to the back teeth of losing to this lot, in this stadium. You're Atletico Madrid and there are 50,000 fans here who'd die for you. For them, for the shirt, for your own pride, you have to go out on the pitch and show that there's only one champion and they're dressed in red and white."

His most significant and historic win was an Intercontinental Cup victory over Independiente. Atletico won the league in 1973 and went to the final of the 1974 European Cup where they lost to Bayern Munich after a replay. This was Aragones' last season as a player but in his first year as manager, the club replaced Bayern in the two-leg final of the Intercontinental Cup. Having lost by the only goal in Buenos Aires in March 1975, the Madrid team and its novice manager turned the tie around a month later with a 2-0 win, the clinching goal scored, ironically, by Argentinian striker Ruben Ayala. Over the years a total of six teams that had been runners-up in the European Cup (Champions League) represented Europe in the tie with the Copa Libertadores winners for world supremacy. Atletico Madrid were the only one of the six to win, providing them with the record of being the only European side to win the Intercontinental Cup never having won the European trophy.

Almost thirty years later in 2004 the now veteran coach, having had a succession of management jobs including a total of four terms at Atletico Madrid, a Copa del Rey win with Barcelona and stop-overs at Sevilla, Valencia, a second term at Betis and two terms at Mallorca, finally became manager of the national team. Although his travels were notably devoid of trophies, it was said of his club career that he never failed to leave a team in a better position than that in which he found it.

Spain qualified for the 2006 World Cup by way of a play-off. They then topped their group before losing 3-1 to France. The European Championships in Austria and Switzerland represented the next opportunity for Aragones and Spain to achieve something. It was at this point that the manager showed his strength of character. He decided to go with younger, less experienced players, the type of players he could mould to his way of doing things.

Dropping Real Madrid stars such as Michel Salgado and the legendary Raul was never likely to play well with the Spanish foot-ball media, especially the Madrid based daily papers. But Ara-gones was not the type to be rattled by some adverse comment. His typical response to media cross-examination demonstrated his determination not to be bullied by anyone: "Do you know how many World Cups Raul has been to? Three. Do you know how many Euros he's been to? Two. Now tell me, how many did we win?"

It would not be his last bout of adverse media attention. The team topped its qualifying group for the European Championship. Then they won their three group games to move into a difficult quarter final against World Champions Italy. Before that game much was being made of Italy's injury problems. Pirlo and Gattuso were out and their loss was being portrayed as disastrous for the world champions.

At a press conference before the game, Aragones was ques-tioned about this Italian problem and asked how much advantage it gave his team, when he responded with his normal directness. "Pirlo, I agree is an important player. But if Gattuso is critical, then I'm a priest."

That played predictably well in the Italian press. The game ended scoreless and Spain won 4-2 on penalties. They moved on to beat, for the second time, the other qualifiers from their group at the finals, Russia. Germany were their final opponents and a Fernando Torres goal was enough to decide that final. Aragones had achieved the championship win that the country craved since its only other win in 1964. They were under achievers no more. And he had done it his way.

The squad and team had a composition which by Spanish standards was quite unprecedented containing four players each from Liverpool and Valencia with only three from Barelona and two from Real Madrid. This was before the rise of Barcelona under Guardiola but Aragones had his own belief in what has been described as 'tiki-taka'. He explained exactly why he favoured this style as well as why he made some of those controversial selection decisions.

"Our work was based on two key concepts. The first was the style of play, which was based around getting our best players on the pitch in order to control possession of the ball. I used to say that our innate physical make-up meant we couldn't compete with the likes of Germany, while now its opposing teams that can't keep up when we get our one-touch game going. And the other key was getting rid of any egos."

His work for Spain complete, Argones retired from international management taking on one final task at Fenerbahce in Istanbul. It did not work out and he left just a year into a two-year contract in 2009. Luis Aragones died in Madrid on February 1, 2014 aged 75.

7

Great European Managers

FOOTBALL throws up some unlikely success stories and some colourful characters. This chapter looks at European greats from different countries and diverse backgrounds. There are two Italians, Giovanni Trapattoni, a former successful player steeped in the game and Arigo Sacchi, a former shoe salesman with no playing career.

An Austrian orphan, Ernst Happel went on to become a successful manager in several countries while a dignified German maths teacher, Otto Hitzfeld, demonstrated that there is no set background or recipe for outstanding achievement in football management. Certainly there are qualities without which success cannot be achieved. A sound understanding of the game, a talent for judging a player, the ability to impose discipline without alienating people, are all desirable qualities. Guy Roux was a man who embodied all of those qualities while also confirming that the only way to become the longest serving manager in history is to start young.

A learned or inherent ability in psychology is also helpful. As with any selection of managers, these differ quite a bit from one another, but each one brought something to the game which worked for them and for many of those who shared their journeys.

A striking aspect of converstions with players who had worked under Happel, Trapattoni and Sacchi was the colossal respect the former players had for these managers.

Ernst Happel

"It is really easy for me. There is no difficulty
in keeping one's mouth closed."

**Ernst Happel answers a question and demonstrates
just one way in which he was different**

Paul Courant had played for seven years at Liege when he made the
move across Belgium to Club Brugge. In his own words; "Happel
was why I came." Already an international and the recipient of a
'Footballer of the Year' award, he would have no regrets. Championships and a Belgian Cup win were to follow. His injury-enforced
absence and that of colleague Raoul Lambert were undoubtedly
significant factors in Brugge's 0-1 Wembley defeat to Liverpool in
the 1978 European Cup Final.

Courant is a widely experienced man within football and in
business, who would later become Director of Football at KV
Mechelen presiding over the most successful years for the little
Belgian club as they racked up a Belgian Cup, a European Cup
Winners Cup and a European Super Cup. He had this to say of
his manager at Brugge: "I have not in my lifetime met three people of the calibre of Happel, both as a manager and as a person.
He was an amazing person with the most extraordinary charisma
and integrity."

The story of Ernst Happel's origins calls to mind the Johan
Cruyff quote: "Every disadvantage has its advantage." Happel's
early life was difficult and lonely. It was the type of experience that
either destroys or makes an individual. Happily for football, it made
Happel the man he became. And the man he became was a superb
footballer and an even better manager.

Happel was born in Vienna on 29th November 1925 at a time
when Vienna was in a very depressed state after the demise of
the Austro-Hungarian Empire at the end of the First World War.
There was a population of immigrant Czechs, so large at 250,000
that made it the city with the second highest Czech population

after Prague. Happel's mother was part of this immigrant group, as indeed were several of the key figures in Austrian football including Hugo Meisl and the tragic Matthias Sindelar.

The Czech immigrants mostly lived in the poorer parts of the city and were employed in the more menial jobs. There were some earlier arrivals who had developed their own businesses but young Ernst was well removed from that grouping. His mother was a single woman who married Franz Happel a year after giving birth to Ernst. Franz was a publican who took on the young boy as a stepson. The birth certificate actually bore the name Ernst Nechiba, but despite the early divorce Ernst would hold onto the name Happel for life.

Step-father Franz turned out to be his own best customer. Ernst's mother left the boy with her mother, his grandmother, in a tenement at Huglgasse Nr.3, a stone's throw from Rapid's stadium. He liked his granny who ran a market stall but times were tough for a small child without a father and whose mother had abandoned him.

The escape or outlet for a poor boy in Vienna of the early thirties was probably quite similar to that available to less privileged children in many cities. The outlet was street football. Young Happel would drop his schoolbag and head into the streets from which his grandmother would end up summoning him as night drew in.

Happel came into the Rapid Vienna team at seventeen in 1943 and stayed with Rapid until his retirement in 1959 apart from a short break in 1955-56 when he moved temporarily to Racing Club of Paris. He was an outstanding central defender and earned fifty one Austrian caps between 1947 and 1958. During his time at Rapid, the team won six Austrian Championships and one Cup Final as well as a Zentropa Cup in 1951.

He maintained that the creation of the European Cup came too late for his club team which he believed could have won such a competition. In 1954 he played in the Austrian team which took third place at the World Cup in Switzerland.

The easiest part of describing Happel is listing his achievements as a manager. He led teams to domestic leagues and cup victories in Netherlands, Belgium, Germany and Austria. In three of those four countries he took his league champions to the European Cup Final, winning twice. His European Cup triumphs with Feynoord, over Celtic and with Hamburg over Juventus were both against the odds as he became the first man to win that august competition, now the Champions League, with two different teams.

His managerial career began in the Netherlands in 1962 with Den Haag where he stayed seven years winning the Dutch Cup in 1968. Then came the short move to Feynoord. Four years in Rotterdam brought a league title, a completely unexpected European Cup and just to show that beating a great Celtic team was no fluke, the Intercontinental Cup. A mistaken acceptance of the job of managing Sevilla was quickly corrected when he departed for Club Brugge and more success between 1974 and 1978. If taking Feynoord to the summit of European football was remarkable, bringing Club Brugge of Belgium all the way to the European Cup Final was arguably an even greater achievement. Three Belgian league titles, one Cup success, a UEFA Cup final appearance and finally that European Cup runners-up placing, were a fair reflection of the domestic dominance and international competitiveness of Club Brugge under Happel.

In 1978 Ernst Happel led a Netherlands team to Argentina. Having broken the hearts of their own people in 1974 when losing the World Cup Final, this team with no Cruyff on board, was much less highly rated. As can happen, they began the tournament hesitantly but grew into it.

The first round in Argentina was a group phase where Netherlands competed with Peru, Scotland and Iran, with two to qualify for a further group phase. Happel's team beat Iran, drew with Peru and surprisingly lost to Scotland in a game memorable for a wonderful solo goal by Archie Gemmill. So Netherlands qualified in second place, on goal difference ahead of Scotland. This second series had two groups of four with the two group winners to meet in the final. The Dutch, performing much better now, topped a group in which all four teams were European, beating Italy and Happel's native Austria and drawing with West Germany. Inevitably, the hosts, Argentina, qualified after a controversial final group game in which they defeated Peru 6-0 to oust Brazil on goal difference.

The final was a dour encounter heading for a 1-1 draw when in the 89th minute Rob Rensenbrink struck the foot of the post. It was a chance that he would usually have put away. That is how close Netherlands and their manager came to winning a World Cup. Extra time brought victory to Argentina but Happel later said he had no regrets and felt that had Rensenbrink's shot gone in, the game would probably have continued for at least ten more minutes. It was that kind of tournament.

The generals were in power and there was a widespread feeling of unease at the way in which Peru had succumbed in what amounted to a semi-final. Unsubstantiated rumours and denials abounded for years about what rewards the Peruvians got for their part. The Dutch had over-achieved in making a second successive World Cup final. Sadly for them, and for their manager, they joined Hungary of 1954 as losers for whom there was universal sympathy and respect.

Happel returned to club management, briefly at Harelbeke before a two-year stint at Standard Liege. He then moved to Hamburger SV in 1981 where he remained until 1987 making it his longest spell in management at one club.

He had been preceded as Hamburg manager by the strict disciplinarian, Branko Zebec. Unfortunately Zebec had a drink problem which forced his early removal in December 1980 after which his assistant Aleksandar Ristic took temporary control until Happel's arrival at the end of that season. Felix Magath had been signed in 1976 from FC Saarbrucken and was a highly influential midfield player, and later manager, at the club. Magath won a European Championship with West Germany and was twice on the losing side in World Cup finals. As a player he is best remembered for scoring the winning goal in the European Cup Final as Happel's team overcame a hotly favoured Juventus side.

Magath had this to say about Zebec and Happel: "Under Branko Zebec we were used to following his instructions to the letter. The game under Branko Zebec was set up in such a way that little or no errors could be made. Ernst Happel was the complete opposite. Happel wanted his team to play the game, play the ball forwards and set up goals. That was very, very good for the team as discipline and conduct were already perfect. With Ernst Happel came a creative moment for the team. Every player was able to live out his place on the field and every player was allowed to bring his own judgement, and this led to the team becoming more successful than under Zebec."

Magath was confirming the truth in Happel's assertion that he would rather win 5-4 than 1-0. Two Bundesliga titles were gained under Happel. The addition of their European Cup as well as the German Cup, the DFB Pokal in 1987 makes Happel the most successful manager in the club's history.

Bearing in mind the strength of the opposition, that European Cup Final win is probably as great as any of the victories achieved by the Austrian coach. If Ernst Happel needed an opportunity to demonstrate his tactical acumen, here it was. Giovanni Trapattoni's side deployed a man-marking defence. Happel saw how his own starting team would suit the Juventus man-marking system. So he moved players and in doing so dragged the right back, the most inappropriately named Claudio Gentile, to the left side of the Italian defence. This created space for Hamburg to attack down their left flank. It was from this space that Hamburg engineered the only goal of the game. Unquestionably the win was not just victory for Hamburger SV but a triumph for their brilliant coach over the highly-regarded and successful Trapattoni.

Although Happel was famous for how little he said, Magath described his speech as not quite his own private language but said his German was inflected with Dutch and Flemish expressions and Viennese was also there. Happel, he said, often made a statement which you had to just interpret.

Magath said: "Make no mistake about this, Ernst Happel spoke rarely, not even to me or the other players. Happel hardly even spoke in the meetings before a game, which were relatively short. It didn't really work via verbal communication, you had to pay attention, you had to keep an eye on him and interpret his instructions."

Paul Courant, elaborated on this approach. He recalled Brugge's European Cup semi-final meeting with Juventus, Courant said the team talk lasted at most five and probably nearer to three minutes. Happel knew that players were not at their most receptive to lists of ideas and suggestions at that point, just before a game.

Courant stressed the really great thing was you did not need a talk at that stage — the work had been done. For a week prior to that game everything in training had been about how you were expected to play in the game. It was repeated over and over with simulation of what way Juventus would set up and consequently how Brugge would play. By game time, he said, there was nothing left to tell any player — they each knew their own function and that of those around them.

Happel's biography, "Genie und Grantler" (Genius and Grumpy Old Man) owes the latter description to this reluctance to speak any more than he felt necessary. The author, Klaus Dermutz, outlines an exchange he once had with Ernst which gives a remarkable insight into how he felt about sharing his views. The interview between Dermutz and Happel goes as follows:

KD: You are interested in factual analysis?

EH: Very few journalists are factual and subjective. Most of them use your own words against you. My principle is the following: If I have said little, then I'll already have spoken too much. If I have already said too much, I'll get it back tenfold. I don't need that at all.

KD: So you must always hold yourself back?

EH: Yes. I surely do hold myself back. What do you think would happen if I always shot my mouth off? Where would I run to in public while all the dirty washing is being washed? I wouldn't get anything out of that.

KD: Is it difficult for you not to make certain developments public?

EH: It is really easy for me. There is no difficulty in keeping one's mouth closed.

At press conferences he bore out this philosophy, making it policy to speak for no more than thirty seconds. It was this approach which earned him the "grumpy" title.

In Happel we see one of the great football men — a man of intelligence and charisma, a man who respected people and who was widely respected. He was a devotee of attacking play and a man who as well as having an extraordinary ability as a leader, could in the words of Courant, "change a game during a game." Remarkably successful substitutions for Feynoord in the Intercontinental Cup Final and for Netherlands in the World Cup final illustrate this point. He was a manager who time and again, in different clubs, even in different countries, turned ordinary teams into extraordinary achievers.

He shared with other great managers the approach to team rejuvenation. "It is necessary to systematically, not radically, make a team younger. That is my principle." He believed a successful club side probably had four years in which to dominate while at international level, a team could be dominant for up to ten years.

One of the tales of his exploits in Brugge is that in a vital game, the team returned to their dressing room 0-2 down at half time, having played well below their capability. Happel was slow to appear and when he did get there, he put his head in the door and uttered just two words: "And now?" The team won 3-2. From such are legends made.

After Hamburg he returned to Austria managing Swarovski Tirol from 1987 until 1991 during which time they won the Austrian League and Cup double in 1989 adding a further league title in 1990. He was then appointed to manage the Austrian national team but he died of lung cancer on 14th November 1992 aged 66. Four days later as Austria played Germany in a 0-0 draw, Happel's cap lay poignantly on the bench for the duration of the game. It was not the final tribute to a great man. Fittingly, the Praterstadion in Vienna was re-named the Ernst Happel Stadion in honour of the man voted Austria's greatest ever manager.

Giovanni Trapattoni

'I may have won yesterday — but that was yesterday.
I want to win today, tomorrow and tomorrow.'
Giovanni Trapattoni

When it came to winning, there were few who could match the record of Giovanni Trapattoni. Perhaps being born on St.Patrick's Day (1939) was an omen in terms of his eventual involvement with the Republic of Ireland team. However, the man from Cusano Milanino had a long and hugely rewarding career before he set foot in Dublin. A playing career from 1959 to 1972 saw him spend all except the last year with his home-town club AC Milan. A short hop up the road to Varese and just a few first team appearances brought the curtain down on a trophy-laden life playing club football. Those successes were as nothing compared with what was to follow.

Trapattoni was an important part of the Milan teams of Nereo Rocco, winners of the European Cup in 1963 and 1969. These famous wins were preceded by Serie A titles. In the second European Cup Final Trapattoni was credited with having nullified the great Johan Cruyff, a critical factor in Milan's emphatic win. His role as a man-marker was one in which he was supremely effective. The name given to this type of player in Italy tells a lot about the Italian mentality where football is concerned. He is called a francobollatore — someone who stuck to his man like a postage stamp/francobollo. The Italian Cup was won in 1967 and in keeping with the Milan way at that time, this win led to European success with a Cup Winners Cup victory in 1968. And to round off the collection, Trapattoni shared in the Intercontinental Cup win of 1969, the never-to-be-forgotten bloodbath against Estudiantes of Argentina.

His playing days over, Trapattoni was encouraged and facilitated by Nereo Rocco to begin a coaching career with the youth teams at Milan. He briefly managed the first team when Rocco went to Fiorentina, finishing third behind Torino and Juventus before being hired by Juventus in 1976 where he remained until 1986 producing one of the most glorious periods in the history of that illustrious and powerful club.

Clearly his arrival at Juventus was greeted with enthusiasm by the players. Marco Tardelli described it as 'a breath of fresh air.' Sergio Brio was hugely impressed by the new coach's willingness to help individual players. He said he had been a young lad of twenty one at the time and it was a new experience to have someone so dedicated to helping you improve.

Roberto Bettega said: "His method was a departure from what other managers were doing at the time, especially in the way he involved himself in the squad." Clearly, Trapattoni had the energy and the man-management skills to win over players who had already known success and who wanted to return to the top, having just lost a League to their deadly rivals Torino. Juventus could and did buy the best players, from Liam Brady to Boniek and Platini.

Brady's own assessment of Trapattoni is highly complimentary. "The times were different. Trapattoni wanted to succeed. He had some of the best players in Italy at the time but no one was treated differently, everyone was treated with respect at all times. As a young manager he was very much in tune with the players and the players responded really well to his honesty, enthusiasm and intregrity."

Juventus had an ability to identify the best managers and this appointment was no exception. Under Trapattoni, the Turin club won six Serie A Championships, two Italian Cups, two UEFA Cups, a Cup Winners Cup, The European Cup and an Intercontinental Cup. The World Club title was played under the newer format with a single game in Tokyo deciding matters. Juventus were taken to penalties by Argentinos Juniors, holders of the Copa Libertadores, winning 4-2 in the shoot-out.

Significantly, this win made Juventus the first football team to have won all official continental competitions and the club world title. Their players Antonio Cabrini and Gaetano Scirea became the first European players to achieve this feat and Trapattoni became the first European manager to do so. Despite building a dominant force and a team capable of scintillating attacking play, it was always believed that Trapattoni reverted to what he knew best when the pressure came on. What he knew best was how to defend and how to set up a defence. His own view on this was simple and predictable: "I have more of a defensive reputation than an attacking one but that does not bother me because my results speak for themselves."

After all the success with Juventus 'Trap' was lured to Inter in 1986 where he remained for five years the highlight of which was a brilliant Serie A Championship win in 1989 with a team powered by the German duo of Andreas Brehme and Lothar Matthaus to be joined a year later by Jurgen Klinsmann. With Argentinian Ramon Diaz up front along with Aldo Serena who had come in from Trap's Juventus team, it was as attack-minded a team as ever had taken to a pitch under his guidance. Walter Zenga was a reliable goalkeeper while the defence had the incredible Giuseppe Bergomi at right back. Bergomi was at that time precisely half way through a twenty year career as Inter fullback. Other Italian greats such as Riccardo Ferri and Nicola Berti helped form a team which finished eleven points clear of second placed Napoli. 'Trap' never felt he was fully appreciated at Inter, despite the League and a UEFA Cup win, their first European trophy in over a quarter of a century. He returned to Juventus from 1991 to 1994 before seeking a new challenge in a new country.

His time at Bayern Munich was cut short and they parted the ways after one season only for the club to come back a year later having re-thought their plans, inviting Giovanni to return. This time he stayed three seasons, winning a League, a German Cup and a League Cup in that time. His term is remembered more for an off-field event than anything else.

There was a famous press conference were Trapattoni appeared to 'lose it' as he turned on his critics in the media, and within the club. Later he claimed he knew exactly what he was doing and that essentially the outburst was staged. Given his propensity for unclear public utterances even in Italian, it is hard to tell whether he was in control or not. The issue was the fact that he was not always playing some of the perceived top names in the club. As he said himself; "sometimes you have to shout!"

After a three year stay at Fiorentina in which a third place finish was the highest achievement, Giovanni Trapattoni was appointed Manager of the national team.

Italy, under Dino Zoff, had reached the final of the 2000 European Championships. In that final in Rotterdam they led until the very last minute of injury time when Silvain Wiltord equalised for France. The rules provided for extra time in which the 'golden goal', the first to score, would decide the game. France through David Trezeguet scored that goal. After the tournament Silvio Berlusconi publicly criticised Dino Zoff for his selections and general approach. Zoff felt he had no option but to resign. Trapattoni was entrusted with the national team. Bizarrely, as the criticism of Zoff had been that he was not bold enough, a master of defensive methods was given the task of replacing him.

Italy arrived to the World Cup Finals in Japan/South Korea having comfortably topped their qualifying group. At the finals, they finished second behind Mexico with whom they had drawn, while losing to Croatia and beating Ecuador. This left them facing joint hosts, South Korea, rather than the United States who managed to defeat Mexico.

Trapattoni expressed grave concern about the game when the other co-hosts were eliminated earlier in the day of the Italy v South Korea game. And based on their initial experiences at this tournament, Italy did indeed appear to have grounds for serious concern. In that first phase they had no fewer than four goals disallowed and all bar one of those seemed incorrect decisions.

Refereeing was now the topic of discussion for every Italian at the finals and at home. From the kick-off the Koreans went at Italy, never giving their defenders time on the ball and clearly upsetting the hot favourites. Within four minutes they had a deserved penalty which was saved by Buffon in the Italian goal. Vieri put Italy ahead inside the first half hour, a lead they held until two minutes from time when South Korea scored as the ball was bundled in after a stumble by defender Christian Panucci.

Extra time proved disastrous for Italy. Francesco Totti tumbled under a tackle in the penalty area and while penalties have been given for less, it was possible to argue that the defender first got a touch on the ball before coming into contact with Totti. But the referee's decision to send Totti off on a second yellow card for simulation was outrageous and justified the Italian protests and claims that he was inept if not corrupt. But the chubby Ecuadorean, Byron Moreno, appeared determined to become a figure of hate in Italy. Almost immediately after the sending off Tommasi broke clean through on goal for Italy only to be called back for a completely incorrect offside decision. Eventually, and it seemed inevitably, South Korea scored a late winner when their player Ahn Jung-Hwan quite improbably outjumped Paolo Maldini to head the decisive goal. Ahn played his club football for Perugia where five goals in two seasons, mostly spent warming the bench, was his unimpressive record.

The Italian press and Trapattoni were convinced there had been a conspiracy but while they had certainly suffered some bad decisions, there was more emotion than reason in most of the post-match analysis. Italy had cause for complaint but they had several chances to win the game. To this day, Giovanni Trapattoni believes in the conspiracy theory, as do many Italians. It was a highly unsatisfactory outcome to a tournament.

Whispers that perhaps a more positive approach would have done the trick when they were a goal to the good were overwhelmed by the roars of conspiracy theories. Trapattoni stayed in charge until the European Championships in 2004 where Italy made an early exit with the coach again claiming conspiracy when, in the group stage, neighbours Sweden and Denmark played a draw which secured their own positions while condemning Italy to third place and an early return home.

This ended 'Trap's time at the helm. Ironically, his successor, Marcello Lippi led the team to World Cup success just two years later, at the height of a new betting scandal in Italian football.

Following his spell as international manager he became manager of Benfica whom he led to their first league title in eleven years. A short return stay at Stuttgart preceded his next League win as he took Red Bull Salzburg to the 2007 Austrian Bundesliga. This made Giovanni Trapattoni only the third manager to win titles in four countries, an achievement since equalled by Jose Mourinho.

Five years managing the Republic of Ireland was the last chapter in the career of a charismatic coach who was extraordinarily successful as a club manager but for whom international management proved more difficult and not always for reasons over which he had any control.

Ireland were not blessed with the talent which he had at his disposal in Italy. Furthermore, many had claimed the coach was too old and working in outdated methods when he took the Italian job. Now some eight years later similar criticisms, perhaps with more justification, were heard as he arrived in Dublin. His time with Ireland drew mixed reactions. Expectations were not too high. Failure to qualify for tournaments was tolerated if there was some evidence of progress. That is where the disputes and discussions centred. Having made the play-offs for qualification for the 2012 European Championships in Poland and Ukraine, Ireland received and availed of the easiest possible draw when they were paired with Estonia.

At the tournament the Republic team lost all three games scoring just once and conceding nine goals. Being placed in a group with Italy, Croatia and World Champions Spain did the Irish no favours. Nevertheless there was criticism of Trapattoni's method and approach with many believing his innate conservatism was never suited to an Irish squad which would normally endeavour to compensate for technical deficiencies with huge effort.

It was also felt that he made the assumption he had no players with any skill or imagination and planned accordingly and that this was not a correct assessment and sold short some of the better players available to the Republic.

Sadly, his time with Ireland saw further controversy when a notorious unpunished handball by Thierry Henry in a Paris play-off game for World Cup qualification brought further misery to Ireland. The thoughts that maybe a more adventurous mentality in earlier games would have dispensed with the need for a play-off or that Ireland had failed to beat France in Dublin were conveniently ignored as the injustice became the only story.

Trapattoni parted with Ireland soon afterwards, returning to a well-deserved retirement at his home outside Milan. He was never anything other than polite and courteous and for this he was hugely respected in Ireland, even by those who would have preferred a more adventurous style, which was never really an option with the master of defence.

Arrigo Sacchi

"I never realised to become a jockey you
should first have been a horse."

**Sacchi, upon his appointment as manager of AC Milan,
answers those who question his lack of playing experience**

There are many tales of how players got their lucky break in football but few can have matched the appointment of Arrigo Sacchi at Milan. Sacchi had not been a player. His managerial experience was limited to four full seasons, none of those in Serie A. The Parma team he managed played and defeated Milan in a home and away cup tie. Milan owner, Silvio Berlusconi, who had just acquired the club in 1986, was highly impressed by the manner in which Parma played.

He was possibly the only owner who had the nerve and the self-confidence to back his judgement and gamble on this virtual novice. Milan had not been a force for many years. Liam Brady described their set-up as decidedly unimpressive when AC Milan were among the clubs seeking to sign him as he departed Juventus in 1982.

But the new owner was determined that a once great club would return to the very top of the game under his guidance and with his resources. Sacchi arrived at Milan for the 1987/88 season. And it is clear, firstly that having been appointed manager he was given complete authority and secondly and crucially, he received 100 per cent support in the early days when things did not go especially well.

His initial appointment was greeted with derision by the Italian sports media who fastened on to his lack of experience as a player, taking the view that this deficiency made managing at the highest level quite impossible. Sacchi reacted with the immortal retort: "I never realised that to become a jockey you should first have been a horse."

Filippo Galli has spent most of his career at Milan, first as a player, later returning to run the youth development programme at the club. Galli holds five Serie A and three Champions League Winners medals. He believes it was the degree of organisation Sacchi brought to the club that made the difference. He said: "It was good at that time because Berlusconi, with his company, had taken over the club and of course he brought the organisation of his company. And so the link between these two mind-sets was very good for the team. Sacchi organised very well the pre-season and all the training sessions schedule. At that time we had had good managers and good coaches such as Liedholm but the organisation that Sacchi brought to the club was unbelievable. And he was part of every decision — every decision, technically speaking, but also about the performance and about the planning of the journeys, of everything. He was not the man who was in charge of just the side, he was part of everything within the organisation."

Sacchi's influences were the attacking sides such as Honved, Real Madrid, Brazil and Netherlands. This set him apart from what had been the prevailing trend in Italian football for quite some time.

Gabriele Marcotti described quite succinctly the basis of Sacchi's radically innovative footballing theory: "One of his core beliefs was that, if you could synchronise movement and positioning, you could get a 'multipier' effect. If your team moved as one, each player continuously adjusting to what was happening, it would be almost like playing with thirteen or fourteen players, rather than eleven. Thus, Sacchi had a countermeasure for every possible scenario on the pitch. So for example, if the opposing fullback passed to the winger on the right-hand side of midfield, the whole team readjusted. And when the winger passed it inside to a central midfielder, they would all readjust again. Always coordinated, always in unison. And it was the same when Milan had possession."

Filippo Galli explained what this was like in practice: "The organisation was outside the pitch but also inside the pitch. And Sacchi was really a maniac in this way because really he was mad about the organisation on the pitch. I remember that he could move you a few centimetres — 'no you have to move here because otherwise you cannot intercept the trajectory of the ball,' so it was unbelievable for us the organisation on the pitch."

When Galli describes Sacchi's appointment and what it was he set about achieving one can only marvel at what was achieved and how quickly. It is one thing to dismiss the scepticism of journalists with a memorable quote. It is an entirely different matter to walk into a dressing room with wall-to-wall internationals and announce that, while you've never played or coached at this level, you have an idea. In effect, he had to convince mature internationals and seasoned professionals that they should buy into a concept of how the game could be played which differed from anything they had experienced before.

The acquisition of three Dutch players, Marco Van Basten, Ruud Gullit and Frank Rijkaard put him in a position to introduce the type of play he had achieved at Parma but with better players and on a bigger stage. Rijkaard could not be used during his first year as the rule allowing only two foreigners applied, changing to three at the end of that season. The team already contained Paolo Maldini, Mauro Tassotti, Roberto Donadoni, top scorer Pietro Paolo Virdis and Franco Baresi.

While Sacchi had strong self-belief there has rarely been a better example of the need for an owner or chairman to support their appointed manager through early tribulations or setbacks. What made Sacchi's preparation different for the players was that every single day of the week became the most important day. There was no slow start to the week, a couple of harder days, and a tapering off. It was flat out intensity of concentration every day. Thursday meant a game against some random opposition, their own second team, a local team, a visiting team, whatever it took to provide opposition so that the full first team side could play together in a game where they had to play, for at least forty five minutes, with maximum intensity and attitude, as if it were a vital league game.

Ruud Gullit recalls his time under Sacchi with respect and affection. "Sacchi was very much focused on how the team had to be in any situation. So it was all about when we were defending we had to have the same shape. The shape of the team was the most important thing. 'Keep that' — 'hold that' — especially in moments when you are in difficulty because the less space the opposition has, the less goals they were going to make. And we were also very much vertical — always forward, backward, forward backward, all the time. That's why a lot of the opposition were all the time offside. Sacchi was trying to make that perfect. He was one of the best managers."

An example of how Sacchi worked was when on one occasion he had been struggling with flu and was confined to bed on the Thursday. That night he phoned everyone involved, coaches, trainers and finally the players. Filippo Galli says by the time Sacchi got to him, the manager knew more about the game than Galli, who had been playing.

Sacchi's four year stay would restore Milan to a position of dominance they had not experienced for some time. They won the League title in his first year, were third in year two and then second in each of the two remaining years. However, on the world stage they made a major impact winning two successive European Cups and two World Club titles.

It is for their exploits in Europe that most neutrals remember that AC Milan team. The very first entry to Europe under Sacchi was disastrous. In the autumn of 1987 Milan were eliminated from the UEFA Cup by Espanol, the small club from Barcelona. That game had been preceded by a home defeat to Fiorentina in the league and these results created a very difficult climate for Sacchi. Filippo Galli said it seemed that Sacchi might not be able to continue, such was the clamour from the supporters. But Berlusconi stood by his man.

Brian Glanville describes a phone call from the owner to a manager whose confidence and morale had been battered. "My dear Sacchi, go on as you are and you'll see in the end we'll both be proved right." Galli described how it changed. The manager continued to drill the team with intensity and then they went to play at Verona. "Like a switch, it worked and we won one nil, Gullit scored and from there it was like a rolling stone." It was indeed a transformation. Milan went on to bring home the first trophy of the Berlusconi regime in a league campaign which saw them lose only one other game besides that Fiorentina defeat. With that league title came qualification for the European Cup and a chance to atone for the disastrous defeat to little Espanol.

An easy 7-2 aggregate win over the Bulgarians, Levski Vitosha, was followed by what came close to being a truly disastrous event in Belgrade. The home player, Vasilijevic, committed the most appalling foul on Roberto Donadoni who lay unconscious on the ground and unable to breathe. It was only the medical knowledge, presence of mind and sheer persistence of the Red Star physiotherapist who had to break Donadoni's jaw to enable him get air into his lungs, saving his life. Both legs finished 1-1 with Milan going through 4-2 on penalties, thanks largely to goalkeeper Giovanni Galli.

A struggle with Werder Bremen in the quarter final saw only one goal scored over the two legs, a penalty from Van Basten. In the semi-final a 1-1 draw away to Real Madrid was the last occasion of tension on the way to Milan's third ever European Cup as they cut loose in the return leg continuing in similar fashion against a flat Steau Bucharest in the final watched by 97,000 people at the Camp Nou. The semi-final second leg saw Sacchi's Milan at their absolute best as they destroyed a Madrid team containing Buyo in goal, Martin Vasquez, Michel, Bernd Schuster and a strike force of Emilio Butragueno and Hugo Sanchez. Once Ancelotti opened the scoring with a long distance exocet inside twenty minutes, the game was up. The three Dutch stars each scored with Donadoni, now thankfully, recovered, making it 5-0. Two goals each from Gullit and Van Basten put paid to Steau in the final. The Intercontinental Cup was then added to the Milan Trophy cabinet as Atletico Nacional of Colombia were beaten 1-0 in Japan, the goal scored by substitute Alberigo Evani, deep in extra time. The Medelin team famously contained goalkeeper Rene Higuita of the scorpion kick and Andres Escobar, so tragically murdered after the U.S. 1994 World Cup.

While Milan could not retain their league title, they returned to a second successive European Cup Final in Vienna against Benfica.

It was a dull, drab affair in which Rijkaard won the game with the only goal scored in the 68th minute. They easily won the Intercontinental Cup in Tokyo where Olimpia of Paraguay were despatched 3-0 with man-of-the-match Rijkaard scoring twice.

At Milan it took a brave or mad man, an idealist, to approach football with such a positive attacking, pressing method as Sacchi devised. Looking back at that era, it was to the great benefit of football in Italy and in the greater world, that such a man was actually granted the opportunity to implement his ideas. It is to his credit that such success was achieved during his four years at Milan. The most notable aspect of his departure was that he had complained bitterly that Berlusconi was not prepared to spend on recruitment of further top players to replace the ageing members of his team such as Tassotti and Ancelotti.

The manager certainly had a point because after the Dutch acquisitions in his first year, the team stayed virtually unchanged during the remaining three years of his tenure. And he was no 'yes' man, never hesitating to make demands of Berlusconi and Galliani, the AC Milan General Manager. For their part, they were critical of Sacchi in those latter days as they contended the last two League titles should have been won, blaming him for exerting far too much pressure, physical and psychological, on the players. Filippo Galli believes that the team became more focused on Europe and that it was simply difficult to compete at the same intensity throughout the league and European campaigns.

Sacchi went on to be appointed Italy manager after the disappointment of the 1990 World Cup. The desired and expected home-win had not been achieved and to make matters worse, their great rivals, West Germany, lifted the Jules Rimet trophy in Rome.

The US finals in 1994 offered a shot at redemption for the national team under its new manager. There were no obvious odds-on favourites. Brazil were considered the most likely to succeed but were regarded as a pretty mundane side. Argentina looked as if they would be without the rapidly disintegrating bloated figure of

Maradona. No other European team promised greatness. So Italy, although showing nothing exceptional themselves, reckoned they had at least a chance in the US.

Once the tournament began, they showed even fewer signs of potential outright success, qualifying for the second phase only after finishing third in a four-team group. Their win over Norway was decisive after a draw with Mexico and defeat by the Republic of Ireland.

It was an inauspicious start for Italy and Sacchi. But his men were resilient. While group winners Mexico exited at the next stage, beaten by Bulgaria and Ireland played poorly in losing to the Netherlands, the Italians beat Nigeria 2-1 both goals scored by the ponytailed Roberto Baggio. Spain were next up in the quarter finals and again Italy went through 2-1, this time both Baggios, Roberto and Dino, doing the damage.

The New York semi-final brought together Italy and surprise package, Bulgaria, ensuring a European team would contest the final. The game was decided in one moment of genius from Roberto Baggio towards the end of the first quarter. He waltzed past a couple of Bulgarian defenders before powering home a ferocious drive for the game's only goal.

So Italy led by the former shoe salesman who had transformed Milan would play in the World Cup Final at the Pasadena Rose Bowl against the favourites, Brazil, who had by way of a single Romario goal, overcome an extremely negative Sweden in the other semi-final.

There was much criticism of Sacchi for the myriad changes to the team during his tenure as Italy manager. To be fair to Sacchi, they seemed to have been plagued by injuries throughout the campaign. Franco Baresi was hurt so badly in the first phase game against Norway that he required surgery and did not re-appear until the final. Again, it was argued he should not have been restored to the team in such circumstances — a direct echo of the Ferenc Puskas story at the 1954 finals. For all the talk of constant tinkering, the team was built around a core of AC Milan players with the three Juventus men, Conte and the two Baggios. There were six Milan players in the starting line-up for the 1994 final.

Italy defended superbly, inspired by the AC duo of Maldini and Baresi. After 90 minutes plus extra time, with neither side giving up a goal, the first World Cup Final to be decided by a penalty shoot-out had arrived. The exhausted Baresi skied Italy's first penalty over the bar but Brazil also missed their first kick. It went to 2-2 before Massaro missed while his opposite number scored to put Brazil 3-2 ahead. It now fell to Roberto Baggio to keep Italian hopes alive. This was the player who had done more than any other to get Italy to the final. Along with Stoichkov of Bulgaria, he had been the shining light of a fairly indifferent tournament which had culminated in an indifferent 120 minutes just concluded. Sadly for Baggio and for Italy, his penalty went soaring over the bar giving the Selecao their fourth and least distinguished World Cup victory.

Arrigo Sacchi continued until Italy's exit at Euro 96 in England where the team was eliminated from a group containing the Czech Republic, West Germany and Russia.

He returned briefly to club management spending a year at Atletico Madrid during which he led the team to the Cup Final and consequent qualification for European football. Clearly, he made an impression during his short stay in the Spanish capital as he was to return some years later in 2004/5 when he was appointed Director of Football by Real Madrid.

This was during club president, Senor Perez's first "gallactico" period when he believed that filling a team with expensive superstars was a guarantee of success. Sacchi was scathing of what he found and stayed only one season. For a man whose philosophy was based on the "multiplier" effect, requiring concentration and workrate from all players, the set-up at Real was anathema to everything he believed. A team full of stars who never tracked back was as far as one could get from the Sacchi way of doing things.

Since then his involvement has been as a pundit and quite a

critical one at that. His football legacy is the AC Milan team of the late 1980s and early 1990s and their swashbuckling style with which they conquered Italy, Europe and the world.

Sacchi's greatest legacy is the change in Italian football which was due primarily to his positive approach. By the time his four years at AC Milan were up, the scoring rate in Serie A had shot up to the extent that more than 100 additional goals were being scored per season in a league where negativity had reigned.

The last word on Arrigo Sacchi is with Gabriele Marcotti who wrote about a former player meeting Sacchi in more recent times and described how his one-time manager was more relaxed. "He was set at eight — and not his normal eleven."

Guy Roux

"When I was seven I said I wanted to play football every day of my life. And I just about pulled it off."
Guy Roux

A story in which a football manager stayed forty four years in his job sounds like a work of pure fiction. Yet it is the tale of an extraordinary football man, Guy Roux, and the club A J Auxerre where he forged one of the most remarkable careers in the history of the game. Auxerre is a small town about 170 kilometres south of Paris with 39,000 inhabitants.

Guy Roux was born in 1938 in Colmar, near the border with Germany. Guy's father was imprisoned by the Germans during the early years of the Second World War and upon his release the family relocated to Appoigny, a village just north of Auxerre.

Roux joined Association de la Jeunesse Auxerroise (AJ Auxerre) as a fourteen year-old, making his first team debut two years later in a local league game. From Auxerre he went to Stade Poitevin but after one year he moved on to spend from 1958 to 1961 at Limoges. This was amateur football. By 1961, aged twenty two, Roux realized he did not have the ability to play at the higher levels in the professional game, and decided coaching was the only route through which he could have a life in football. Arthur Rowe at Crystal Palace accepted his request to come and spend a brief internship at Palace to observe coaching and managing at a professional club, albeit in England's Fourth Division.

With no other experience Roux then applied for the vacant manager's job at Auxerre and was duly appointed player-manager. What prompted the club to go with such a young man was money. Roux would work for a ridiculously low salary and he committed to develop the team, not by spending non-existent funds on transfers but by developing young players. His offer to 'always balance the books' was what swung the decision. He would do things on the cheap and at that particular moment, 'the cheap' was about all AJ Auxerre could afford.

If there is an upside to working as a football manager for virtually nothing, at an impoverished club, it is that patience must be higher than expectation because finding a replacement to work under similar conditions is nearly impossible. True to his word, Roux was a model of frugality, even famously persuading local farmers to donate manure for the Auxerre training ground.

National Service between 1962 and 1964 proved an early unwelcome interruption but once Roux returned to the club, progress was made. He continued to play through the 1960s but it was his organization and leadership that put Auxerre on the road to success. In 1970, a landmark year, Auxerre were promoted to the Third Division of the national league system. Ten years later on July 24, 1980, Auxerre made their debut in the first division (Ligue 1) having reached the second tier in 1974.

Under Roux progress was steady. Every aspect of the club was important to the manager. Players learned quickly that hard work was the minimum requirement. Roux was a tough task-master, an obsessive disciplinarian, but a man capable of convincing players that his methods worked for the team and for the players' own long-term careers.

Basile Boli may be best known for scoring a winning goal in a Champions League final for Marseille (albeit they were later stripped of that title) or while playing for France, for head-butting Stuart Pearce, but his formative footballing years were at Auxerre. When Roux was tipped off that Boli liked to climb the academy wall at night and buzz about the town on his moped, Roux had a quick solution. Boli not only found his machine chained and locked to the railings but also had the cost of the lock deducted from his next pay-cheque.

Roux established a network of informants who helped him keep a tight rein on his players. Probably the most ingenious ruse was his enlisting of the toll-booth attendants on the nearby Autoroute through whose tollgate cars would have to pass going to or coming from Paris. No player could take what he thought was a discreet night out in the city without his manager learning next morning of the precise times he had gone through the toll barriers.

So great was Roux's belief in developing young players that in 1980 he rejected the opportunity to sign an international striker who had been offered to the club, in favour of investment in a new and greatly improved youth academy. It was a decision that said much about the long-term mentality of both manager and club.

The Coupe Gambardella is the prestigious French Under-19 competition played between teams from the professional clubs. Auxerre won this cup for the first time in 1982 and went on to win it on a further five occasions up to 2000. That run of success through the latter years of the 20th century indicates how Guy Roux and Auxerre operated, developing youth, building on that development, sometimes selling players for huge profits, replacing them with more youths or players who cost much less, balancing the books and competing at the highest levels.

By 1983-4 Auxerre, having finished third in Ligue 1, were playing European Football. High league placings in the following years led to regular nights in Europe. As the team was rising in stature so were some Auxerre players. The French squad that won Euro

1984 included goalkeeper, Joel Bats and midfielder Jean-Marc Fer-reri while Patrice Garande took Olympic Gold in a great year for French football. In 1989-90 Auxerre reached the quarter finals of the UEFA Cup. In 1993 it took a penalty shoot-out before Dortmund managed to knock them out in a UEFA Cup semi-final. In an earlier round Auxerre had eliminated Louis Van Gaal's Ajax, a team that would within two years win the Champions League.

And Roux's side had by now become a model of consistency on the home front. Third place in the league in 1994 was not even that season's greatest achievement as the team went on to win the Coupe de France. Fourth place in 1995 was followed by the most successful season in the history of the club.

In season 1995-6 Auxerre, with an average attendance of just 11,000, finished on seventy two points, four ahead of both P.S.G. and Monaco, to take their first ever league title. To complete this extraordinary season, the little club from Burgundy went on to beat Nimes in the Cup Final 2-1 having trailed by a goal at half time. To illustrate how far Auxerre had come, their nineteen-man squad in the double winning year was laden with players who had become or would soon be capped by their countries. There were nine French internationals, two very experienced multi-capped Algerians, one Madagascar international and Taribo West who made it an even more memorable year by winning Olympic Gold with Nigeria in Atlanta.

As well as Lilian Laslandes and Alan Goma, the French stars on the team included Laurent Blanc whose career was effectively put on track by Roux. Blanc had an outstanding season for Aux-erre as the double was won. Johan Cruyff was so impressed he negotiated Blanc's transfer to Barcelona and Blanc arrived at that club on the day Cruyff was so ignominiously sacked. The double winning team also included another World Cup winner, Stephane Guivarc'h, the man later regarded as the worst striker ever to play in the Premier League where he had represented Newcastle Unit-ed.

Auxerre finished top of their group in their maiden Champions League campaign, with victories over Ajax, Grasshoppers and Rangers. It took that season's ultimate winners, Dortmund, to end their involvement.

Eric Cantona had come to Auxerre as a youth player in 1981 remaining until 1988 when he was transferred to Marseille for a healthy FF22million. His play had been outstanding but his disciplinary record had not. Roux bided his time and did a brilliant piece of business.

Enzo Scifo came to prominence with Anderlecht in his native Belgium, winning three league medals before a lucrative transfer took him to Inter. That did not work out nor did his next move to Bordeaux. Still only twenty three when he arrived in Auxerre in 1989, his two years there under Roux got his career back on track. Club and player benefitted greatly as the reincarnated player moved to Torino, where he won a Cup and on to Monaco where he won a league before returning to Anderlecht for yet another league win.

Philippe Mexes would come later to win a Coupe de France before adding two Italian Cup medals with Roma. Djibril Cisse got his break in football at Auxerre under Guy Roux where he won a Coupe de France in 2003 before moving to Liverpool. Bacary Sagna was another Roux protégé who would achieve success in England with Arsenal and Manchester City, having first won a Coupe de France medal in 2005 in the final game of the forty four year reign of Guy Roux.

In all, an astonishing array of talent passed through this tiny French club with its famously badly dressed manager. Roux cultivated the image of the country bumpkin in a baggy tracksuit and funny bobble hat. His amazing record shows he was no bumpkin. Awarded the 'Legion d'Honneur' in 1999, and on first-name terms with Presidents and Prime Ministers, despite the string of world famous players who passed through the club during his time there, Guy Roux was always the most important figure at AJ Auxerre. To have managed a club for such a long number of years through all the changes in football and in the wider world is a truly unique achievement. Roux started out as Auxerre manager a few months before construction began on the Berlin Wall. He was still managing the same club some sixteen years after the wall came down.

His decision to announce his retirement immediately after the 2005 Cup final victory, the fourth in his long career, did not go down well. Players felt he might have waited until they had enjoyed their moment of glory and the wily Guy was accused of hijacking the attention as his announcement meant Roux was the focal point during the victory parade with the cup.

Bill Shankly said: "Liverpool was made for me and I was made for Liverpool." Without doubt, Auxerre was made for Guy Roux and Guy Roux was made for Auxerre. As if to prove the point, he surprisingly came out of retirement to sign a two-year contract with Lens. Four games later, he quit, realizing he was not and never would be ready for a challenge away from the club he took from absolute obscurity to the very top of French football.

Ottmar Hitzfeld

"In football you are judged only by results — there are no style points."
Ottmar Hitzfeld

Ernst Happel was the first manager to win the European Cup/ Champions League with two different teams. The next to do so was a man whose career followed a steady incremental rise from the bottom to the very top of the game. It was a rise which eventually had him voted Bayern Munich's greatest ever coach, World Soccer Magazine's World Manager of the Year, UEFA Coach of the Year, IFFHS World's Best Coach (twice) and the "Best Coach of All time" in the Bundesliga. And these were just some of the individual honours bestowed on Ottmar Hitzfeld.

In 1949 Ottmar Hitzfeld was born, the youngest of five children in Lorrach, West Germany, close to the Swiss border and the city of Basel. His senior playing career began at Basel in 1971 and apart from three years at VfB Stuttgart, Hitzfeld played all his club football in Switzerland, moving back to Lugano and finishing at Luzern.

Having qualified as a teacher of mathematics and sports while playing for Basel, he planned to return to teaching once his twelve year playing career ended in 1983. He was shocked to be told he would have to re-sit his teaching exams because of the length of time which had elapsed since he had qualified. Hitzfeld refused to accept this ruling and decided he would try coaching and managing before dealing with a return to his first choice of work. His time as a player had been thoroughly enjoyable, the highlights being six appearances for the national team at the Munich Olympics in 1972, finishing as top scorer in the Swiss League the following year and winning two Swiss Super Leagues and a Swiss Cup with Basel.

He spent a year in his first coaching job at FC Zug whom he led to promotion before moving to FC Aarau for the next four years, during which time he had his first triumph as a coach when his team won the 1985 Swiss Cup. Explaining the pressing game he introduced at Aarau, he said it was considered unusual at that time but his reasoning was: "If you're with a smaller club you have to play with bigger risks to be successful."

In 1988 Hitzfeld was appointed coach at one of Switzerland's strongest clubs, Grasshoppers of Zurich. His three years with Grasshoppers brought the Cup in his first year, followed by a double and then retention of the league championship. Four major trophies in three years attracted the interest of Borussia Dortmund who had just had a poor season in the Bundesliga and were seeking a new manager. Hitzfeld joined Dortmund and retained the existing coach Michael Henke as his assistant, initiating a long and fruitful working relationship.

Hitzfeld's description of the Dortmund team at that time is revealing. "The team was very insecure. They weren't playing well at home. They were afraid to play at home. My main task was to instil confidence and assertiveness back into the team — to make them a force at home once again and to give them the ability to dominate every opponent."

In the first season, Dortmund were within two minutes of a league title. Stuttgart scored in the 88th minute on the last day of the season to snatch the title leaving Hitzfeld's team in a very creditable second place. This earned the club a place in the UEFA Cup, an opportunity grasped enthusiastically as they made it all the way to the final of that competition. A heavy defeat over two legs against Juventus was taken by Hitzfeld as a lesson in football and in life. He realised there had been progress and that his task was to build on that. And the building took a little longer.

In 1995 Borussia Dortmund won their first Bundesliga in thirty two years and only their fourth ever. The fifth title was added in 1996. Michael Henke, Hitzfeld's assistant manager and coach, described the 1997 Champions League victory as the greatest ever achievement in Ottmar Hitzfeld's managerial career. It is a difficult statement to contradict, as Borussia Dortmund won their first and only Champions League and in doing so avenged that UEFA Cup final mauling by Juventus. The Italian hot favourites were well and truly beaten by a superb Dortmund side in which recent signings Paulo Sousa and Paul Lambert excelled, the latter playing Zidane out of the game to win 3-1.

The steady advance to the top of the football world had culminated in that Champions League win for Dortmund. But the manager was not done. In 1998 he was hired by Bayern Munich. At the time of his arrival, he himself felt he had a big advantage over many of the players as he had already won both the Bundesliga and a Champions League. In six years at Bayern he would lead them to four Bundesliga wins and two Cups. This included the double in 2000. There were a further three League Cups.

It was the pursuit of the Champions League that brought the greatest disappointment and then the greatest joy. The final of 1999 in Barcelona will be remembered for the amazing Manchester United win with two injury time goals after 90 minutes in which they were outplayed and apparently on their way to defeat. According to Michael Henke: "The team was on the floor, we were ruined. But I believe even at that moment we saw the quality of Ottmar Hitzfeld. He remained calm and objective and managed to pull the team together. He had won the Champions League with Dortmund and he could have won the Champions League with a second team and he did really win it after 90 minutes, but he could not hold the cup in his hands."

Hitzfeld held what he described as his longest team meeting ever, in which he explained to the players that it was not just bad luck that they lost and that if they were to come back and win this competition they would need to eliminate the errors and retain concentration to the very last.

Within two years they were back in a final against Rafa Benitez's Valencia. At full time it was 1-1 both goals coming from penalties. Extra time came and went. The shoot-out was dominated by Oliver Kahn who saved three times to ensure victory. The Intercontinental Cup was a further landmark achievement for the manager as Boca Juniors were beaten by a single goal.

The season 2002-3 brought yet another Cup and Bundesliga double for club and manager. By 2004 as Bayern were going through a period of indifferent form, finishing a season without a trophy, Hitzfeld left the club.

He returned to Switzerland where he took time to recover from exhaustion and what he described as feeling a bit depressed. In February 2007, he returned to Bayern after the sacking of Felix Magath. It was too late to rescue the league.

The following season after the team had been renewed through some frantic transfer activity, Bayern and Hitzfeld were back to winning ways. Toni Kroos had come through the club's development system. Among the incoming transfers were, Franck Ribery from Marseille, Luca Toni from Fiorentina, Miroslav Klose from Werder Bremen and Ze Roberto from Santos. The double was won yet again. Hitzfeld resigned but said the year and a half of his return had been the happiest time he had spent in football. Free from the pressure, or perhaps better able to cope with it following his time away from the game, he was more relaxed than for many years. The return was a personal triumph for a man who had always respected his players and who always received respect in return.

After his second term at Munich, Ottmar Hitzfeld was appointed manager of the Switzerland team. So from 2008 until 2014 he managed the country from just down the road from his home place, the country where he had started out in senior football at Basel. During his time in charge, he, quite remarkably, led the Swiss to consecutive World Cups in South Africa and Brazil. They topped their qualifying group for the 2010 tournament and had a 1-0 win over eventual champions Spain. The 2014 qualifying campaign ended with Switzerland unbeaten and on their way to Brazil.

Players who played for him spoke of his calm demeanour and of how he earned their respect through his knowledge and ability to communicate that knowledge without ever raising his voice or losing his temper, no matter the circumstances. And the team he picked off the floor after their shattering defeat by Manchester United found themselves a year later needing a draw to win the league. In the 90th minute of the final game of the season against Hamburg, they conceded the first goal of the game and with it the league... apparently. But in the fourth minute of injury time, Bayern scored the equaliser for the point that gave them another Bundesliga title. It was the completion of their recovery from the cruellest of defeats — a lesson truly learned from a master teacher.

Hitzfeld's stated simple philosophy, and one he clearly lived by, was: "You can't be satisfied just because you have achieved something. Satisfaction is the biggest enemy of an athlete."

8

Netherlands

IN the long history of Association Football, until the 1970s Netherlands never really figured as a power in the game. They had played their first International game against Belgium in 1905. They were one of several European countries which refused to travel to Uruguay for the inaugural World Cup Tournament of 1930. Netherlands, Italy, Spain and Sweden had all expressed interest in hosting that tournament. When 1928 Olympic Champions, Uruguay, were awarded the honour there was an immediate withdrawal by these four nations as well as by Austria, Germany, Hungary, Switzerland and Czechoslovakia. England was not a member of FIFA so their participation did not arise for a competition at which the hosts would add the World Cup to their Olympic title.

Italy 1934 saw a return of the Europeans but for the Netherlands it was to be the briefest experience. Having qualified along with Belgium from a group comprising just those two teams and The Republic of Ireland, they made it only as far as the first game in Milan where they were beaten 3-1 by Switzerland.

Qualification for France in 1938 seems to have been even easier. Once more the Netherlands and Belgium emerged from a group, again containing only one other team — this time Luxembourg. The Dutch World Cup odyssey to France lasted no longer than their initial tournament participation in Italy, as they made a prompt exit losing to Czechoslovakia in Le Havre. Following the devastation inflicted by World War II, the country did not even participate in the World Cup qualifiers for Brazil in 1950 or Switzerland in 1954. Their 1958 qualifying games were against Austria and Luxembourg.

By now only one team could emerge from the three-team qualifying group and this was Austria. The pattern continued with failure to qualify for Chile in 1962, for England in 1966 or for Mexico in 1970.

So how could a country with such an abysmal record up to that point arrive at the 1974 World Cup as the most exciting team in the world, as the team that every football-loving neutral wanted to see win? They were a team of all the skills, a team that rivalled Hungary of 1954 as the most unfortunate beaten finalists.

And four years later they would go to Argentina, this time without their best player, only to finish runners-up again, losing unluckily to the host nation. What transformed a nation which was not even competitive into one of the best and most attractive in world football? The astonishing change in the fortunes of Dutch football is a study in itself. Here we look at the men, the coaches and managers who played such a key role.

Jack Reynolds

"For me, the attack is and remains the best defence."

Jack Reynolds

The story of a transformation begins with club football in the Netherlands decades earlier with the arrival of an Englishman, Manchester-born Jack Reynolds, at the small Amsterdam club, Ajax. As a player. Reynolds had no career worth speaking of. From Manchester City reserves as a twenty-one-year-old in 1902, he moved to Burton Albion for a year and to Grimsby for two years. He spent the next two years at Sheffield Wednesday where he made two first team appearances, then had a short stay at Watford before finishing at New Brompton where he stayed from 1908-1911 playing 108 times and in doing so doubling his career total of first team games.

Reynolds was yet another of those English coaches who had a vision for the game, a vision notably not shared by those in control of football in England. So to coach he went first to St. Gallen in Switzerland before arriving at Ajax of Amsterdam in 1915. He did double-job to manage the Dutch national team briefly in 1919, left Ajax in 1925 returning for a further thirteen years in 1928. This term was ended in brutal circumstances in 1940 as the Nazi invasion of the Netherlands resulted in Reynolds and other non-nationals being interned for the remainder of the war.

His internment was spent at Upper Silesia, now part of Poland where P.G. Wodehouse was among his fellow prisoners. The war over, he came back for a third and final stint from 1945 to 1947. In all, that amounted to twenty seven years as Ajax manager for Jack Reynolds. Within that time, he led them to their first ever Dutch Championship and by the end of his managerial career he had presided over eight championship wins as well as one KNVB Cup in 1917.

In his book "Brilliant Orange", David Winner quotes historian Harke Groenevelt on how Reynolds laid the foundations at Ajax for what would eventually follow. He worked from early morning until 10.00 p.m. coaching teams of every age group in the same style. Reynolds is credited with establishing what would become the Ajax way; attacking football based on utilising the wings with quick passing by skilful players and on a tactical system that did not change from team to team at every level within the club. In 1965 three years after his death, a stand at the De Meer stadium was named after Jack Reynolds, further testimony to the regard in which he was held within the club.

It has been suggested that he created "total football" but perhaps it is more accurate to say he created the environment in which it was possible to develop the concept of total football, something which will always be associated with the Ajax team that won three consecutive European Cups between 1971-1973 and the wonderful Dutch team of the 1974 World Cup. Never was the adage about success having many fathers as applicable as when attempting to establish the origins of "total football". Ajax had nine English managers in all and a successor and compatriot of Jack Reynolds has also been credited in some dispatches with having created the concept.

Vic Buckingham

"I thought: 'he's a useful kid.'"

Vic Buckingham on his first sight of a very young Johan Cruyff

Just as Reynolds was greatly and quite rightly respected for his hard and intelligent work with his charges, Vic Buckingham who led Ajax from 1959-1961 and from 1964-1965 was recognised as a great coach and manager. His subsequent recruitment by Sevilla and Barcelona was indicative of the respect in which he was held in Spain. Indeed, in joining Barcelona he began a trend which would continue for decades and bring great benefits to the Catalan club, as the path from Ajax was followed by Rinus Michels, Johan Cruyff, Louis Van Gaal and Frank Rijkaard.

Buckingham's reputation in Britain was badly affected by the emergence of a betting scandal in 1964 at Sheffield Wednesday, the club he had just left to return to the Netherlands. Three of his former players earned life bans from football but apart from having been in charge when the corruption took place, there was no evidence linking the manager nor was there any indication that he had knowledge of a plot that involved players betting against their own team.

Buckingham was a proponent of the type of football preached by Reynolds and demonstrated by Ajax. Among his discoveries was a young player called Johan Cruyff. Once more Ajax had a manager who helped provide that environment necessary for creativity to flourish. And finding one of the games' most creative geniuses amounted to putting another building block on the wall that would soon be complete for all to see. Buckingham's Ajax career ended as do so many in football management. On January 21, 1965 after a drawn game against DWS, a rival Amsterdam team, Buckingham was sacked. It had been a difficult and inconsistent season with some bad results including a 4-9 defeat at Feyenoord in the game before the DWS derby. In his first season in football, young Johan Cruyff was in a team too close for comfort to the relegation zone. The manager paid the price and was replaced by, of all things, a Dutch manager.

Rinus Michels

"He'd chase them in the city, he'd chase them on the bike.
If people went out he was on top of them."
**Ruud Gullit describes how the young disciplinarian Rinus
Michels enforced curfew on his Ajax players**

Football never ceases to amaze and to throw up some quite strange statistics, but statistics taken at face value can sometimes mislead. In Vic Buckingham's last seven games as boss of Ajax, they won four, drew one and lost two. In Rinus Michels' first twelve games in charge, only three were won, five were drawn and the remaining four were lost. But the team avoided relegation. On the face of it, not much had changed in that year apart from the name of the manager. However, the changes for the players were dramatic. The Ajax players were part-time footballers in 1965, reliant on other jobs to keep them afloat.

Training began at 7.00 a.m. after which players ate food and departed. Those who could do so returned for ball-work at 2.30 p.m. while everyone assembled for further football coaching after 5.00 p.m. Michels' first priority was success in domestic competition. If he could achieve that he would be better positioned to pursue the next objective, persuading the club's board to agree to pay the players sufficiently well so they could become full-time professional footballers.

Marinus Jacobus Hendricus Michels was steeped in the Ajax club from an early age. Born in 1928 and raised in the shadow of the Olympic Stadium, there could only ever be one club for Michels. By nine years of age he had his own Ajax jersey, something quite uncommon in pre mega-marketing replica days.

By 1940 he was a junior member of the club but once again, we see a player whose career was interrupted by war. In this instance it was his teenage years which were lost to football but showing no ill effects, Michels made his senior Ajax debut in 1946 aged eighteen. As debuts go this one was pretty impressive, the young forward scoring five times in an 8-3 win. He was considered a strong and forceful player rather than a particularly skilful one and would go on to play thirteen seasons for Ajax winning league championships in 1947 and 1957 and quite impressively scoring on average just under one goal in every two games. His career ended by a back injury in 1958, Michels became a gymnastics teacher and remained so until summoned by Ajax to replace Buckingham.

And it was as a coach/manager that his reputation was earned. Ajax, relegation candidates when he arrived in 1965 would within the next six years win four League Championships and the KNVB Cup three times. His tenure in charge from then until 1971 would prove to be the most important development in the history not merely of Ajax but of Dutch football.

Ruud Gullit spoke about Michels approach to managing the great Dutch team to the European Championship in 1988. He contrasted the more mellow approach of Michels at that time to his early days managing Ajax. Michels had a reputation for strict discipline and Gullit painted a picture of the young manager in Amsterdam: "He was always on top of that group when he was with Ajax. He'd chase them in the city. He'd chase them on the bike if people went out. He was on top of the team."

In 1965 Michels' initial focus was on improving the team and team spirit but above all achieving a balance within the team which he perceived to have been badly lacking and to which he attributed huge significance. His second season saw Ajax win the League title. Full-time professionalism followed.

The games which told Michels and indeed the rest of the football world that Ajax were on their way came in the tie against Liverpool in the second round of the 1966/7 European Cup. The first leg in Amsterdam ended 5-1 to Ajax. After the game Bill Shankly was predicting the return would be a 7-0 win for Liverpool, suggesting it had been one of those freak results which would soon be corrected at Anfield. The return was a 2-2 draw with Ajax comfortable at all times with Johan Cruyff scoring both goals.

Following the Liverpool success, Ajax drew their next European Cup home tie, a quarter final against Dukla Prague and then lost the second leg. Michels was furious at losing to what was clearly an inferior team. The captain who had conceded the winning own-goal was immediately transfer-listed and never again played for the club.

The changes introduced by Michels applied to every aspect of club life at Ajax and not merely to the recruitment of the right players. Training methods were improved. The physiotherapist was recognised as a critical member of management and the one person in whom players would confide. His station was moved from the open area of the changing rooms to a private office.

Michels worked diligently, constructively, intelligently but ruthlessly to turn a team of relegation threatened part-timers into an all-conquering force. Anyone considered unsuitable was jettisoned. New young players were brought in. The Ajax of legend was gradually taking shape and just four years after the bitterly disappointing Dukla Prague defeat, Michels' Ajax had been moulded into a team to conquer Europe for the first time.

There is a pragmatism under the surface of every winning manager, no matter how much of an idealist he might appear. Rinus Michels was no exception. David Winner describes a conversation he had with Barry Hulshoff the Ajax defender. "Michels wanted me to be harder, meaner, to foul forwards if they beat me. He wanted me to kick a man, just take him out. But I couldn't and didn't do it. Maybe some little holding, but not enough. It wasn't in my character." As an alternative Hullshoff learned to read the game so effectively that fouling along the lines described proved unnecessary.

Michels' first major recruitment decision was to prove critical. He recognised that the team lacked the steel to become winners and he had a good idea how to fix that. Velibor Vasovic was the sweeper for Yugoslavia and Partisan Belgrade. He had captained that club and scored their only goal as they lost the 1966 European Cup Final to Real Madrid. Vasovic had won five Yugoslav League medals, four with Partizan and one with their deadly rivals, Red Star, with whom he controversially spent a season. He was hard as nails, an experienced winner with a winning mentality and as a trained lawyer he was well capable of making his point in any company. His signing by Ajax demonstrated Michels' pragmatism and determination to achieve the ultimate successes with his Ajax team.

Vasovic has been described as being "unburdened by false modesty" and while he does appear to have had an unlimited belief in his ability and in his contribution to the Ajax success story, one would find it hard to argue against most of his claims. Success came pretty quickly to Ajax. Vasovic came in to a team which had already won a championship in 1966 but his leadership helped that evolving team win further league titles in 1967, 1968 and 1970. Throw in KNVB Cup wins in 1967, 1970 and 1971 to see how dominant this team had become domestically.

In 1969 Ajax reached the European Cup Final losing 4-1 to an A.C. Milan side managed by Nereo Rocco and containing stars such as Fabio Cudicini in goal, Karl-Heinz Schnellinger, Kurt Hamrin, Giovanni Trapattoni and as captain, the iconic Gianni Rivera. Ajax had their stars in Barry Hulshoff, Piet Keizer and Johan Cruyff. It was their first shot at stardom. They lost. But they would be back.

It was ironic that another Dutch team, their deadly rivals Feyenoord of Rotterdam would beat Ajax to the European Cup Winners rostrum with a 2-1 extra-time win over Celtic in the 1970 final played at Milan's San Siro stadium.

It has been said that losing might not be a disaster if lessons are learned in defeat. There have been few examples of a lesson being as well learned as that which Michels had at the hands of the mighty A.C. Milan.

The European Cup final defeat taught Michels that despite their massive progress at home, success in Europe required a further step-up. He needed to replace several of the older players with younger more energetic and talented men who would play to his instructions. In came players like Gerrie Muhren from Volendam, the brilliant young defender Ruud Krol and later, the supremely talented and hard running Johan Neeskens. That defeat also taught him that his favoured 4-2-4 formation left them too open and that a system which enabled better defensive work was necessary. The change was made to 4-3-3.

The most interesting aspect of the type of game Ajax played is that Michels by his own admission, did not have any clear vision of how they might play. He did not set out with the idea of total football in his head. It was as the team matured that the system began to develop. No doubt, the introduction of Vasovic played a part. The arrival of such players as Ruud Krol and Johan Neeskens was also vital. But the single most important element in this team's evolution and in the evolution towards what became known as total football was Johan Cruyff.

It was Cruyff who dictated matters on the field. Possessed of an extraordinary instinctive understanding of space and how to use it when in possession and close it when not, he more than anyone, was the fulcrum around which the position-changing and high pressing revolved. The team became known for playing offside. Again, this was not part of a pre-determined plan but something which occurred as a consequence of the positional inter-changing and relentless pressing of the opposition. When Ajax lost the ball, the objective was to press the other team quickly and aggressively and to do this as far up the field as possible. With quick defenders such as Krol minimising the risk of counter attacks, this became a highly effective part of the Ajax game.

Attacks could come from anywhere on the field. Defenders could break forward, central players could come down the wing. Every player knew he had the freedom to go forward and that someone would slip into his position so that the shape of the team did not change. It was predicated on all team members being skilful and quick. It was football born of intelligence and an enormous amount of hard work and discipline.

By 1971, Ajax were hitting their stride as the new power of European football and Michel's vision and dreams of European glory were realised. It had been an amazing journey from a relegation battle in 1965 to the summit of European football. Ambition became reality when on June 2, 1971 at Wembley Stadium Panathinaikos were beaten 2-0.

On their way to total football, to three European titles, Ajax may have won friends and admirers around the world of football but the ruthlessness in Michels approach, was the element without which the same success would not have been possible. Once the European Cup had been won, Michels' objectives at Ajax had all been achieved. Before the team went in search of a second European title, the coach was on his way to Barcelona. The parting was quick but it would not be the last time many of these players played for Rinus Michels.

When Barca won the last ever European Fairs Cup in late 1971 credit for this victory went largely to the departed Vic Buckingham rather than the recently arrived Rinus Michels. Indeed, Michels found the whole experience of managing Barcelona extremely difficult and stressful. The man who had been able to shape and build a great team in Amsterdam was finding a radically different football culture in Catalonia.

His disciplinarian approach was not received by the players as it had been at Ajax. Two years of struggling were his lot until something changed at the start of the 1974 season with the arrival of Cruyff. With the Dutch ace pulling the strings, Barcelona was a transformed team and players who had appeared to lack confidence were suddenly looking like world beaters.

Even with a technical hold-up over the ratification of the transfer, making Cruyff unavailable for the first seven league games, the team's form improved so much once he took the field that they became unstoppable on a march to the club's first league title in fourteen years. Michels stayed in Catalonia just one more year before returning to Ajax. In 1974 he took the Netherlands team to a

World Cup in West Germany and with his team playing some of the finest football ever seen, powered by six Ajax or recently ex-Ajax players, "total football" found a worldwide audience as Netherlands reached the World Cup Final.

This was the first of four spells in charge of the national team. His persistence could never be faulted and in 1988 Netherlands finally won its first and to date only major tournament when taking the European Championship in West Germany. Their defeat of the hosts in the semi-final was heralded by Michels himself as redemption for that terrible defeat in 1974. This time the team was inspired by top scorer Marco van Basten and the charismatic Ruud Gullit.

A country whose national squads earned a reputation for dissent and division was indebted to Michels who singularly appeared to have the status to command the respect of his players and to bring out the best in what was widely seen as a virtually unmanageable group of individuals. This was achieved despite heart surgery in 1986. Surprisingly, it was not achieved by ruthless discipline but with superb man management by a mature and intelligent coach.

Gullit described him as 'quite mellow' in his approach to this national squad, a changed man from his earliest days in management. Gullit said: "I asked him years later why? He said because you guys, when you were with PSV, with Ajax, with Milan, you were already winning things, you were already professionals — I didn't need to do anything for you — you just did everything by yourselves."

Gullit's own reaction to the manager's approach was telling in that he felt Michels' recognition that he had winners on his hands which enabled a calmer attitude, was great. At this time, PSV had won the European Cup, Ajax had won the Cup Winners Cup in 1987 and lost the final in 1988. Milan powered by Gullit and Van Basten had won their first league title in an age, so Michels did have winners all around him with five PSV players in his regular starting line-up.

Ruud described Michels as: "A great tactician as well — he knew exactly what the team needed and where he could harm the opposition. He always said 'never underestimate the opposition, because they want to hurt you as well. So we must be prepared for what they are good at.'"

Rinus Michels died in Belgium in 2005 aged 77 after further heart problems.

Johan Cruyff

"You don't have to understand. If I wanted you
to understand, I would have explained it better."
**Johan Cruyff grows tired of being asked the same question,
which he has made clear, he does not wish to answer.
Barend and Van Dorp TV Show**

Johan Cruyff was a truly fascinating person, a visionary on the football field and a man who managed his life in a manner rarely seen in any sport let alone football. His early rise with a young Ajax team was meteoric. Under the guidance of Rinus Michels he became at nineteen the key man in the Ajax team that went on to win four Dutch Championships in five years from 1966 leading to their first European Cup in 1971.

After the third consecutive European Cup win Cruyff moved to Barcelona. A number of events converged to bring about his decision to leave his home-town club where he had been since the age of ten. Cruyff was the third different Ajax captain to lift that European trophy and remained captain when a meeting took place at pre-season training camp. A coach who might have known better decided to put the captaincy up for grabs by calling for a vote.

Teammates who felt Cruyff had been considering a departure voted to change the captaincy. That moment had come, which comes to all great teams — the moment when what has gone before will be no more. Cruyff went on to his next challenge. "The meeting was winding to its dull conclusion when Knobel (the manager) remembered something. 'There is one last thing. The captaincy. We'll have to decide who's the captain.' If there was a single instant when Ajax's golden age ended, this was probably it." (David Winner–Brilliant Orange)

Without question Cruyff knew his own worth and was unapologetic in seeking the best deal available in all circumstances. Showing a Dutch pragmatism he drove a hard bargain with chairmen and sponsors but reasoned that he was a professional footballer which by definition means behaving professionally and maximising his income. His quote while still a young player at Ajax sums up his philosophy quite well "When my career ends, I cannot go to the baker and say, I'm Johan Cruyff, give me some bread." Here was a player who knew he was hugely talented but also realised his career could end with one bad injury. Also he loved to argue! And as recently as 2015, in a wide-ranging interview in which, incidentally, he gave all the credit for what became known as total-football, to Rinus Michels, Cruyff declared that ultimately: "The most important thing is not money, it is self-esteem."

Cruyff became a Barcelona legend as he inspired the team to its first La Liga title in fourteen years, the 5-0 away win at Real Madrid the highlight. His performances had him crowned European Footballer of the Year for the third time. Barcelona also won a Copa del Rey during his five years at the club.

Nothing describes Cruyff's character like the ending of his playing career in Holland. After Barcelona, now thirty one and having lost three quarters of his money in an ill-advised venture, he went to the U.S. where lucrative contracts were to be had and played one season each in Los Angeles and Washington before returning to Spain for a very brief time at Levante. Ten games in, it became clear this was a mistake so club and player parted company.

He then returned to Amsterdam and Ajax where he completed two years from 1981 to 1983 adding two more Erevidisie titles to the six from his early career plus a Cup medal in 1983. Now came a defining moment in his life. Ajax told him they would not offer him a further one-year contract; they believed he could not play sufficiently often to make a contract viable, that in effect he was too old; finished.

He then signed for rivals Feyenoord who were heading towards ten years without a league title. In his final season as a player in Holland, Cruyff wore the colours of Feyenoord, playing in every league game except one. Feynoord won the League and KNVB Cup double and Cruyff was named Fotballer of the Year for 1984, his fifth such award, the first having come in 1967. It was not a bad way to end a playing career.

Having had an incredible playing life, his coaching career spent at just two clubs, Ajax and Barcelona, was pretty impressive and included some landmark achievements. He coached/managed Ajax from 1985 until 1988 winning the KNVB Cup in 1986 and 1987 and more significantly the European Cup Winners Cup in 1987. The Cup Winners Cup was highly regarded and was considered very important although less prestigious than the flagship competition, the European Cup.

One of the features of his move into management was that he could now implement a playing system in which he believed and which was a variation on what had been the Ajax method from the days of Jack Reynolds. There were still two wingers wide on the touchlines but at the back Cruyff believed in three mobile players supplemented by a defensive midfielder. He wanted two strong and skilful midfield players who would control the game and a centre forward who could score goals and do a lot more besides including making space when appropriate for the supplementary attacker.

At its best, the system was not far off the total football concept of which Cruyff, the player, had been a key component. With Marco Van Basten in the number nine role, attacking assistance came from the even more prolific, in that European campaign at least, John Bosman. They were supported by wide players Aaron Winter, later to go to Lazio and Inter, Arnold Muhren later to star for Ipswich Town and a young Frank Rijkaard. It was an attractive attack oriented team. Cruyff was a rookie manager, but this was a rookie with a difference. To be named World Soccer's "Manager of the Year," as he was in 1987 in just his third year in charge at Ajax was quite an amazing achievement and is indicative of the manner in which his team played. As a player Cruyff had always shown an awareness of how the team should play. His teammates talked about his extraordinary feel for where everyone should be positioned to the extent that he would shout at his fellow players to get five metres forward or three metres to the left. It was as if he could be on the pitch playing but also seeing the big picture as if removed from the field and watching from the stands.

The extent to which he was the thinking footballer, long before he ever managed can be gleaned from an article written in 1972 when Cruyff was twenty five and at his peak in a great Ajax team. This piece is from a book by two Dutch journalists, Frits Barend and Henk Van Dorp which consists of some articles but mainly interviews with Cruyff throughout his career.

"Cruyff is a proponent of the theory that the three different lines of a team (defence, midfield and attack) should play closely together. He prefers to see one or two people from the midfield or defence appear in the front line. That gives him the opportunity to go to the wing knowing there will not be a gap in the centre. In the Ajax line-up, he is not stranded on an "island" and expected to chase every lost ball. The way Ajax played last year, it was easy for him to receive passes and play the ball to someone else. It was often visible in his game."

For someone so relatively young to have such a clear vision of how the game should be played is highly unusual but explains how his move into coaching and management was so natural and so likely to be successful. The system of play which Cruyff had propounded at Ajax was so successful that as late as 1995 when the club won its last European Cup, it was acknowledged that this team was still playing the Cruyff way. That is close to twenty five years after this article was published.

Johan Cruyff's return to Barcelona as coach came on May 4, 1988. Club President Josep lluis Nunez was as fine an example of a political animal as could be found in any boardroom. A chairman with a will to mould a club to his ways, he succeeded in stuffing the board with his acolytes, thereby protecting himself from any possible coup and doing so sufficiently well that he stayed in power for an astonishing twenty two years. It must be acknowledged that Nunez, a successful building contractor, brought about serious infrastructural change at the club such as the expansion of the Camp Nou, the development of the mini-stadium alongside the Camp Nou, the FC Barcelona Museum and the construction of La Masia, the most famed apprentice base in Europe.

A look at how Barcelona handled the hiring and firing of its coaches around that time is quite revealing: Rinus Michels completed his second stint of exactly two years in May 1978. He was followed by Frenchman, Lucien Muller, who did not quite make the twelve months, exiting in April 1979 just a month before his successor Joaquim Rife would take the team to its first European triumph by winning the Cup Winners Cup. Rife lasted about as long as Muller, not quite making it a year and he was replaced, on an interim basis, by the returning and readily available Herrera for just two months to the end of the season. Given their earlier history, it was ironic that Herrera should be replaced in May 1980 by Ladislao Kubala. By November of that year Kubala was gone, to be replaced by Herrera until June 1981. The German, Udo Lattek, followed in June 1981 and actually stayed on board for almost two years until March 1983. During Lattek's time the club won a second Cup Winners Cup as well as a Spanish Cup and League Cup.

Lattek will not have been shocked by his early dismissal once the league title was seen to be out of reach. He had described his earlier experience at Bayern Munich — "I told the President, Wilhelm Neudecker, we need some changes. 'That's right', he replied, 'you're fired.'" After Lattek, Jose Luis Romero came and went in March 1983 to be followed by World Cup winning manager Cesar

Luis Menotti who was gone by June 1984. Terry Venables followed Menotti and managed to jam the revolving door for a little while before it all went wrong. He lasted until September 1987 by which time he had brought the club its first league title in eleven years as well as a League Cup but the 1986 European Cup Final loss in Seville to Steau Bucharest would haunt him and become the beginning of the end of his Spanish adventure.

The European Cup was the real ambition of all Barcelona presidents, players and supporters or cules as they are called. Failure to win the ultimate European trophy was a source of frustration and reflected on every single manager who tried and failed to win this great prize.

Less than one year and two more temporary coaches later, Nunez would make the best decision of his entire twenty two years as president of FC Barcelona. He would appoint as coach a man who as a player had two loves, Ajax and Barcelona. The Catalans were hiring someone whose three years in coaching had been a resounding success. They were hiring a man who had been an idol as a Barcelona player and who was fully aware of the culture of the club and its supporters and of the politics which were never far from the surface at FC Barcelona.

The autocratic trigger-happy president was hiring the man described as the "obstinate maestro." It should have ended early and in tears. But Johan Cruyff went on to become, and still remains, the longest serving manager in the history of Barcelona.

Taking over when things are at a low ebb can have its advantages. Attendances at FC Barcelona had dropped to between 20,000 and 25,000. This compared to Cruyff's time there as a player when the average home crowd was between 90,000 and 100,000. Those had been good times indeed. However, a 25,000 attendance was a derisory figure for Barcelona as well as being financially disastrous.

The fallout from a players' mutiny against the club president Nunez meant the incoming Cruyff got funds to bring in replacements of his own choosing. Amazingly, he never enjoyed a relationship with Nunez and rarely spoke with the president, having decreed in the early days that he would not countenance any directors, the president included, entering his dressing rooms. His view was quite simple. "If you want me, I will come to your office. You don't come to my dressing rooms."

The need to develop a style of play and to ensure this style was adopted across all club teams, youth and reserves in particular, was a recurring theme for Cruyff. He reasoned that players could be brought through much more easily this way and that their progression would not be impeded by changes in playing systems. It was the Ajax way and indeed the Herbert Chapman way and the Bill Shankly way from decades earlier.

Prior to Cruyff's arrival, Nunez had cleared out ten of the squad. Steve Archibald who had been a resounding success during the championship win under Venables, but who had later suffered bad injuries, was among those transferred. So too was Mark Hughes brought in by Venables but never able to win over the supporters. Cruyff demanded that the skipper Alexanco, who had been spokesman for the recalcitrant players, be retained and he proceeded to re-appoint him as captain.

The rebuilding began with the signing of a core of good Spanish players such as Jose Maria Bakero, Txiki Begiristain, Ion Andoni Goikoetxea and Julio Salinas. Five players from the youth team were promoted to the senior squad, among them Pep Guardiola. Gary Lineker's experience under the Dutchman was less than satisfactory as he saw no benefit to either the team or himself in Cruyff's wish to play him wide on the wing. Long time Barca player Carrasco was another who found the new coach's positional requirements a complete and most unsatisfactory mystery. Both players were moved on at the end of the first season. If there was concern that their departure would deplete the side this was soon replaced with great optimism when Ronald Koeman and Michael Laudrup were signed. Both would go on to become Barcelona legends. Others to follow in the door, in time, were Romario and Ghe-orghe Hagi.

Cruyff took with him to Barcelona his trusted ally from Ajax, Tonnie Bruins Slot and the management team was completed by Carles (Charlie) Rexach, a hugely respected and popular former player and former Cruyff teammate. Year one saw the European Cup Winners Cup return to Barca and the following year a Copa del Rey was secured with a 2-0 win over Real Madrid in the final.

Cruyff was still not happy with his squad and after further changes which included letting popular players go, his own ratings took a tumble with the supporters and the sense of unease was pal-pable as the new season began. Year three, 1991, saw the arrival of Hristo Stoichkov, the volatile Bulgarian. Having won three league titles in Bulgaria he arrived at Barcelona where he played a mas-sive role in the club's success.

Barcelona under Cruyff won four league titles in succession. Stoichkov completed what became known as "The Dream Team" and ended up European Footballer of the Year in 1994. Ronald Koe-man, who had been one of Cruyff's first signings was also critical to the team's success. At that time a limit of three foreigners was imposed on teams. The wealthier clubs like Barcelona would usu-ally have four in their roster but only three could take the field at the same time.

This was how Michael Laudrup slipped down the pecking order behind the newly arrived Romario in the final year of the four-in-a-row. As significant as the four consecutive league titles were, the crowning glory of the Cruyff era was the completion of the great dream of winning the European Cup. In a tense final at Wembley Stadium in 1992, a goal by Koeman finally freed Barca from the tyranny of failure in Europe's main event, as Sampdoria were over-come.

Of the twenty two squad members in 1991 when that first title was secured only thirteen were still in the line-up for the fourth win in 1994. Among those were both goalkeepers, Zubizarreta and

Busquets, whose son later came through under Pep Guardiola, himself one of the thirteen constant members of the dream team. The three foreigners who survived those years were Koeman, Laudrup and Stoichkov while apart from Guardiola and Busquets, the remainder of the squad, including Bakero and Goikoetxea were all players brought in by Cruyff.

After the fourth title, the team began to disintegrate at a faster pace. Cruyff's relationship with the president also deteriorated. It had never been great but as long as there was success on the field, Nunez was happy to stay out of the manager's way. Now Johan wanted to rebuild and found he was not getting any positive response to his requests for specific targeted purchases.

Eventually, Nunez and his vice-president, Gaspart, met with Bobby Robson and then leaked to the media that Robson was taking over from Cruyff. As a way to do business or as an act of gratitude, it certainly left a bit to be desired. Jimmy Burns in "Barca — A People's Passion" explains how Gaspart came in search of Cruyff at the technical staff's dressing rooms. All hell broke loose as a furious Cruyff told him what he thought of him and Nunez and the row ended with Gaspart threatening Cruyff and saying: "You no longer belong here."

Burns sums it up about as well as it ever could be summed up: "Johan Cruyff, one of the greatest footballers of all time, who had won Barca more titles than any other coach in its history, had been given his marching orders like a part-time lavatory attendant who had overslept."

The question often asked is why Cruyff never managed the Dutch national team. He did come close on at least two occasions, both the players and the public indicating they wanted him, but it was not to be. Johan was seen as a difficult man to deal with but he was a man of principle and this, more than anything, came between him and the only other management job he really desired apart from Ajax and Barcelona.

It is the winter of 1992. The Barend and Van Dorp show deals with an issue around the 1994 World Cup in the US for which the Dutch team is expected to qualify without difficulty. There is strong rumour and support for the idea that if and when that happens, Cruyff should take charge at the finals. It would mean ending his contract with Barcelona just slightly early that summer and becoming manager of the national team only for the tournament finals.

In November of that year, Paul Boels, a senior member of the Dutch football authority (KNVB) while on the programme of Barend and Van Dorp says: "Don't worry about Johan Cruyff, Everything is all right. He will become national coach if Holland qualify for the World Cup in America in 1994". In December Cruyff is on the programme. The hosts, picking up Boels phrase, ask Johan: "Is everything all right?" Cryuff equivocates.

The interview continues with the hosts endeavouring to find out just what it is that has arisen in the four weeks between interviewing Boels and Cruyff, that has the latter insisting:

"A couple of things have happened that I don't want to discuss in any detail. Things I don't like." Cruyff makes it clear he does not want to discuss what it is that has got him bothered about whether he will become Dutch manager in the U.S. The hosts, undeterred, press on, asking him what it is he doesn't like and if it relates to Rinus Michels being appointed as a technical adviser to the KNVB. (At this point Cruyff's relationship with Michels is not perfect but his real antipathy is towards Leo Beenhaker). Johan is clearly unwilling and unable to discuss in public something which he wants to sort out with the KNVB in private. But, hell this is television so the two boys press on.

They ask him is it about salary. "No".

Does he actually have a contract at home, as has been speculated. "I might have".

They even take to asking him are the dykes too high.

They press on: "But you have a contract at home."   "Yes, I'm sure I do."

"What don't you like then? Will you or will you not go to America if Holland qualify?"

"If they qualify! You're always running ahead aren't you? There's time for everything. There's just a couple of things I don't like."

"We still don't understand."

And it was at this point of the interview that Cruyff came back with the classic response:

"You don't have to understand. If I wanted you to understand I would have explained it better."

The subsequent trajectory of the KNVB-Cruyff negotiations was downwards only. The team, led by Dick Advocaat, qualified as expected. But the negotiations between Cruyff and the KNVB could only be described as shambolic. It would appear the KNVB did their business in a way which will be familiar to students of how similar bodies in other countries work — when at their worst. Eventually, the discussions, such as they were, broke down in recriminations and with blame being hurled in all directions. The final word went to Professor Harry van Mens, who had participated in the negotiations for Johan Cruyff: "You, the KNVB, have a lot of explaining to do to the Dutch people."

After Barcelona, Cruyff did not return to coaching. He had involvements with Ajax in an advisory capacity but had a fundamentally different view of how the club should develop than that of the then manager, his own protégé, Marco van Basten. His influence at Barcelona has been more important where another protégé, Guardiola, appears to have been far more receptive and committed to the Cruyff way of playing. Cruyff has been widely credited with the rise of Barcelona under Guardiola and the effectiveness of the Masia as a development centre for young players.

As the world has changed and the old "three foreigners" or as it sometimes was in Italy "two foreigners" limitations have long since yielded to freedom of movement, the Celtic 1967 achievement of fielding a European Cup winning team all from the general area around Glasgow seems a quaint anachronism. In early 2013 something happened which it had been thought could never happen in modern football.

Barcelona, already champions elect in Spain, fielded a team, all of whom had come through the clubs youth system. Some such as Jordi Alba and Cesc Fabregas had moved elsewhere but had been bought back to become part of an all home-grown line-up, making them part of a great club with a great culture and for which Cruyff has to be recognised for his enormous and positive contribution.

Simon Kuper and Stefan Szymanski go a step further in their book "Soccernomics" in which they insist a line can be drawn from Cruyff straight to the Spain team which dominated European and World football from 2008 but especially in 2010 and 2012. With the Barcelona spine and a playing system mirroring that of the Catalans, there is total logic to their assertion that the team which defeated Netherlands in the 2010 World Cup Final is a direct result of the adoption of the Cruyff way of playing or as they term it "Cruijffism."

And as a person, what was Johan Cruyff like? Paul Courant told a story from his and Cruyff's playing days. He and Johan Cruyff had finished providing their post-match comments on television immediately after a Belgium V Netherlands international, Courant asked Cruyff if he would swap shirts. Johan apologised saying he had already agreed to swap with the Belgian goalkeeper, Jean-Marie Pfaff. Courant thought no more of the episode until five days later a package arrived at the Club Brugges office addressed to Courant. It was a Johan Cruff shirt, signed and posted by the man himself — a gesture which will forever remain with the Belgian.

Johan Cruyff, who had long relinquished his chain-smoking habit, died of cancer on March 24th 2016 just a month short of his 69th birthday.

Ukraine

FOOTBALL always had a position of importance in the old Soviet Union. Such were the structures and culture that interaction with the outside world was restricted. The great Dynamo Moscow goalkeeper, Lev Yashin, was the first internationally recognised star player, winning the Balon d'Or in 1963.

The club that broke the mould and eventually emerged on the European stage was Dynamo Kyiv. While Ukraine was still part of the USSR, Viktor Maslov became coach and with a revolutionised approach to football, took Dynamo Kyiv to new heights. His approach was further developed by Valeryi Lobanovskyi, a former player at Kyiv who brought scientific thinking to football as no one had ever done before. Lobanovskyi teamed with a statistician, Anatoliy Zelentsov to write a book with the exquisitely Soviet title of "The Methodological Basis of the Development of Training Models."

The club's achievements and that of its three players who became Balon d'Or winners is testament to the extraordinary men who provided exemplary leadership, in Lobanovskyi's case through the emergence of an independent Ukraine. Despite their inability to access what would have amounted to basic information for coaches elsewhere, these men demonstrated incredible management and leadership in their world of football.

Viktor Maslov

"Man-marking humiliates, insults and even morally oppresses the players who resort to it."

Maslov outlines his philosophy

Moscow 1970. Dynamo Kyiv player and 1966 Soviet Footballer of the Year, Andriy Biba, gave an interview to Soviet Daily Sport Express in which he let his views be known on the brutal dismissal of his manager Viktor Maslov, right there in Moscow where Dynamo were to play CSKA.

"The dismissal of Maslov was simply disgusting. Can you imagine? They were scared to tell him in Kyiv! Unexpectedly, Mizyak, a member of the Ukrainian Sporting Committee who had nothing to do with football but was responsible for overlooking Winter Sports, arrived at the hotel Rossiya where the team was staying. Our cowardly football chiefs entrusted specifically this person to let Maslov know that Kyiv no longer required his services......how we managed to play the next day, I can't remember. We're leaving for the airport and he's staying. There was anguish in Maslov's eyes. And tears, that no one had ever seen before."

No student of football could be surprised at the calculated ugliness of a manager's termination. But Viktor Maslov's contribution, not just to Kyiv but to the game of football, made his undeserved treatment especially nasty. Maslov was a man who brought something lasting and worthwhile to the game of football. He was an innovator, a man with a new idea that worked. He was a pleasant and amiable man who knew how to get the best from his players, who had jokingly and affectionately christened him "Grandpa", a name based on his rotund shape and prematurely balding head rather than his actual age.

Having enjoyed a relatively modest career as an intelligent midfield player, almost all of it at Torpedo Moscow, his move to coaching and managing followed directly on his retirement from playing in 1942. The leagues in the Soviet Union were suspended from 1942 until 1944 because of the war. His first spell as manager at Torpedo ended in 1948. Following equally undistinguished spells in charge of other clubs he returned to Torpedo for a second term from 1957 to 1961.

This time, his team made it to second place in the Soviet League in 1957. Then came his first big achievement, the 1960 league title which was followed by a runners-up placing again in 1961. A short stay at FC SKA Rostov was followed by what was to become by far the most productive period of Maslov's career, his seven seasons at FC Dynamo Kyiv. Dynamo had won their first ever championship in 1961 but the following two seasons saw them slip back to fifth and then seventh place. Maslov's arrival in 1964 heralded a new era and new thinking.

The capability to communicate and discuss football management was extremely limited within the Soviet structure. Although the development of relationships and dialogue was impossible under the Soviet system, Maslov had made efforts to study the Brazilians as they announced themselves to the world at the World Cup Finals in 1958. His conclusion was that while he liked their 4-2-4 formation, he believed a solution would be to bring back an extra man into midfield. He quickly decided that a better balance was achievable with two men withdrawn. The 4-4-2 system was born. Maslov's vision of how his team would play coincided with a new awareness of a more scientific approach to preparation. Proper diet and a greater understanding of physical preparation would play a key role in the development of a system which could be successfully deployed only by a team of supreme fitness.

Many of the Dynamo supporters were less than happy when Maslov dropped Valeriy Lobanovskyi, Yuriy Voinov and Oleg Basilevish, some of their most respected players, all of whom had been important contributors to the 1961 inaugural league title. Maslov believed there were cliques at the club and that these players were largely responsible and he harboured doubts that they would be capable of adapting to the changes. His system was the basis for the "pressing" game which would take the team to unprecedented glory. The idea of pressing was radical because up to that time, teams were allowed time on the ball, especially in their own half of the field.

The first requirement was physical superiority. The intense

training regime saw to this. The objective in games was to be able to both attack and defend with the maximum number of players at all times. The opposition would be hunted down, harried and dispossessed in all areas of the field.

The "pressing" method would later be utilised by Rinus Michels and Arrigo Sacchi among others. The club was famed for the ethos of unity and openness encouraged by Maslov and involving tactical discussions among players and coaches at which everyone was allowed, indeed encouraged, to contribute. Considering the prevailing culture in which this was happening, Maslov truly was a remarkable man. When one of his players was asked how Viktor had come to know so much about coaching he replied: "From God. Some people are born musicians, poets, painters. Maslov was born a coach."

Dynamo dominated Soviet football in the late sixties. Since the creation of European football competitions, the Soviet authorities had absolutely forbidden their teams from having anything to do with their cold-war enemies. Interestingly, once Kiev began to succeed, they were permitted to participate in Europe albeit with KGB chaperones on board. Having equalled a record by winning three championships in a row and a domestic double in 1966, Dynamo became the first Soviet club to experience European football.

Andriy Biba explained: "Why the decision to allow Dynamo to compete was made, I don't know, but in the squad we thought that we were being used essentially as lab rats. For the celebrated Moscow clubs this was very useful; they could take a look at the tournament, without risking their reputations. We had to play "blindly". We did not have access to any tapes of our future opponents. As for the idea that the coaching staff could travel and see their matches live, this was the realm of fantasy. Everything was new and unknown"

Entry to Europe was a monumental event for Dynamo Kyiv, its players and management. The closed nature of the U.S.S.R. made participation in European competition an unfulfilled and probably unrealistic dream for the leading clubs. So the opportunity to compete against teams from the west, whatever the motivation of those providing the permission was warmly welcomed by Dynamo.

The 1965-1966 European Cup Winners Cup saw Kyiv start with a 10-1 aggregate win over Coleraine of Northern Ireland. This was followed by an impressive 6-1 outcome over two legs against Rosenborg of Norway. The quarter final brought opponents in the shape of Celtic, who proved too strong for Dynamo, drawing 1-1 in Kyiv and winning comfortably 3-0 in Glasgow.

Two years later, Kyiv would have their revenge on the Scots, who as holders were eliminated by the Ukrainians in the first round of the European Cup. Unfortunately, Dynamo would go no further than the following round, falling to Gornik Zabrze of Poland. By then the Kyiv side had achieved as much as it would under Maslov's tutelage. And indeed what had been achieved was significant, shifting the balance of power from Moscow where it had rested for some three decades to Kyiv in the Ukraine.

Maslov was 60 and returned to his roots at FC Torpedo Moscow where he managed from 1971-1973. Losing the cup final on penalties after a replay was as near as he got to silverware. His final posting was at FC Ararat Yerevan where in 1975 his team would win the Cup Final on a 2-1 scoreline, ironically defeating Dynamo Kyiv. Maslov, the father of the modern game, died on May 11, 1977 aged 67 years

The next great era for Dynamo Kyiv awaited a new master, and ironically, a man and former player with whom Maslov had fallen out.

Valeryi Lobanovskyi

"A path always remains a path. It's a path during the day,
it's a path during the night and it's a path during the dawn."
Valeryi Lobanovskyi defends his decision to stick to his principles

While there was speculation at possible sinister reasons for the falling out between Maslov the coach and Lobanovskyi, the player, all the evidence points to the fact that Maslov did not have the time or space for a player given to ostentatious displays of dribbling, no matter how good that player's ball control. Later, Lobanovskyi, now a coach, would admit that he would not have time to indulge Lobanovskyi, the player, in his side.

Born in 1939, he joined his home town club, Dynamo Kyiv at seventeen and was in time to play a key role in that first League Championship of 1961, also winning a Cup medal in 1964 before leaving the Maslov-led club to play less than two years each at Odessa and at Shakhtar. Then, at twenty nine he announced his retirement citing his disgust at playing what he deemed anti-soccer. The player who had been the ultimate individualist was to become the manager whose philosophy was entirely based on the primacy of the team and the team ethic. The flamboyant forward was to become the most scientific of managers.

While a player he won two international caps in addition to the league and cup titles enjoyed with Kyiv. However, it was as a coach that he would achieve world recognition due to his unprecedented success. He was regarded as the first coach to take an almost mathematical approach to organising his team. Players were fed detailed data on individual opposition players. Elaborating on the system created by Viktor Maslov, he increased the fitness levels even further and introduced a built-in flexibility, with defenders over-lapping and forwards dropping deep where necessary — it was a tactical fluency which might well have been described as "total football."

Lobanovskyi's first managerial appointment was at Dnipro Dnipropetrovsk, lasting four years until 1973. Andriy Biba was signed from Kyiv and the team made progress, achieving promotion to the top division of Soviet football and finishing sixth in that league the following year. The young manager was learning that his methods could work. To realise his goals and ambitions required a better resourced club which took Lobanovsyi back to Dynamo Kyiv in 1974, this time as manager/coach.

Dynamo Kyiv under his guidance, emerged as a truly dominant force in the Soviet Union during the period 1974 to 1990. Eight Soviet Super Leagues, six Soviet Cups, the UEFA Cup Winners Cup twice, the UEFA Super Cup in 1975 was the haul of trophies but it was the power and athleticism married to superb technique that earned Dynamo and their manager admiration and respect in the game.

As a young man Lobanovskyi had been a brilliant student of mathematics. It was against this background that his application of maths and science to the preparation of football teams and to the playing of the game, made him unique. An indication of the type of obstacles provided by the political system of the time is that he had to call in all sorts of favours to obtain a computer for Dynamo Kyiv.

His use of statistics on opposition as well as his own players and team was a new development. Diet and fitness preparation were taken to a higher level and were monitored consistently. An idea of what he expected from players may be gleaned from the quote: "There is no such thing as a striker, midfielder or defender. There are only footballers and they should be able to do everything on the pitch."

Lobanovskyi could and did, therefore, make demands of players — but as long as the outcome was constant improvement and success, he had the complete loyalty and respect of his players. There is evidence that he was a deeply-thoughtful, highly-intelligent person with a clear view on how he wanted his teams to play. He treated his players with respect but as with all successful managers there is more than one side to the story.

Another former Kyiv player, Oleksandr Khapsalys had this to say: "Better not joke with Lobanovskyi. If he gave an instruction and the player said 'But I think..,' Lobanovskyi would look at him and scream 'Don't think! I do the thinking for you. Play!' "

Throughout those first glorious years in charge of Dynamo another ever-present element in all the success was Oleg Blokhin. Any player who can score, on average, a goal every second game at the highest level over almost twenty years, truly is to be cherished. Blokhin was a huge player in the life and successful times of Valeryi Lobanovskyi, scoring so consistently and scoring when it mattered most, in both UEFA final wins. To crown his achievements Blokhin, on his way to collecting the 1975 Ballon D'or, scored all three goals when Dynamo beat Bayern Munich 3-0 adding the UEFA Super Cup to their Cup Winners Cup.

Lobanovskyi took the pressing game, the brainchild of Maslov, and developed it further. His Kyiv teams utilised it to the full at home while deploying a variation more rooted in counter-attacking in difficult away games. It was for their brilliant clinical counter-attacking style that Dynamo are best remembered as the first Soviet team and the best East European team to have graced European competitions.

The manager's career at Kyiv was interrupted briefly as he took sabbatical leave on three separate occasions to manage the national team. On the first of these breaks he led his team to bronze at the 1976 Olympics. His second short spell at the helm did not yield success as they failed to qualify for the 1984 European Championships, although some blamed this failure on poor refereeing in a crucial game. The third term with the USSR national team was by far the most interesting.

While Lobanovskyi had been on his brief period of leave in 1984, things took a turn for the worse with the Kyiv team struggling to a tenth place finish and the loss of European competition. Valeryi quickly turned things around. The team, now featuring the emerging talent of Igor Belanov would win the double in 1985 proceeding to add a second Cup Winners Cup victory in 1986 with victory over Athletico de Madrid. By the end of that year, in the magazine World Soccer, Dynamo would be named second best team in the world behind World Cup winners Argentina. Lobanovskyi was named second best manager in the world and Igor Belanov became the second Dynamo Kyiv player to receive the Ballon D'Or.

Lobanovskyi, following the win over Athletico de Madrid, had again been persuaded to take charge of the USSR team, this time at the Mexico World Cup. The team came through the initial group stages comfortably before losing very controversially to Belgium 3-4 after extra- time. Questions surrounded two of Belgium's goals, both of which appeared to have been offside. This Soviet team was made up for the most part of Kyiv players.

At the European Championships of 1988, Lobanovsyi's USSR team, again powered by Kyiv players did better, finishing runners-up to Netherlands. By 1990 Lobanovskyi had taken Kyiv to their final title and his record eighth in the old Soviet Union.

He moved to the Middle East to UAE and then Kuwait, each job ending with his sacking. His sojourn in the Arab world is an indicator of how complicated an endeavour management can be and how so many factors dictate whether a manager succeeds or fails. Many of the greatest managers the game has known have had their failures. This should not alter their status as great managers.

By 1997 he was back at Dynamo where, this time, he remained for five seasons winning five Ukrainian Championships and three Cups. This was the post Perestroika era. Dynamo were now winning Ukraine Championships but any suggestion that such wins were no longer proof of quality in the Kyiv side can be knocked on the head. In the 1998/99 season Kyiv reached the semi-finals of the Champions League, losing agonisingly to Bayern Munich on an aggregate score of 3-4.

The 1999/2000 season brought yet another league title but a heart attack in 2001 seriously impaired Lobanovskyi's ability to function. Worse was to follow. A stroke on the 6th May 2002 proved fatal. The greatest manager produced in the Ukraine or indeed in the Soviet Union died on May 13, 2002 aged 63.

By then a third player developed by Lobanovskyi had been awarded the Ballon D'or — this time in the new era of freedom of movement while playing for another club to which he had been transferred. The player, Andriy Shevchenko along with Oleg Blokhin and Igor Belanov were among the crowd of more than 60,000 people who filed past the coffin of Valeriy Lobanovskyi.

Today an enormous monument incorporating a statue of the seated Lobanovskyi greets visitors to the Dynamo Stadium. In 2003 when Shevchenko won his Champions League medal with AC Milan, he made a pilgrimage home to Kyiv and the grave of Lobanovskyi, a man to whom he believed he owed a great debt and a man whose great ambition had been to bring that greatest of European Club trophies back to the Ukraine. Andriy Shevchenko placed his Champions League medal on the grave of Lobanovskyi, a fitting tribute to a manager and coach who had brought Soviet and Ukrainian football to unprecedented heights.

10

Brazil & Argentina

OVER the years it would have been easy to believe that all Brazilian football was 'samba football' and that all Argentinian football was tough and hard. The images suggest flamboyant players and coaches in Brazil and pragmatic, cynical figures in the Argentinian game. Beaten to World Cup success by their tiny neighbours, Uruguay, Brazil's breakthrough finally came in Sweden in 1958, Argentina's at home, more controversially twenty years later.

Mario Zagallo, Brazil's most successful manager had teams playing with enduring brilliance but with an awareness and capability in defence. Cesar Luis Menotti, like Zagallo, the first coach to bring the World Cup to his country, showed a greater appreciation for the finer points of the game than did many of his countrymen who managed club or national teams.

Not only that, but Menotti also showed a great sense of responsibility towards the players under his care. In this respect he stood out, especially in comparison with a few of his countrymen.

The hugely successful Carlos Bianchi, strangely had all his managerial high points in South America, failing to get any success on his ventures into management in Europe where he had excelled as a player. It can be difficult to define what has led to success or failure for a manager. Often we see the ten per cent of the iceberg that shows itself above the waterline. The bigger piece, or the bigger story below the surface frequently is complicated or beyond our comprehension.

Mario Zagallo

"Those who saw it, saw it.
Those who didn't will never see it again."
Midfielder Gerson describes Mario Zagallo's team's
World Cup winning display in Mexico 1970

Most records are beaten over time, but being the first to do something can never be equalled. Mario Zagallo will always be known as the first man to win World Cups as both player and manager. As a player he was on the left wing as Brazil racked up World Cups in 1958 and 1962. Being on the left wing on a team which had Garrincha on the right wing was a unique experience. Mario Jorge Lobo Zagallo had not started out as a winger but showing excellent judgement, soon opted for that position as he believed, quite rightly as it turned out, that it gave him the best chance of making the national team.

With "the little bird" Garrincha on the other wing the left sided player had to be committed to tracking back and to emptying the tank in every game. Zagallo won three state championships with Flamengo before adding two more after a move to Botafogo in 1958. One of the few players to play all games at the finals in Sweden and again in Chile, he scored in that 1958 final, best recalled for a wonder goal by the seventeen- year-old Pele. His contribution in Chile in 1962 was even greater as Brazil, without the injured Pele beat Czechoslovakia 3-1 in the final. These two teams had emerged from the same group having played a scoreless draw at their first meeting. Zagallo played a total of thirty three times for his country, finishing in 1964.

Of Zagallo's thirty three caps, six were gained at the Sweden World Cup Finals, and a further six in Chile in 1962. Certainly two World Cup medals and at club level five State Championships was a decent return by any standards His initial move into coaching and managing followed a very logical path. He began with the Botafogo youth team, graduating to the first team in 1966 and leading them to consecutive Rio State Championships from 1967 and the "Taca Brazil" Cup in 1968. He quickly developed a reputation for tactical astuteness, which would not have surprised those who had paid attention to his performances as a player. His appointment to manage Brazil came very late in the run in to Mexico 1970.

Joao Saldanha had managed the team through the qualification process where comfortably they won all six games, ensuring their presence in Mexico. Brazilian president, General Medici was a strong Flamengo supporter and let it be known that he wanted that club's player, Dario, in the national football team. Saldanha refused point blank and pointed out that he would not pick the General's cabinet. He was then criticised by the Flamengo coach, Dorival Yustrich. In 1967 Saldanha, while working as a journalist, had had a confrontation with a goalkeeper from Bangu whom he accused of match-fixing. This argument concluded when Saldanha fired two shots in the air. This time round he pursued Yustrich to a hotel where he was staying. Fortunately, as Saldanha came armed with his handgun, he missed the Flamengo manager in every sense of the term, as the latter had gone out. Clearly there was a problem but then Saldanha started openly to discuss his plans to drop Pele from the squad because he could not be prevailed on to track back and the team, having qualified, had then stumbled through a couple of preparatory games.

Brian Glanville provided the most apposite description of Saldanha, calling him a "gifted lunatic." Enough was enough and Saldanha was replaced by Mario Zagallo.

There is a point of view that Zagallo inherited an extraordinary bunch of players. That is undeniable. But within that crop of players there were several examples of duplications, of situations where it appeared certain players were so similar that only one of the pair could be selected. This is not an uncommon occurrence and has manifested itself with many top teams over the years. Mostly the managers decided to opt for one or other avoiding trying to fit both into a system which could not function with both.

Zagallo, uniquely, had another idea. He would play them all. Again, there are those who would say he simply wrote down the names of his best eleven players and that was his teamsheet, no thought to potential duplications or misfits, and that the attacking abilities contained within were so great that they could not lose. The truth is it was never as simple as that.

The widely held view in Brazil at the time was that Pele and Tostao could not play together as they fulfilled the same role. The sceptics were equally concerned that Gerson and Rivellino offered the same type of choice — pick one or the other as they can't go in the same team.

Zagallo, quite rationally, started with a solid defence as the basis for everything. What made the system so brilliant was its fluidity. This has frequently been misrepresented as great players just playing by instinct and making it work. But while Carlos Alberto charged down the right flank the other three back four players held their positions and Clodoaldo on the right of midfield was ever vigilant. Jairzinho would come infield off that right wing and the whole pattern worked. It worked so well it was repeated time and again. Jairzinho scored in every game in those World Cup Finals in Mexico.

The individual brilliance of Pele, Tostao, Gerson and Rivellino was there for all to see, flourishing within a team structure. For once the slogan: "They said it couldn't be done" ... would end with the words..."and they were wrong". Mexico 1970 was a tournament where no one doubted that the best team won. The phrase "the beautiful game" was never more appropriate than in Brazil's play. They inspired and thrilled and showed football at a level rarely seen to the extent that this team has become the benchmark for evaluating greatness in football. As Gerson put it: "Those who saw it, saw it. Those who didn't will never see it again." Mario Zagallo was still seven weeks from his 39th birthday when that memorable final took place.

After the high of 1970, Zagallo returned to club football taking

Fluminese and Flamengo to championship titles. He later moved to the Persian Gulf and after brief but lucrative spells at Kuwait, whom he led to Gulf Cup success, and Saudi Arabia, he took the United Arab Emirates to qualification for the World Cup finals of 1990 in Italy.

Spiritually Zagallo was never far from the Brazil national team and by 1994 he sat as Technical Director alongside Carlos Alberto Parreira, in the Rose Bowl at Pasadena as Brazil once again conquered the world. Functionality had replaced exuberance in this squad and a penalty shoot-out final 3-2 win over Italy typified that.

When Parreira departed the Brazil Federation inevitably turned to Zagallo who managed the team to the Paris final of 1998. This time there would be no happy ending as the hosts won 3-0. Brazil's performance was overshadowed by the mysterious illness that befell Ronaldo on the eve of the game, news of which began to emerge shortly before kick-off. When the players took the field, Ronaldo was among them.

It was a clearly out-of-sorts Ronaldo and if ever a team could be said to have incurred negative inspiration, this was the team. Back in Brazil, the criticism was saved for Zagallo for having persisted with fielding Ronaldo when he was unfit to play. Later it was revealed that the young Ronaldo weighed down by the expectations had suffered convulsions or an emotional fit. Zagallo then decided to leave him out. Shortly before kick-off Ronaldo arrived in the changing room declaring himself fit. Zagallo then reversed his decision leaving out Edmundo. Describing Edmundo as volatile is like calling Big Ben a clock. Not for nothing was he known as "the animal". He was said to have thrown punches at other players when informed of his late withdrawal.

Despite his earlier achievements, Zagallo was subjected to stinging criticism for the events in Paris. However, his record stands up well to scrutiny. He managed Brazil in 154 games winning 110, drawing thirty three and losing just eleven times. He holds two World Cup winners medals as a player and two more as manager and technical director. Add the club championships as player and coach and few will argue that he is up there among the best of all times. But if Zagallo did nothing else but bring the world the beautiful team of 1970, he deserves a place in football history.

Tele Santana

"Tele was one of the greatest Brazilian coaches of all time.
He was a coach who prioritised technique,
touch and the beautiful game."
Nelinho pays tribute to his manager

That the most popular Brazil manager of all is one who failed to win at two successive World Cup tournaments says much about how Brazilians see their football. Tele Santana da Silva, described in Brazil as "the last romantic," certainly brought excitement if not trophies during his time as Brazil boss. His playing career as a forward lasted ten years at Fluminense, followed by three final years between Guarani and Vasco da Gama. He then managed Fluminense and in what was regarded as a great achievement, took Atletico Mineiro to their first ever championship before, in 1980, taking over the reins of the national team, the Selecao.

After the break-up of the famed 1970 team Brazil went through a period where functionality replaced imagination in their football teams. The performances as much as the outcomes led to constant criticism of the 1974 and 1978 World Cup appearances.

Then came Santana, a man whose football philosophy was never in doubt. He would rather lose playing great football than win playing mediocre stuff. As Zico put it: "I think that group of footballers didn't know how to play any other way.........even when we were behind we never tried to win ugly." Brazil and Santana arrived at the 1982 finals in Spain with a collection of amazingly gifted players, many of whom were lured to Italy after the tournament. As one of them, Luizinho, declared: "It was the last great generation we had, full of world class players in Brazilian football."

In addition to Zico and Luizinho they had Falcao, Junior, Socrates, Oscar, Cerezo and Eder. The team had been assembled by Santana over the two years leading up to the tournament. Their European tour in 1981 had included wins in Germany, England and France. Everyone who had been privileged to see them play had been enthralled by the style and sheer class of the team. It was why they arrived in Spain, overwhelming favourites to win another World Cup. People around the world were not just looking forward to the World Cup — they were looking forward to seeing this fantastic Brazil team of all talents win the World Cup.

It was widely known that Santana had no time for on-field violence or bad behaviour. If a player fouled repeatedly he would be substituted. This was the beautiful game as it was meant to be. Explained Zico: "What he wanted was for us to play with creativity, to play for fun and to play in a way that would get results but in a clean, disciplined and correct way, respecting the laws of the game"

With two points for a win and one for a draw, Brazil stormed through their opening group finishing on six points with a goals tally of 10-2. Then it became four groups of three, each of which would produce a semi-finalist. The 'group of death' was that containing the holders Argentina, the favourites Brazil and the still mis-firing Italians. Italy's 2-1 win over Argentina was not as good as Brazil's 3-1 win over their South American rivals. As a consequence, a draw would suffice in the final group game to see Brazil through. Italy had to win. Italy led through Paolo Rossi. Brazil equalised. Italy led again through Rossi and again Brazil equalised. With twenty minutes left Brazil just needed to put up the shutters and move on to the semi-final. After an Italian corner the ball was heading goalwards when Rossi deflected it to the net. A third equaliser was not forthcoming against a determined Italian side.

It was with an air of sadness that this Brazilian team left the stage to return home to a tumultuous reception. The reality is that this defeat had more widespread repercussions than simply the one-off eclipse of a bunch of great players by a more utilitarian side. Eder, the scorer of some wonderful goals for that Selecao said: "We all look back on that game with great sadness. It didn't just change Brazilian football, it changed world football."

It is true that the Brazil team that won the World Cup in Pasadena in 1994 in a penalty shoot-out over, of all teams, Italy, was not nearly as well received upon their return home nor as lauded and respected as the great players from Spain 1982. Thew great Number 10 from that 1982 team, Zico, still says evcery player who played on that team is proud to have done so.

In the 1986 World Cup in Mexico, Brazil's exit again would be dramatic and again it would be in a game widely held to be a classic. They dominated France in the quarter-final in Guadalajara but having gone ahead, Brazil missed chances culminating in a penalty miss by the great Zico, who was unwise to even attempt the kick as he had barely entered the fray as a substitute when the penalty was awarded. Zico, with virtually his first touch, put Branco through on goal only for French goalkeeper Joel Bats to take him down for a penalty. The game went to extra time and finally to penalties where Socrates missed for Brazil before Platini did likewise for France. The French won out and Santana's second World Cup ended in a second glorious failure. Despite not reaching even a semi-final in either 1982 or 1986 Santana was appreciated, even loved, at home in Brazil for the manner in which the team played.

The last word on Tele Santana as national team manager comes from Nelinho; "Tele was one of the greatest Brazilian coaches of all times. He was a coach who prioritised technique, touch and the beautiful game."

After a two-year break Santana returned to club management first with Flamengo before achieving his greatest successes with Sao Paulo where championship success was followed by two Libertadores Cups which had eluded Brazilian clubs for the previous ten years. Two Intercontinental Cups in 1992 and 1993 were added through victories over Johan Cruyff's Barcelona dream team and Fabio Capello's Milan. So he finally gained ultimate success, a World Championship, albeit with club rather than country. Surprisingly, or perhaps not, the team Santana most admired was the Dutch side of 1974 with Cruyff at his peak

But as time went on, Santana's all-out attacking philosophy was increasingly vulnerable to more tactically astute teams. As Italy showed at the Spain finals, a team with the capability of containing the more individualistic Brazilian attackers while counter attacking effectively, was more likely to succeed than Santana's outfit filled with skill and creativity but perhaps lacking in defensive steel or maybe just lacking in cynicism. .

Santana suffered a stroke in 1996 which left him in very poor health for the remaining years up to his death in Belo Horizonte in 2006 aged 74.

Osvaldo Zubeldia

"Glory is not reached by a path of roses."
Osvaldo Zubeldia — the father of anti-football

As a football nation, Argentina dramatically entered the consciousness of those in Britain, during the 1966 World Cup. Alf Ramsey's famous "animals" quote lives long in the memory and in the history of that era.

It was the era of major breakthroughs for Celtic in 1967 and Manchester United in 1968 as the European Cup finally came to Britain. The 'reward' for winning a European Cup was a tie against the champions of South America to decide which club was the World's best. The Intercontinental Cup was a home and away affair and after Celtic won 1 — 0 at Hampden they went to Argentina to play Racing Club de Avellaneda and lost 1 — 2 leading to a play-off in a neutral country, in this case Uruguay. In the second game Celtic needed to call on their reserve goalkeeper as Ronnie Simpson was struck by an object thrown from the crowd, before the kick-off.

A Paraguayan referee quickly lost control of the third game, which achieved the near impossible by exceeding the levels of cynicism and violence witnessed in the previous games. While Racing won by the only goal, the result was incidental. There were six sendings off.

The bad taste from that tie had hardly vanished when Manchester United found themselves competing with Estudiantes de La Plata who had just won the first of their three-in-row Copa Libertadores. The first leg was played at Boca Juniors Stadium and was won 1 — 0 by Estudiantes. A newspaper interview at the time with the Benfica manager, the Brazilian Otto Gloria, was re-printed in the match programme. Since it consisted of a pretty crude attack on the character and sportsmanship of Nobby Stiles, a key player when England beat Argentina and indeed when Manchester United beat Benfica, it was highly inflammatory and set the tone for the tie. Gloria had described Stiles as 'an assassin.'

The fact that Estudiantes eventually won the tie by virtue of a 1 — 1 draw at Old Trafford was again incidental to the broader impact the game had. 'Holding the ball out there put you in danger of your life' was Matt Busby's view of what it was like to play against a real assassin, the midfield general of Estudiantes and Argentina, Carlos Bilardo. Racing had shown how to go about winning at all costs but Estudiantes took matters to a new level.

In the first leg, in Buenos Aires, Stiles was kicked, punched and head-butted. When he finally retaliated he was immediately sent off, conveniently incurring a suspension for the second leg. Bobby Charlton would require stitches to a head wound. At Old Trafford, Denis Law went off with an eye injury and a player from each side was sent off in the final quarter, the Estudiantes number five, Medina, and George Best of United. Ironically, the visitors goal at Old Trafford was scored by Juan Ramon Veron, a man whose son, Juan Sebastian Veron, would in time play for Manchester United before returning to South America to emulate his father by winning a Copa Libertadores in 2009 while playing for Estudiantes.

While future national team manager Carlos Bilardo was the destructive force on the field, all of the credit for the manner in which Estudiantes approached the game, went to their manager, Osvaldo Zubeldia. Regarded as the first manager in South America to focus on and analyse the opposition so that he knew them as well as he did his own players, he also brought about tactical change. He regarded Brazil's 4–2–4 as too open in midfield and introduced a more defensive formation, with three defenders and five in midfield.

He was a proponent of the offside trap. His philosophy was that being frequently ruled off-side, 'morally crushes the enemy' so he becomes reluctant to make the forward runs. Is it any wonder he was accused of creating 'anti-football'? And could there have been a greater clue as to their modus operandi than the fact that most of the Estudiantes de La Plata side had come through the club's youth team, known as La Tercera que Mata — The Killer Juveniles?

Zubeldia was an early mover in terms of pre-planned free kicks, believing much more could be achieved if sufficient work was done on the training ground. This is normal practice today but was new in the 1960s. He also believed in tactical fouling, in screens at corner kicks, in stopping the opposition by any means at his team's disposal.

Passing back to the goalkeeper was something you did as frequently as you felt would help the team retain possession and frustrate the opponents. If that meant passing it back to the point where the crowd objected, well that was too bad — for the crowd. If you were not breaking any law of the game, why would you not persist with such an idea until such time as someone in authority got so frustrated they changed the law?

This was the Zubeldia mind-set. He once took his squad of players to the train station at 7.00 a.m. so they could see nine thousand commuters going to work. His point was that if they worked hard at football they would never need to work hard like these people catching early morning trains. Twice daily training sessions brought to reality the concept of hard work.

Above all he wanted hard-working players in an organised structure. It will come as little consolation to those who remember 1968 in Old Trafford to learn that Estudiantes 1967-1971 were once voted among the three most hated teams in history. Their goalkeeper, Poletti, as much as admitted sledging, long before that term entered the lexicon of sport. He talked about calling a player a cuckold and seeing the reaction as the player became 'destabilised'. The Intercontinental Cup win was the first for Estudiantes but by retaining the Copa Libertadores for the next two years they were back competing against the Champions of Europe in 1969 and 1970.

It was in 1969 that matters came to a head for the team of Osvaldo Zubeldia. A.C. Milan were champions of Europe and their first leg win by 3-0 at the San Siro virtually ended the tie there and then. A fortnight later, Milan walked onto the famous La Bombonera pitch in Buenos Aires but few of them were fit to walk off when the final whistle was blown. And the last part of the short journey was unprotected from home fans hurling cups of hot coffee at the visiting players. The hostility, the spitting, the kicking and punching were clear indications that Milan were centre stage in one of the most violent games in history. After thirty minutes Milan captain, Gianni Rivera even managed to score the ties fourth goal. Estudiantes came back with goals either side of half-time but the Italian team members were in far greater danger in terms of their personal safety than they were of losing the tie.

Alberto Jose Poletti, the goalkeeping proponent of "destabilising" opposing players, came from his goal and proceeded to kick Prati in the back, while the Italian was down receiving treatment. The Milan player was forced to go off for attention but was able to return to the fray. Nestor Combin who had scored one of the goals in Milan was singled out for extraordinary treatment including a hefty kick from Poletti and had his on-field involvement ended when Ramon Suarez punched him so hard in the face, Combin's septum was smashed and his cheek bone damaged. The photo which was published across the world was of the Milan player receiving treatment as his white shorts and shirt were literally covered in blood. Nestor Combin's bloody image became the motif, the logo, for this Intercontinental Cup Final. Milan midfield man, Giovanni Lodetti said Combin was the problem, the main reason for the aggression and nastiness from Estudiantes. He said: "We talked with some journalists and players. They told us they considered him a deserter."

Combin was Argentinian but had left his home country before his twentieth birthday to join Olympique Lyonnais with whom he remained for five years, eventually taking French citizenship and playing football for France. The farce reached its unpleasant height when the blood-drenched Combin, while being stretchered off La Bombonera, was arrested. The Argentinian regime were accusing Combin of desertion and insisting he would now remain and fulfil his army service.

Fortunately Milan were led by Nereo Rocco, as tough and calm a man as was needed in this crisis. The Italian embassy was called into action in what was now a serious diplomatic incident. Rocco had the team at the airport but insisted they were going nowhere until all their players were ready. Argentina blinked and Combin was released to join his team-mates on their journey home with the Cup. The entire episode caused consternation in Argentina particularly in view of their bid to host the 1978 World Cup. Three Estudiantes players were arrested. The goalkeeper Poletti was handed a life ban, later rescinded. Ramon Suarez was banned from international fixtures for five years.

Despite these developments, Estudiantes and Zubeldia went on to complete their three-in-a-row Copa Libertadores triumphs. In 1970 they faced surprise packet, Feynoord of Rotterdam, who had shocked Celtic in the European Cup Final. By now, there was no Poletti in goal and no Suarez at the back. Two other defenders had also been replaced in an Estudiantes team showing four changes from the side that had brought football to a new low against Milan. The first leg was played in Argentina. So Feynoord managed by the Austrian genius Ernst Happel, went into the lion's den and found themselves two goals down. But the resolute Dutch side clawed their way back and scored twice to give themselves an advantage in the return at the De Kuip Stadium.

Their defence stood strong in that return but goals were proving hard to come by in the first half. Happel then made the decisive change replacing his reliable striker Coen Moulijn with Joop Van Daele who delivered the only goal, clinching for Feynoord and Happel, an Intercontinental Cup which had eluded both Jock Stein's Celtic and Matt Busby's Manchester United.

Having had huge success with Estudiantes, winning three Copa Libertadores titles, Zubeldia went on to win a championship with San Lorenzo before moving to Colombia where he led Atletico Nacional to two championships, the second in December 1981, a month before his sudden death of a heart attack aged 54. His most noted disciples were Francisco Maturana who played under him at Atletico Nacional and who led that club to a Copa Libertadores success in 1989 and Carlos Bilardo whose greatest achievement was to lead Argentina to World Cup glory in Mexico.

Alejandro Sabella and Diego Simeone are regarded as worthy successors, coaches who have lived by many of the principles of Zubeldia. On one of the many occasions Rinus Michels was asked about "total football" and who had been its creator/instigator, he replied "Osvaldo Zubeldia." There still exist reports which take this reply at face value. One can only assume these were written by people devoid of the irony gene and unable to understand Michels' humour. Zubeldia was far more accurately credited with being the instigator of "anti-football." But he is rightly described as the "father" of many coaches and even the "grandfather "of some. It explains a lot.

Cesar Luis Menotti

"To be a footballer means being a privileged interpreter
of the feelings and dreams of thousands of people."
Cesar Luis Menotti

Born in 1938 some eleven years after Zubeldia, Cesar Luis Menotti, happily does not fall under the heading of Zubeldia acolyte. In complete contrast to Zubeldia and his philosophy, Menotti saw the bigger picture and had an infinitely more balanced view of football and how it should be played. He began his career with Rosario Central, the team of his birthplace, moving to Racing Club before spending a couple of seasons with Boca Juniors. A brief spell in New York was followed by an even briefer sojourn at Santos of Brazil, the club of Pele, where Menotti made one first team appearance. He also collected two international caps during a career more interesting and varied than spectacular.

The end of his playing career coincided with the Mexican World Cup in 1970 which he attended as a spectator. He was so taken with Brazil's play that he decided he would follow a coaching path. Commencing at Newell's Old Boys in Rosario, he then moved to Huracan with whom he had his first success, the Metropolitano title in 1973. The national team had a poor World Cup in 1974 having gone to West Germany as one of the tournament favourites. They stumbled through the first group stage, advancing on goal difference before being routed by the up and coming Dutch team when Johan Cruyff scored twice in a facile 4-0 win. A 1-2 defeat to Brazil was the final indignity as Argentina went home early.

The critical element in Menotti's appointment was that the driving force behind the Huracan club, surgeon David Bracuto, became President of the Argentine Football Association (AFA) in 1974. But Argentina, at this time was like no other country in the world. The military junta wanted the World Cup to become an emblem of their brilliant organisation, an example to the world of how Argentina under their rule would reign supreme. Menotti liked to present himself and to be depicted as a left-wing intellectual, an image which did not fit with a right-wing military leadership. Jonathan Wilson makes the point that: "(Menotti) with his unapologetic theorising, has always seemed emblematic of a particular form of South American left-wing intellectualism. Part of it is his relationship with the junta, which wasn't as oppositional as has at times been claimed but certainly wasn't close."

One of Menotti's first demands upon being appointed was to place a ban on the transfer abroad of any players under the age of twenty five. It made perfect sense especially in a country that produced technically good players, in great demand particularly in Europe and where most alternatives offered better options than living in Argentina in the mid 1970s.

This is the problem with assessing Argentina's football performances and achievements in the period up to and including the 1978 World Cup. It is widely acknowledged that Menotti, popularly known as "El Flaco", the thin one, was a decent coach and manager. He certainly talked sense and advocated a neat attacking style of play, based on skill and eschewing the type of approach made infamous by Zubeldia and his followers. There had been something emblematic in the emphatic victory of Rinus Michels' side over Argentina in Germany. The new total football, to the delight of football lovers everywhere, thrashed the disciples of anti-football. The convenient fact that a Huracan man was in a position to influence the appointment of Menotti should not take away from the sensational attacking football that Menotti had brought to Huracan in the first place. His affection for Brazil 1970 and his friendship with Pele were genuine influences on the kind of football he espoused.

It can be difficult at this remove to comprehend how Argentina functioned in the 1970s. Between 1976 and 1983 some 30,000 people became 'desparecidos' — the disappeared. The mothers of the disappeared began a vigil in Plaza de Mayo, in the heart of Buenos Aires. The Montoneros were left-wing guerrillas fighting a war against the hated Military junta. However, their actions far from endearing them to the populace, simply persuaded people that they were one more cause of the oppressive rule. Against such a background, preparations were under way for the hosting of a World Cup.

General Carlos Omar Actis was the President of Autarquico Mundial '78, a body which had been set up by the generals as the organising committee for the World Cup. On August 19, 1976 while on his way to a press conference, General Actis was ambushed and murdered. The Montoneros were immediately blamed but they issued vehement denials claiming they were of the people and had made it clear they would not interfere with any aspect of the forthcoming World Cup. This was at a time when concerns were being expressed throughout the football world on the advisability of proceeding with a World Cup in view of the unstable political climate in Argentina.

Next morning there occurred one of the worst incidents in the 'dirty war' as it was called. Thirty prisoners were taken from the dreaded, notorious holding prison and torture centre in Buenos Aires, the Intendencia. While many episodes of the war may be disputed, what happened next is not disputed even by the lawyers representing those accused, decades later, of being the perpetrators. Thirty people, held illegally, were taken at dawn by truck to a place some forty miles away near a town called Fatima. There they were unloaded, blindfolded and their hands tied. They were each shot in the head at close range. Their bodies were piled together over a dynamite charge and they were blown into kingdom come. The Fatima massacre was believed to be a reprisal for the murder of General Actis.

The replacement for the dead general as head of the organising body for Mundial '78 was a Navy captain, soon to be a general, Carlos Alberto Lacoste, a relation of the President, General Jorge Rafael Videla.

Preparing for a World Cup or even trying to concentrate on football, cannot have been easy but Menotti stayed with the task and despite initial non-co-operation from a couple of the major clubs he persevered with his selections until finally he had a squad with which he was happy as the tournament drew near. Among his more controversial decisions was to omit a seventeen year old wonder boy called Diego Armando Maradona. The final squad had five players from River Plate but only one, Alberto Tarantini, from Boca Juniors, the two clubs which had initially been unhelpful. This is even more amazing when one considers Boca were Copa Libertadores champions in 1978.

In the last ever sixteen-team tournament, Argentina beat Hungary and then France, both by 2-1 before losing 0-1 to Italy. The second round had two groups of four with the winners of each group going directly into the final — no semi-finals. The Netherlands, beaten finalists from 1974 and without Johan Cruyff, with Ernst Happel replacing Rinus Michels at the helm, beat Iran, drew with Peru and risked elimination as they went down 2-3 to Scotland. They qualified for the second stage behind Peru, on goal difference over Scotland. Their performance then improved as they beat Austria 5-1 and drew 2-2 with West Germany. A win over Italy by 2-1 was sufficient in that second stage to see them top their group by two clear points and qualify for their second successive final. The hosts beat Poland and played a scoreless draw with arch rivals Brazil. Their neighbours played their final game against Poland, which they won comfortably enough by 3-1. It would now come down to goal difference between Argentina and Brazil, to decide who would meet the Netherlands in the final. Argentina had to beat Peru but as Brazil's game was over before Argentina kicked off, they knew by how much they needed to win — a four goal margin would do it.

And so began one of the most controversial games in World Cup history. The game was played in an electric atmosphere before a crowd of 37,000 in Rosario. Argentina pressed but were still just a goal to the good as half-time approached. Just before half-time left back Tarantini made it two. Within five minutes of the restart

Luque and Kempes scored to open up the necessary four goal lead. Two further goals by Houseman and Luque against a clearly tired Peru team, made it 6-0 and comfortable qualification for the final.

Years later all kinds of allegations arose. The result had been arranged between the Generals in Peru and those in Argentina. The fee was money. The fee was corn. The fee was co-operation in dealing with some Peruvian dissidents. And so it went. The game showed all the indications of one between two teams, one of whom had nothing to play for while the other was highly motivated. Once it settled down after an initial tentative period Argentina looked like they could get the necessary goals and quite frankly Peru looked like they did not need to be bribed to lose a game where they were clearly second best. Whether they were bribed or not, the evidence on either side is inconclusive, and the claims have been made principally by those with agendas. If it did happen, Menotti certainly had nothing to do with it. If not, his team's win has been unjustly undermined.

The World Cup Final brought a different challenge for the home side. They met a vastly experienced Netherlands team which had been desperately unlucky to lose four years earlier to hosts West Germany. The atmosphere inside the Estadio Monumental in Buenos Aires, home to River Plate, was incredible as 70,000 fans unleashed what seemed like tons of streamers and confetti onto the pitch before and during the game.

The Dutch came close to scoring twice with a Johnny Rep header floating narrowly wide and goalkeeper Fillol making a wonder save from a Rep volley on twenty five minutes. Just as it seemed the tie would reach half-time without a goal, a move involving Osvaldo Ardiles, Leopoldo Luque and Mario Kempes, ended with Kempes eluding a defender and scrambling the ball home to an explosion of noise. On the hour mark, with little indication of either side scoring again, Happel, the master of the astute substitution replaced Johhny Rep with Roda JC striker, Dick Nanninga. The substitute delivered a late equaliser before Rob Rensenbrink saw his last minute strike come back off an upright. It was his and Netherlands last chance, a cause for eternal "if onlys" as Argentina seemed to grow stronger in extra time eventually scoring twice to win 3-1.

Happel was less than impressed by the hosts and the atmosphere in the competition but was typically philosophical about that Rensenbrink effort saying had it gone in, they would probably have found enough injury time for Argentina to score. He had that inescapable feeling Argentina were destined to win, no matter what.

Menotti, on the other hand was a confirmed hero. He resented the victory being used by the regime as evidence of their greatness but was also pretty philosophical, asking what he could have done. "To coach teams that played badly, that based everything on tricks that betrayed the feelings of the people? No. Of course not." Argentina's captain, Daniel Passarella described Menotti's ability with words, the basis for that surge in extra time in the World Cup Final. "He always knew exactly what to say to motivate his players. And he was always very calm. We only saw him get really angry once: just before extra time in the final against Netherlands. He looked at us and said, 'Look around you. There are 80,000 of us and eleven of them. We're not going to lose, are we?' It was the type of shock tactic that the team needed. We took to the field again certain we'd win and we made the title ours."

In 1979 Menotti led Argentina to win the World Youth Championship in Japan. It was only the second such tournament, the first having taken place in 1977 in Tunisia. His and the tournament's top scorer was Ramon Diaz, who starred for River Plate, winning five championships, later adding a Serie A title with Inter and a French Cup with Monaco. Diaz's managerial career was even better as he led River Plate to six championships as well as a Copa Libertadores in 1996 while he added a further championship while managing San Lorenzo. The player of the tournament in which the Soviet Union were comfortably despatched 3-1 in the final was Diego Maradona.

The 1982 World Cup could be best described as a tournament too far for Menotti. With several ageing players and Maradona well below form, it was not a good tournament for the reigning champions. They qualified for the second phase without impressing, beating Hungary and El Salvador and losing to Belgium. Then successive defeats, 1-2 to Italy and 1-3 to Brazil spelt the end of this World Cup for Argentina and the end of his time as national team manager for Menotti.

However one views the 1978 win, it is unarguable that Menotti brought a dramatic change to how Argentina played football and to how the people of that country saw football. He claimed to have returned the game to what it once had been, to have saved it from the desperate negativity and spoiling tactics which had pervaded the game in Argentina before his arrival as coach. While those negative elements were not entirely removed from their game, the team under Luis Menotti certainly played with more skill, with an immeasurably more attack minded attitude and for that he deserves great credit.

He went on to manage Barcelona, very briefly, staying just one season, 1983-84, during which they won the Copa del Rey and the Spanish Copa de la Liga. Returning to his homeland he seems to have become a restless soul, taking up several high profile coaching appointments as well as moving overseas on a couple of occasions but never settling long in any position. He took both River Plate and Boca Juniors to runners-up spots in the championship and did the same with Independiente several years later. In between there were spells at Atletico Madrid, Penarol of Uruguay and Sampdoria.

A return to international management with Mexico, like those later club appointments, lasted just a short time, in this case fifteen months. The tall, gaunt, iconic chain smoking Menotti had some health issues in later years. As a coach he did not always win — but true to his own beliefs and doctrine he lived by the principle: "what possibility of growth did I give to my footballers?"

Carlos Bilardo

"In this life you need a measure of good luck — in football even more so. Whether a ball hits a post and goes in or comes back out can permanently change a coach's career."

Carlos Bilardo

Menotti took Huracan to a championship and made them a million friends. Menotti took Argentina to a World Cup which was meant to make the Generals a lot of friends. While it is not clear what help, and there was certainly some, Argentina and Menotti received in 1978, his football philosophy was hugely attractive and it took a brave man to advocate such style at this troubled time for the country. The scheduling of the final group games certainly gave Menotti's team a major advantage over Brazil. When the Menotti way was found wanting in 1982 it was time for change.

The change consisted of Carlos Salvador Bilardo MD. A city boy from Buenos Aires, Bilardo was born in 1939 and broke into the San Lorenzo team while still a teenager, winning a Primera Division title in his first year. Within two years he was transferred to Second Division Deportivo Espanol where he remained for five years while continuing to study medicine. Bilardo started his football life as a goal-scoring forward but eventually moved to become a midfield anchor man. By 1965 he was back in the big time with Estudiantes with whom he won a League Title followed by three Copa Libertadores and the World Club (Intercontinental Cup) against Manchester United.

Upon retirement from playing Bilardo took over from his mentor Zubeldia as coach of Estudiantes de la Plata. He took the club to the final of the Copa Libertadores in 1971 but lost that final to Nacional of Uruguay after a playoff. Seven years later as coach of Deportivo Cali of Colombia, he repeated the experience, this time losing comprehensively to Boca Juniors. Bilardo had been one of two Estudiantes players who had studied medicine together. Their playing days ending, Raul Madero became physician to the national football team, while Bilardo went into football coaching and management, having retired from medicine in 1976.

His first international post was not with Argentina but as coach to the Colombia team as they set about trying to qualify for the 1982 World Cup. Failure to qualify cost him his job and he returned to Argentina to be hired once more by Estudiantes. The team won the Metropolitano title bringing Bilardo to the attention of the AFA as they began the task of finding a replacement for Menotti.

The new regime saw Bilardisme, an approach containing much of what Zubeldia had practiced but cutting back on some of the more objectionable excesses. Bilardo introduced a 3-5-2 system after a series of unimpressive performances which had begun to trigger questions about his suitability for the job. When he first announced a selection with three centre backs, eyebrows were raised and some assumed this was an error; that he had just called out the wrong name by mistake. The system proved successful and was seen as a scheme which particularly suited Diego Maradona who now received the support and service he required from a five-man midfield.

The 1986 World Cup would demonstrate the wisdom of making sure whatever formation would be deployed had to accommodate Maradona. When a coach is gifted with a player that good it would be unforgiveable to fail to optimise his talents. Bilardo was smart enough to see this and the result was a World Cup which has become synonymous with one player.

The twenty four team tournament began in Mexico with six groups of four. After each team had played the others in their group the top two qualified as did the best third placed teams in four of the groups. This meant after twenty four games, there were still sixteen teams left in the competition. Mercifully it now went to straight knockout. Argentina qualified comfortably, beating South Korea before playing a 1-1 draw with Italy and then beating Bulgaria.

A tense local derby against Uruguay was won 1-0 and England were up next in the quarter finals. The 2-1 win is remembered not only for his outrageous hand-ball goal but also for the equally extraordinary goal as Maradona slalomed through half the England team before sliding the ball past Peter Shilton for one of the greatest goals ever scored. Undoubtedly, England were hard done by when a piece of treachery like the handled goal was allowed but with Maradona at his peak, it is reasonable to assume he would have done whatever it took to win the game by fair means if not foul. The final of this tournament provides ample support for this argument.

A strong Belgium team was undone by the Argentina captain in the semi-final as he scored a pair of near identical goals in which, twice, by dropping a shoulder he threw an entire defence off balance before planting the ball low in the corner of the net. The final against West Germany had Lothar Matthaus shadowing Maradona with support from whichever colleague was nearest, the clear intention being to neutralise the man on whom Argentina depended. He or Bilardo determined he would drop deeper leaving others to do the damage. Now in a changed role, that of provider, he would undo West Germany despite their best efforts. Matthaus fouled Maradona on the left. The free kick was headed to the net by Jose Brown rising above everyone. Maradona released Jorge Valdano with a perfect pass after he had first pulled the defence the other way. Two late goals from Karl-Heinz Rummenigge and Rudi Voller, both resulting from corner kicks, brought the Germans level but within three minutes of the equaliser and with only six minutes remaining, Maradona released Jorge Burrachaga with a perfectly weighted through ball putting him into the record books as the scorer of a winning goal in a World Cup Final.

How much of this success was down to Bilardo's management or Maradona's genius is a moot point. It was a strong Argentina side and the expertise with which those two passes were tucked away on such a big occasion was testimony to the calmness and ability of the two goal scorers. Bilardo has to be respected for the manner in which he brought a unified team to the tournament and on to glory.

They were tough, skilful and functional and had the best player in the world in his absolute prime. The last of these points was a gift but the other three required intelligent planning and management skills. Bilardo showed all of these characteristics when four years later he brought a lesser team all the way to the final before they succumbed to a German team now reaching its peak.

While his teams were never as attack minded as those of Menotti, they were sufficiently well organised to make it to two finals before the coach, reprising the path taken by his predecessor, appeared to stay for short periods with the teams over which he was subsequently in control, Sevilla FC, Boca Jumiors, Guatamala, Libya and once more, Estudiantes. Restlessness would appear to be an affliction of former Argentina managers. He engaged in some teaching, some journalism and a radio show and even became General Manager of the national team, a background role removed from coaching but with a big influence on who got to coach the squad. His legacy is two World Cup Finals, one victory. More than that, he brought a unity and stability and if his football, Bilardisme, was not as attractive as Menottisme, he did move away from some of the worst traits associated with that country's coaches and players.

Carlos Bianchi

"With Boca Juniors, for example, you knew that half the country was willing you on. But to think that a modest Buenos Aires side like Velez Sarsfield, with no more than 200,000 supporters, could become world champion! That truly is the stuff of dreams."
Carlos Bianchi

While Menotti and Bilardo enjoyed the glory of having led their country to World Cup victory, a third Argentinian is the man who has the amazing record of having managed teams to win the World Club Championship/Intercontinental Cup on three out of the four occasions his teams contested the final. His achievements begin with eight national titles and four Copa Libertadores, with Velez

Sarsfield and Boca Juniors. His name is Carlos Arcecio Bianchi and he is widely known as the Viceroy, El Virrey.

Born in 1949 in Buenos Aires, Bianchi began his career with Velez Sarsfield on a freezing cold Sunday in July 1967 and in the six years that followed he scored 123 goals in 165 games including one run of thirty six goals in as many games. As a player, Bianchi's only Championship success came at Velez when he was a mere nineteen years of age. He would go on to win many awards, principally for his phenomenal goal scoring but never again, as a player, would he win a championship in a career that lasted all of eighteen years.

As Juan Peron returned from exile in Spain in 1973, Bianchi headed in the opposite direction landing at Stade de Reims in the champagne region of France. This was a club that had twice contested European Cup Finals while Real Madrid were on their initial run of victories. Stade de Reims had fallen on hard times since then, including spending time in the Second Division. Hiring Bianchi was seen as an attempt to restore the great days of Just Fontaine, their legendary goal machine. And Carlos Bianchi did not disappoint. Thirty goals in thirty three games was a good start. His second season was injury interrupted but fifteen goals in only sixteen appearances showed his capability. Thirty four in thirty eight games in Bianchi's third year at Reims made it impossible for the club to hold on to their prolific scorer.

Bianchi was Paris-bound by the summer of 1977. There were doubters and sceptics who were quick to question his ability to continue scoring goals once the pressure of playing for a big city club began to have its effect. Bianchi responded with thirty seven goals in thirty eight games for Paris Saint-Germain, becoming France's Division 1 top scorer for the fourth time. And he made it the fifth time the next year. He moved for a brief stay to League Champions Strasbourg scoring only eight times in twenty two games as he prepared at thirty years of age to return to his home country. Among his colleagues in that Strasbourg team was Arsene Wenger, later to make his own name as a manager. Back at Velez Sarsfield, the striker continued to perform at the highest level, becoming Argentina's top scorer in 1981 and continuing to average better than a goal every two games until 1984, his final season.

A comeback in Europe, inevitably with Stade de Reims, now in Division 2, although short-lived proved to be the door to a life in coaching and managing. Four years at Reims and two further years divided between Nice and Paris FC were more an apprenticeship than a period of great achievement. It was an apprenticeship well served and a return to Velez Sarsfield as coach brought instant and unprecedented success to the club and to Bianchi. Velez Sarsfield was anything but a major power in Argentinian football. Now, in four seasons they won three Championships, and for the first time the Copa Libertadores in 1994 and the Intercontinental Cup and Copa Interamericana in the same year. Their opponents in the Intercontinental Cup in Tokyo were the star-studded AC Milan managed by Fabio Capello and playing in the final for a sixth time. But victory by 2-0 went to Bianchi's novices.

This achievement alerted the ambitious A.S. Roma President, Franco Sensi. The appointment proved a notable disaster for both club and coach. Roma struggled in the lower half of Serie A and inside twelve months Bianchi was fired. It was believed he had difficulty with the more frantic pace of football in Italy. It was also a fact that he clashed with a number of Roma players including a young Francesco Totti and Argentinian striker Abel Balbo.

Bianchi took a twelve month sabbatical in Argentina which ended with Boca Juniors hiring him and proving that despite the Roma experience his stock was still high at home. Bianchi's ability not to hold a grudge was impressive. Balbo, showing no sign of nationalistic loyalty, had led a players' revolt to have the coach removed at Roma. Later, Boca Juniors, now managed by Bianchi, was the chosen destination for Balbo after he and Bianchi met and sorted out their differences facilitating the transfer of the forward to his home country after he had helped his strike partner at club and country, Gabriel Battistuta, to a Serie A title with a Roma side managed by Fabio Capello.

And Bianchi picked up where he had left off. In three years in charge he led the powerful Boca to three successive Championships, two Copa Libertadores, and the crowning glory of this era, an Intercontinental Cup win over Real Madrid. The Champions of Europe were hot favourites as they brought to Tokyo a truly formidable line-up which included Iker Casillas, Roberto Carlos, Claude Makelele, Luis Figo, Fernando Hierro and Raul. But Bianchi again proved the master as his slightly more defensive structure got the better of Vicente Del Bosque's side through two goals from Martin Palermo against the one from Roberto Carlos.

After another one year break, the coach returned to Boca to lead them to a further championship, followed by his fourth Copa Libertadores and his third Intercontinental Cup in which AC Milan were once again his victims. This time the game was decided by a 3-1 penalty shoot-out having finished 1-1. Carlo Ancelotti's Milan team was every bit as populated with world class players as had been the Real Madrid side three years earlier. Dida, Cafu, Maldini, Costacurta, Pirlo, Kaka and Shevchenko were all in the starting team.

Astonishingly Boca Juniors team in 2003 contained only one player, Sebastian Battaglia, who had played in the 2000 Final. It was an extraordinary level of player turnover and a truly amazing achievement to win the ultimate prize despite so much change. Their bench contained goalkeeper Willy Caballero and a young Carlos Tevez, both to do well in Europe in the years that followed. Tevez is among a select number of players to win both Copa Libertadores and European Champions Leagues. Another of Bianchi's protégés to do so was Walter Samuel who followed his win with Boca Juniors by winning in Europe with Inter Milan.

Their title may be unwieldy but the IFFHS (International Federation of Football History and Statistics) awards the very prestigious World Coach of the Year award. It was won by Carlos Bianchi in 2000 and again in 2003. It is hard to argue with the 2000 decision but after such drastic change to a team, no one could argue with the 2003 award to the man who brought that new team back to the pinnacle of world football within so short a time.

Amid the usual fanfare, Bianchi was recruited by Atletico Madrid in the summer of 2005 but the experiment turned out little better than that carried out by Roma a decade earlier. By January of 2006 with the team struggling in the league, a 0-1 home defeat to Real Zaragozza in the Copa del Rey did the trick. Bianchi was fired.

He was eventually brought into Boca, one more time, in a new role carrying the title Manager but in effect General Manager. He had no involvement in coaching and his role appeared not to be particularly well defined, designed or thought through. Carlos Ischia was the coach and team selection and tactics were his responsibility. It seemed as if Bianchi was to be the link between the coach and the board but it did not work out and the "Virrey" was fired in April 2014 less than eighteen months after his much-heralded return, the victim of indifferent results, over which he did not have much control, at a club to which he had brought championships, Continental (Copa Libertadores) and Intercontinental Cups on a scale never witnessed anywhere in world football.

11

Alex Ferguson

"I can't believe it. I can't believe it. Football. Bloody hell."
**Alex Ferguson after Manchester United scored
two late goals to win the European Cup**

ALEX FERGUSON retired as manager of Manchester United at the end of the 2012-13 season, the club having won the Premier League for the thirteenth time under his stewardship. Add two Champions Leagues, five F.A. Cups, four League Cups, ten Charity/Community Shields, a European Cup Winners Cup, a European Super Cup, an Intercontinental Cup and a FIFA Club World Cup and you get what amounts to a truly amazing record. He is the most successful manager in the history of the British game, a driven obsessive with an incredible work ethic and a deep understanding of what it takes to succeed and no compunction about who or what may need to be sacrificed in the pursuit of victory.

In the immediate aftermath of his retirement, a frequently heard view was that the 'fear factor' had left the Manchester United dressing room. His first managerial job was to last all of 117 days at little East Stirling. Short as that spell was, a player from those days was quoted as saying: "he was a frightening bastard from the start."

His initial experiences at his next club, St. Mirren featured a couple of parallels with the early days of two other great managers, Michels and Clough. He had already determined that publicity was vital if St. Mirren was to become a bigger club. He would talk to the local press, give them a story, and in a manner reminiscent of Clough at Hartlepools, he would visit neighbourhood housing estates in a car equipped with a PA system, exhorting the locals to come out and support their team.

He persuaded local businesses to find part-time jobs for the players, enabling them to train more frequently and achieve better levels of fitness. For Alex Ferguson, promotion to the top division of Scottish football was the first necessary step in developing a thriving club and as the incremental improvements continued under his reign, St. Mirren were promoted as Division One Champions in 1976-77. The first season in the upper echelons saw survival and consolidation but the relationship between the chairman and manager deteriorated to the point where Alex Ferguson was fired for the only time in his career.

His next appointment as manager of Aberdeen truly was the transformative change in his football career. He inherited a good squad of players from Billy McNeill. There were current and future internationals aplenty. Willie Miller, was the prototype Ferguson captain, strong physically and emotionally with powerful leadership qualities. Among others of note in that Aberdeen dressing room were goalkeepers, Bobby Clark and Jim Leighton as well as Doug Roughvie, Gordon Strachan, Joe Harper, Steve Archibald and Drew Jarvie.

However, the move to Aberdeen was anything but an easy one. At Pittodrie he found himself managing several players against whom he had played, at a club where his combative and somewhat aggressive playing style would not have been appreciated. He had moved a wife and young family to what was a relatively remote part of Scotland, over three hours drive from Glasgow. And he had the personal anguish of his father's illness and death during that first year. Battles with players, not least with Miller but with others of note, including Joe Harper, did not make for a comfortable introduction to the north of Scotland.

Somewhat surprisingly, discipline was an obsession. For a man who had had more than his share of early baths in the recent past, and who had already fallen foul of the authorities resulting in a ban on talking to referees, before during or after games, this unequivocal approach was not an easy concept for some of the older players. But there was no tolerance of indiscipline on the field. Michael Crick quotes the then Aberdeen manager: "They will be fined heavily and I mean heavily... Bookings for talking back to referees, not standing ten yards away at free kicks and kicking the ball away will just not be tolerated. And they will be punished severely by the club... I want to see our 'crime rate' become the best in Scotland."

St. Mirren had given him his first taste of winning a trophy but it was at Aberdeen that he developed the habit. The club, although perceived as strong and well respected, had won one Scottish Championship since its foundation in 1903. Alex Ferguson managed the club from 1978 to 1986. To this day Aberdeen has won sixteen domestic trophies, four Leagues in all, seven Scottish Cups and five League Cups. Alex Ferguson brought the club three of those Leagues, four Cups and a League Cup. So in an eight year stay, he brought half of the domestic trophy haul from their entire existence of more than one hundred and ten years. His Aberdeen team also won the European Cup Winners Cup, defeating Real Madrid in the final, and the European Super Cup. It is an astonishing record, an amazing statistic that confirmed Ferguson had what it took to succeed at the highest level in football management.

The experience of encountering problems initially and coping with them by sticking to his principles and not panicking would serve him well in the future. The creation of a siege mentality would also prove a useful tool. At Aberdeen it was the Glasgow media that became a convenient target in Alex Ferguson's contrived persecution complex. He persuaded the players that the Glasgow-based media had no time for them, only wanted to see the old firm win and couldn't actually be bothered coming to some of their games. "But we'll show them!" was the gist of his message. And show them, they did.

Whatever chance there was of attributing Aberdeen's domestic success to a period of transition or a dip in form by Celtic and Rangers, winning in Europe put an end to any such thoughts by Ferguson's doubters, by now becoming fewer in number. And lest anyone doubt his consistency of behaviour, it was with good reason that his Aberdeen players called him "Furious Fergie."

Meanwhile he had been recruited to help Jock Stein with the preparation of the national team as they strove to qualify for the 1986 World Cup Finals. On the night of 10th September 1985 Stein died tragically at pitch-side in Cardiff as Scotland qualified for a play-off game against Australia. Alex Ferguson stepped up to take control of the team for that play-off which was won 2-0 on aggregate and for the subsequent World Cup Finals. The Mexican adventure was a short one with two defeats to Denmark and West Germany and a scoreless draw with Uruguay seeing Scotland make an early exit.

In November 1986 Ferguson was appointed manager of Manchester United. It wasn't just his initial days that were difficult but his early years. By December 1989 the club was still a mile away from winning anything with the team not far off the relegation zone and fans calling for his dismissal. In the New Year United were drawn away to Nottingham Forest in the F.A. Cup and were given little chance because of the respective teams' current and recent form. There was an expectation that it would prove the Scot's last game in charge. Subsequently this was widely denied and it does seem that the then United board were behaving untypically for such bodies who rarely show a manager these levels of patience. But this was a club whose last championship win had been in 1967.

Matt Busby had brought them five titles but finding a successor to win even one was proving more difficult than might have been imagined. The surprise win at Nottingham Forest through a Mark Robbins goal took United on a Cup run which went all the way to the final. A 3-3 draw with Crystal Palace provided the manager with an opportunity to show his ruthlessness as goalkeeper

Jim Leighton whom he had brought from Aberdeen was deemed at fault for at least one goal and was famously dropped for the replay which United won. That 1990 F.A. Cup was Ferguson's first trophy in England, coming three and a half years after his arrival.

The Cup win took United into the European Cup Winners Cup which they won, following up with the European Super Cup. The 1992 League Cup came next as United beat Nottingham Forest in the Wembley final. Then the notable signing of Eric Cantona preceded and many would say, led to, the bridging of a twenty six year gap as Manchester United won the inaugural Premier League. The next year saw the arrival of Roy Keane as long-term replacement for Bryan Robson and Manchester United won their first double of League Championship and F.A. Cup, only the fourth time this double had been achieved in the twentieth century. Within five years United would do the double on two more occasions. Further League titles were added in 1996,1997,1999,2000,2001,2003,2007,2008,2009,2011 and 2013. This took Ferguson's count of League titles to thirteen and Manchester United's to twenty.

Following more than a quarter century without a league title Manchester United now became extraordinarily consistent. From 1992, the year prior to the inaugural Premier League, when United finished four points behind Champions, Leeds United, they never fell below third place throughout Ferguson's reign. Indeed they either won or came second in all years except 2002 and 2005 the two years they finished as low as third.

The year 1999 will always be remembered for the unprecedented achievement by an English team of winning their domestic double as well as the European Champions League which they snatched with dramatic goals in injury time to deny Bayern Munich a title which seemed all but wrapped up with the clock ticking down. That never-say-die attitude was synonymous with Ferguson. Getting an equaliser in those final seconds would have been seen as a great achievement by any team. To score two goals so late and to win in this manner was simply ridiculous. That the goals should come from Teddy Sherringham, the replacement for Cantona and the aptly described super-sub Solksjaer made the events seem as if they had been scripted by the manager.

Once a team or club has reached a peak, it becomes difficult, almost impossible, to maintain the levels of performance, to maintain the dominance. Where Alex Ferguson's real genius is very evident is in his ability to defy this world-view of sport. By maintaining his own savage work ethic, 7.00 a.m. starts and God-knows-when finishes to the working day, a refusal to accept less than 100% from his players and an unforgiving attitude towards anyone who crossed him, he succeeded where no other manager had done before. Teams were re-built as needed. Youth was given its chance, but that chance had to be taken because nobody would be indulged. The greatest players, the greatest servants to the club were unceremoniously dispatched once they became expendable. And Alex Ferguson ploughed on relentlessly, delivering.

There is no doubt that the legendary hairdryer treatment had its effect on players throughout his career. But there is evidence from his early days that this was often contrived by Ferguson for effect. He was known to have been found rehearsing a tongue lashing and to have agreed with a senior player that he would give him a roasting in order to intimidate the younger members within that dressing room who would leave thinking if the boss would do that to a senior international what chance did they have, should they step out of line. It was an approach stright from the repertoire of a Ferguson hero, Jock Stein.

If ruthlessness is a necessary characteristic in a successful manager, it was rarely more evident than in Alex Ferguson. In his early years at Manchester United, international players still in their prime, such as Paul McGrath and Norman Whiteside, were given short shrift because of perceived off-field behaviours which were not compatible with Ferguson's philosophy. Later fallings out with people who had been close to him, drew plenty of attention. Brian Kidd, Gordon Strachan and Roy Keane were three people on whom he had depended and who had served him well. Each was considered expendable when it suited the manager. A colleague from an earlier era was Ricky McFarlane who had served Ferguson for four years as trainer and physiotherapist at East Stirling and St.Mirren. For family reasons the man declined an offer to continue their relationship at Aberdeen. McFarlane was literally written out of Ferguson's life, never mentioned in either of two autobiographies.

The ownership of a club is a matter of huge importance, especially to those who support that club. Apart from phenomenal on-field success, the strange legacy Alex Ferguson has left his club is a dramatic change of ownership.

Ferguson had a keen interest in horse racing through which he became friendly with John Magnier and J.P.McManus, two highly successful men in the world of horse breeding and racing. While the two began acquiring a stake in Manchester United through their vehicle company, Cubic Expression, John Magnier made a generous gesture towards his friend, Alex Ferguson. The horse, "Rock of Gibralter" was registered in Dublin in August 2001 in the names of Mrs. John Magnier and Alex Ferguson.

For no outlay and no training costs, the football boss now had a half share in the prize money as the horse won ten times including seven successive Group One races. When that run ended with a second place in the Breeder's Cup Mile at Arlington Park, Illinois, John Magnier decided to retire the stallion to stud. The horse had run in Ferguson's colours and he had been happily photographed leading the animal into the winner's enclosure during the string of victories. And he received 50% of the £1,164,804 winnings achieved in under two years.

It was speculated that this horse could generate stud fees as high as £50m. Alex Ferguson held the view that he would also be entitled to 50% of this future income. John Magnier saw it differently. He was quite clear on what had been put in place. Ferguson had been given a gift, a nominal honour and of course 50% of the winnings. When attempts to resolve the matter failed, Sir Alex Ferguson (as he now was) initiated legal proceedings in the High Court in Dublin against John Magnier and Coolmore Stud. The response was prompt and clear: "Coolmore Stud and John Magnier consider the action to be without merit and it will be vigorously defended." Magnier was said to have been incensed that his word was being called into question, his reputation being that of a man of the highest integrity, a man whose word was his bond. To suggest that he had reneged on an agreement was about as insulting as it could get.

Clearly, John Magnier's Cubic Exprssion colleague, J.P.McManus, who had no involvement with Rock of Gibralter was less than impressed. Cubic Expression, with a 29% stake in the football club, began asking some serious questions of the Manchester United Board, questions to which they demanded and were perfectly entitled to have full disclosure. They sought details of payments to players, payments to the manager and details of transfer deals. Serious Corporate Governance questions including the relationship between the club and Jason Ferguson, the manager's son, who ran Elite Management, a sport agency which dealt with the club on player transfers, were now before the Club's Board.

The conclusion to the disagreement was outlined by Matthew Norman in the Daily Telegraph as he described Ferguson's actions: "He was luckier still to survive the only grave misjudgement of his career — one that illuminated a monstrous arrogance, avarice and sense of entitlement... For the first time he found himself swimming with bigger and deadlier fish than himself, and although they eventually paid him off with a tiny fraction of what he believed he was due, he was beaten and humiliated."

There was only one winner in this row. Cubic Expression proceeded to sell its share in the football club to Malcolm Glazer, netting an estimated £80m profit in doing so. The irony of the Glazer family, owners of the Tampa Bay Buccaneers taking control of Manchester United is that in effect they did so, using the club as colatteral. Manchester United which had been floated in 1990 was now taken private. Red Football Joint Venture Ltd. and Red Football Ltd. were the vehicles used in the purchase. The estimated total cost was £800m. This was made up mainly of loans or other financial instruments. The loans were secured against the club assets.

The new ownership has proved deeply unpopular with supporters, particularly those with sufficient awareness to realise a club which had little or no borrowings is now deeply in hock and paying generous fees and salaries to those who arranged this coup.

The former manager has come away virtually unscathed from these circumstances and developments for which he was solely responsible. It would appear, his unrivalled successes and phenomenal leadership of the club, often winning championships with what semed to be average teams, has provided insulation from serious scrutiny of how the business of the club evolved to what it is today.

Sir Alex Ferguson has remained a director of Manchester United, something seen as a reward for his fantastic achievements at the club but also for his unwavering support for the Glazers even during widespread protests at their intrusion.

He has published another autobiography in which he took the trouble to criticise several people and settle scores. It is recognised and accepted that an autobiography should avoid being anodyne but several questions arise in relation to this highly successful book. Why does someone who has made millions from the game need another payday? Why does someone who has been such a success need to attack people like Owen Hargreaves for his failure to return from injury? A psychologist expressed the view that it was just Alex Ferguson continuing a life in which he drove himself to be the best in his sphere, now wantuing to have the football's most successful autobiography.

Perhaps it is that simple. His second post retirement tome on Leadership provides a classic example of how to achieve more than one objective with what seems an innocent observation. He claims to have had only four world-class players during all his years in Manchester, naming Ryan Giggs, Paul Scholes Eric Cantona and

Cristiano Ronaldo. It is a masterpiece. In one claim, he settles scores with all those omitted while establishing that because of the lack of players of that calibre, all that success must have been due to some other factor or perhaps some other person. One wonders who that may have been.

The Premier League and Superstar Managers

Postscript Season, 2016-17

"It's Money That Matters"
Randy Newman song from "Land of Dreams"
Reprise Records 1988

THE 2015-16 season in England's Premier League was exceptional, even sensational. Since the initial Premier League was won by Manchester United in 1993 it has been hard to argue with the findings of Stefan Szymanski as described by Simon Kuper, that it's money that matters.

The summer of 2016 saw the coronation of a team from outside the elite and wealthy group which had come to monopolise the top positions in English league football. Leicester City, a 5000 -1 pre-season bet won the League with games to spare. They were managed by a man who had just lost his job managing the Greek national team because of a failure to beat the Faroe Islands. Claudio Ranieri, famed as the "tinker man" for his inability to leave well enough alone while managing Chelsea, led Leicester to a title based on the managerial principle of leaving well enough alone and not interfering too much with what his predecessor had set in place.

What made Leicester's win so universally popular was that a team which had not cost silly money to assemble, played consistently, chalking up a succession of narrow wins with several players performing far beyond expectations. As the season came to a close, only Tottenham offered a challenge and that ended when they were held to a draw by the previous year's champions, a Chelsea team now under a caretaker manager.

Guus Hiddink had held the fort and stabilised matters after the sacking of Jose Mourinho at Christmas 2015 with champions Chelsea one point above the drop zone. Mourinho had provoked a confrontation with the club doctor and a physiotherapist who had gone onto the field to treat an injured player by invitation of the referee but without discussion with the manager. The dispute did nothing to enhance the reputation of club or manager and ended up costing significant money. Meanwhile, just prior to his sacking Mourinho accused his own players of betraying him in a 1-2 defeat to Leicester. The club's stated reason for his sacking was a "palpable discord with the players." Under Hiddink Chelsea finished in 10th place.

Apart from Leicester City, the teams to qualify for lucrative Champions League Football were Arsenal, Tottenham Hotspur and Manchester City. Leicester players were recognised with individual awards as striker Jamie Vardy was named Football Writers Player of the Year while Riyad Mahrez won the PFA award. Claudio Ranieri was named Premier League Manager of the Season.

In January Claudio Ranieri completed a dream period for him when he was announced as FIFA's world coach of the year, ahead of Zinedine Zidane and Fernando Santos who had led their club and country, respectively, to European glory. But this is football and dreams sometimes die pretty quickly. By 23rd February, with Leicester City still in the Champions League but just a point above the Premier League drop zone, Ranieri was fired. It is estimated the cost of relegation is in the order of £100m. The team, previously united, determined and hugely effective, now appeared disunited and lacking in leadership on and off the field. The struggle had gone on for several months and looked like getting worse rather than better. Faced with this situation, boards of football clubs will take whatever action they feel might protect their investment. It's money that matters.

Ranieri's assistant, Craig Shakespeare, was appointed on a temporary basis until the end of the season, to save the club from relegation. He immediately got the team playing in a manner reminiscent of their previous form and in doing so hauled them well away from what had looked like a potential catastrophe. But Leicester City's 2015-16 League success was the prelude to a season in which the bigger wealthier clubs would do all within their powers to reassert their superiority.

Manchester United, long the dominant force under Sir Alex Ferguson, had struggled as David Moyes quickly failed, to be replaced by Louis Van Gaal. What the Dutchman liked to call his 'football philosophy' was not appreciated by the fans and although the FA Cup was won, the final whistle had hardly been blown when Van Gaal was sacked. Boring football and non-qualification for the Champions League were his crimes. Jose Mourinho was announced as the next manager of Manchester United, a job reputedly he had craved for some years.

Manchester City sacked Manuel Pellegrini who was replaced by Pep Guardiola, a move that had been flagged months earlier when Guardiola announced he would end his time at Bayern Munich and Pellegrini who had brought a league title and two league cups in his three years at City, was forced to confirm that he was headed towards the exit.

Liverpool appointed Jürgen Klopp manager on 8th October 2015 but it was widely accepted that 2016-17 his first full season, would be the time to assess the appointment. Klopp was hugely respected for his time at Borussia Dortmund where he won two league titles and a German Cup and was twice named Manager of the Year.

Chelsea had lined up Antonio Conte when the Italy manager had made it clear before the 2016 European Championships that he was headed back to club football. Conte had enjoyed great success

THAT'S RIGHT: YOU'RE FIRED!

with Juventus winning three leagues in three seasons and clearly he missed the day-to-day involvement of club football.

Arsenal had been consistent Champions League qualifiers during the twenty-year reign of Arsene Wenger. But the manager was now coming under increasing fan pressure because of the failure to actually win trophies. A large section of the support wanted cups rather than the financial security of prudent management. There may have been Champions League income from consistent progression beyond the initial stage but there was also consistent failure to look like winning the Premier League.

Mauricio Pochettino, the young Argentinian coach at Tottenham was widely held to be doing a good job but must have been kicking himself at allowing Leicester get away in a season when for various reasons the clubs with greatest resources were struggling or in transition, with his own team the only realistic challengers from a long way out.

The 2016-17 season promised much as some of the world's top managers set out in pursuit of the Premier League. A look at the list of the most highly paid managers confirms the extent to which English football has become, thanks to gigantic TV deals, the wealthiest football arena on the planet.

WORLD'S HIGHEST PAID FOOTBALL MANAGERS 2017
(Total Sportek)

1	Pep Guardiola	Manchester City	£15.0m
2	Jose Mourinho	Manchester United	£13.8m
3	Carlo Ancelotti	Bayern Munich	£9.0m
4	Arsene Wenger	Arsenal	£8.3m
5	Zinedine Zidane	Real Madrid	£8.0m
6	Jürgen Klopp	Liverpool	£7.0m
7	Luis Enrique	Barcelona	£7.0m
8	Antonio Conte	Chelsea	£6.5m
9	Unai Emery	PSG	£5.65
10	Mauricio Pochettino	Tottenham	£5.5m

These figures represent salaries only. They do not take into account the sometimes enormous sponsorship arrangements of which Mourinho is the doyen. He has either currently or recently had deals with companies dealing in among other products and services, cars, mobile phones, casinos, watches and televised sports coverage. The other big name managers are similarly popular with suppliers of beer, wine, cars, sportswear, footwear, electronic products etc.

Transfer market activity was considered key in determining who might succeed Ranieri and Leicester City as Premier League Champions. And the competition would extend beyond just the four. Meanwhile, this is how the clubs of the four superstar managers spent in advance of the season.

	Transfers in	Transfers Out	Net Spend
Manchester City	£171.5m	£28m	− £143.5m
Manchester United	£145m	£46m	− £99m
Liverpool	£61.9m	£76.5m	+ £14.6m
Chelsea	£118.2m	£103m	− £15.2m

Manchester City's big ticket purchases were John Stones, Leroy Sane, Ilkay Gundogan, Claudio Bravo, Nolito and the headline writer's dream, Gabriel Jesus.

They recouped £23m from the sales of Stefan Jovetic and Edin Dzeko. Meanwhile several players who had been first team squad members were sent out on loan. These included, Eliaquim Mangala to Valencia, Samir Nasri to Sevilla and Wilfried Bony to Stoke City. The most controversial loan move was that of Joe Hart to Torino. England goalkeeper Hart had been the No.1 choice while City won 2 Premier Leagues, 2 League Cups and an F.A. Cup, since 2011. Guardiola's wish to have his keeper play out from the back and his obvious lack of belief in Hart's ability to do this meant the incoming transfer of Claudio Bravo and Joe Hart's exile.

Manchester United acquired four players for their first team squad. Ranging in cost from a free transfer for Zlatan Ibrahimovic to Paul Pogba at an astronomical £89m with Eric Bailly and Henrik Mkhitaryan setting them back a combined total of £56m. United sold or released nineteen players in all. Morgan Schneiderlin went to Everton for £24m and Memphis Depay cost Lyon £16m. A further £6m came from the sale of three younger players most of which will have been secured for Paddy McNair. But five of the fees are "undisclosed" including that of Bastian Schweinsteiger to Chicago Fire, in March 2017. Nine players were sent out on loan and Wayne Rooney's career at the club was under serious threat as Mourinho appeared to be of the view that the player had little to offer.

Chelsea's £118m brought them Michy Batshusyi, N'Golo Kante, David Luiz and Marcos Alonso. Their sales included Mohamed Salah £14.5m and the really big deal, the sale of Oscar to Shanghai SIPG for a cool £60m. Kante had played a significant part in Leicester's glorious campaign and was considered a great buy for Chelsea. Marcos Alonso is a young man with a horrendous off-the-field experience of driving a car too fast, while over the alcohol limit, on bad road conditions in which a young woman died. The Spanish authorities regarded a €61,000 fine as an appropriate substitute for 21 months in detention. Alonso was at Sunderland on loan from Fiorentina when Chelsea bought him. The most astonishing statistic around Chelsea's acquisition and retention of players is that they have forty nine players out on loan in ten countries apart from England. It must be fun keeping track.

Liverpool bought six and sold or released sixteen players. Their main signings were Joel Matip, a free transfer from Schalke 04, Sadio Mane for £30m, and Giorgino Wijnaldum £23m. They received £27m for Christian Benteke, £15m for Jordan Ibe and £11m for Joe Allen and took in £14.6m more than they spent. It was still unclear how much control the manager had over transfers, an issue during the reign of his predecessor. Matip came with an excellent reputation while Mane promised goals.

So in the transfer market before and during the 2016-7 season, the two Manchester clubs were the net big spenders. The theory is that money ultimately determines results. These two clubs were certainly buying in to the concept. No expense was spared in providing the manager with what many would consider a ridiculously high salary. With the two best paid managers in the world and a heavy outlay on players, not to mention salaries, those controlling the clubs had every right to demand what all great chairmen have always felt their due — instant success.

After six rounds of Premier League football this is how the table read:

	P	W	D	L	F	A	Pts
Manchester City	6	6	0	0	18	5	18
Tottenham Hotspur	6	4	2	0	10	3	14
Arsenal	6	4	1	1	15	7	13
Liverpool	6	4	1	1	16	9	13
Everton	6	4	1	1	10	4	13
Manchester United	6	4	0	2	12	7	12
Crystal Palace	6	3	1	2	10	7	10
Chelsea	6	3	1	2	10	9	10

Champions Leicester City were on 7 points in 12th place.

Much was made of how Chelsea and Liverpool did not have European commitments, something which gave them an advantage over the clubs who were engaged in Champions and Europa Leagues.

Manchester United as FA Cup winners and Tottenham, following a dismal group stage performance in the Champions League, qualified for the Europa League a competition the Londoners quickly exited at the first hurdle as they appeared to choose to focus on the Premier League.

Manchester United progressed to the point where by the quarter-final stage in April, the media began highlighting the fact that the Europa League winners qualify for the following season's

Champions League, the Holy Grail for all big clubs. Jose Mourinho himself acknowledged that he was targeting the European competition, this at a time when his team was in a struggle to make fourth place in the league but in a Europa League semi-final. This newly discovered regard for the Europa League contrasted with his previous dismissal of the competition.

Arsenal, Manchester City and Leicester City all came through the initial group stage to the knockout Round of 16 in the Champions League. Here Arsenal lost 1-5 in each of their games against Bayern Munich, heralding massive criticism of team, club and Arsene Wenger. Manchester City, in what was widely regarded as confirmation of their inability to defend lost to Monaco on away goals. Their 5-3 home win was followed almost inevitably by a 1-3 away defeat. So only Leicester City made it as far as the quarter-finals at which stage they were edged out 1-2 on aggregate by Atletico Madrid, having performed quite creditably.

In the Premier League the next thirteen games would bring the League to its mid-point and conveniently enough the nineteenth round of games was completed on New Year's Eve. The space-travelling football follower who looked at the table and the form of the big teams after those first six games would have had some difficulty grasping what exactly had happened on his return from outer space on 1st January 2017.

Premier League table at half-way point

	P	W	D	L	F	A	Pts
Chelsea	19	16	1	2	42	13	49
Liverpool	19	13	4	2	46	21	43
Arsenal	19	12	4	3	41	19	40
Tottenham Hotspur	19	11	6	2	37	14	39
Manchester City	19	12	3	4	39	21	39
Manchester United	19	10	6	3	29	19	36
Everton	19	7	6	6	25	23	27
West Bromwich Albion	19	7	5	7	25	23	26

What had happened was that after those first six games, Antonio Conte identified a problem in his team, fixed it and reaped the rewards in the shape of thirteen consecutive wins. A gap had opened up, a gap which would soon become ten points. While Tottenham later embarked on a run of their own making them Chelsea's only challengers, they reduced the gap briefly to four points before it became seven again as they were overcome at West Ham. A Cup semi-final between Chelsea and Tottenham must also have had a psychological impact on both sets of players as Chelsea prevailed looking a far better side than their London rivals.

Premier League Final Table

	P	W	D	L	F	A	Pts
Chelsea	38	30	3	5	85	33	93
Tottenham Hotspur	38	26	8	4	86	26	86
Manchester City	38	23	9	6	80	39	78
Liverpool	38	22	10	6	78	42	76
Arsenal	38	23	6	9	77	44	75
Manchester United	38	18	15	5	54	29	69

The simple interpretation of the final table is that it is hard to finish ahead of a team that wins 30 of 38 games although Tottenham made a decent effort to do so. Manchester City, Liverpool and Arsenal need to defend better. Manchester United defend extremely well but need to score goals.

Arsenal had stood an outside chance of continuing their remarkable record of top four finishes but their late sprint was too late and their hopes that either City or Liverpool would stumble on the final day were not realised as both teams won comfortably. Manchester United finished sixth having had a long unbeaten run which consisted of more than a few draws, something which amounts to points dropped two at a time, no matter how much gloss people try to put on an 'unbeaten' run such as this.

Jose Mourinho's gamble on Europa League success paid dividends when his team beat a disappointing, very young, Ajax side in the Stockholm final, a game overshadowed by a devastating suicide bombing at a Manchester concert just two days earlier. A sombre Mourinho spoke about the events after the game but could not prevent himself from claiming three trophies for the season. The League Cup is a trophy but only the deluded regard the Community Shield as something to boast about.

Jose Mourinho
Manchester United

Jose Mourinho's achievement in qualifying for the Champions League is creditable but it perhaps covers some deep problems at Manchester United. It is possible those problems may be overcome by spending more money before the new season kicks in. As with all such matters, how the money is spent will be critical in dictating what progress United make as they desperately seek a return to the glory days they enjoyed under Sir Alex Ferguson.

Paul Pogba's arrival at Old Trafford was a win for the marketing department if not for the football team. £89m is an extraordinary amount of money but the club were happy to have it reported that Twitter went into overdrive with 615,000 interactions, itself some kind of social media achievement. It is hard to conceive of a more shallow perspective on the importance of a transfer. On the field Pogba was no disaster but neither was he the sensational leader and match-winner that a fee this size should capture. It could be argued that the structure of the team and its playing formation differed dramatically at United from that in which he had played at Juventus. But that reflects on United, their manager and on the player himself, if at that value, he has difficulty adjusting to a changed tactical formation.

By May news broke about Pogba's enormous transfer fee. Allegations from an operation called Football Leaks made claims which were supported by the Danish newspaper, Politiken. It appears

Manchester United were keen to make a splash in the transfer market, to herald a new era, with a new manager of renown and some high profile spending. To this end they engaged Mino Raiola the brash Dutch-Italian agent, who acts for, among others, Zlatan Ibrahimovic, Henrikh Mkhitaryan, Mario Balotelli and Paul Pogba. This is the same Paul Pogba who moved from the Manchester United of Sir Alex Ferguson to Juventus in 2012 for next to nothing. That move, by all accounts, was prompted by Ferguson's distaste for dealing with Raiola.

According to the Football Leaks allegations, Juventus paid Raiola €27m for services provided around Pogba's transfer. United, allegedly paid him a further €19.4m in addition to €100m they paid Juventus. Finally, Raiola, clearly being a man who misses no opportunity to be rewarded, apparently collected €2.6m from the player for his assistance in negotiating Pogba's €8.6m annual salary.

Regardless of these numbers, which it must be said are pretty difficult to disregard, the conflicts of interest are so obvious and so outrageous, as not to be tolerable in any remotely ethical environment. FIFA operates a data collecting process under the heading Transfer Matching System. FIFA's spokesperson, acknowledged that its Transfer Matching System had sought more information but helpfully pointed out that this does not amount to an investigation and such a request should not be interpreted as a disciplinary matter.

It was Jose Mourinho's treatment of other players which brought much attention to the manager and the club over the season.

Bastian Schweinsteiger was instructed to train with the under 23 team. Clearly the manager did not want the player but the former Germany captain and World Cup winner, a model professional, did whatever he was asked to do and continued to offer his wholehearted support to his club colleagues via social media before departing for the U.S. in March 2017. Within days of the player's departure, Mourinho said he regretted how he had treated Schweinsteiger.

Before the season was through the manager would engage in publicly criticising several of his players, most notably Luke Shaw, a player attempting to come back from a shocking leg break. When Shaw came into the team during a game in April, a post-match interviewer commented to Mourinho that the player he had been publicly criticising had performed well. This prompted what was probably the most outrageous reply of the year when the manager stated that the reason the player had done well was because he was playing on the side of the pitch which housed the United dugout and that Mourinho had been telling him what to do. The suggestion was that the player was incapable of making any decisions. It was crass. It was bullying. It was hard to understand how this was considered acceptable at any level, by club, by PFA or by Premier League administration.

United's forwards were regularly collectively and individually subjected to public criticism by the manager, Ibrahimovic being a notable exception. But then the big Swede was scoring goals consistently until incurring a dreadful knee injury in a Europa League quarter final against Anderlecht at Old Trafford. At 35 it is possible the ligament damage may end the player's career. He has pledged to return and refused to take further wages to which he was entitled, because he was no longer in a position to contribute on the field. The Manchester United forwards did have a case to answer. At home they scored fewer goals than either relegated Hull or struggling Swansea City. It was United's lowest goal scoring season at home since the inception of the Premier League.

Apart from Mourinho's frequent public criticism of players and a mediocre performance over the season, a feature of Manchester United 2016-17 was the high incidence of injuries, something which contrasted with Chelsea's exceptionally low level of absences through injury. It remains to be seen whether United were unlucky or if some other element of their physical preparation and training methods had a part to play in what was a major problem for the club, highlighted inevitably by the manager who joked at one point that he himself was ready to play, as he used the situation to declare he was focusing on the Europa League at the expense of chasing a higher Premier League placing.

In the final analysis of the season, the manager can claim credit for the defensive solidity of the team, even with regular injuries to virtually all the first team defenders. He can claim to have won 2 trophies in his first season and to have led the team to Champions League qualification. It is only fair that he be judged on what happens next. United will need to make the right purchases, to ensure there is a squad good enough to compete in Europe and at home. It appears this will happen without Wayne Rooney who is expected to depart over the summer. The man who has captained England and Manchester United is a shadow of his former self, a player whose career appears to be grinding to a halt although he is exactly four years younger than Zlatan Ibrahimovic.

The season over, Mourinho was asked about the possible signing of Antoine Griezmann. His surly reply was that it had nothing to do with him and that Ed Woodward would now need to do his job having been told some months ago which players Mourinho wants. Clearly, it will be someone else's fault if the targets are not bought just as it was the players fault when anything went wrong all season and Jose's achievement when Luke Shaw played well! It must be said that should Jose Mourinho continue to publicly criticise players on whom he depends, there is every chance that his Manchester United career will end in a manner very similar to his latest departure from Chelsea.

Antonio Conte
Chelsea

The first question Antonio Conte was asked in the aftermath of Chelsea's Championship clinching win at West Bromwich Albion, related to the change he introduced as Chelsea toiled in eighth position, eight points off the lead after a mere six games. His immediate response referred to the balance of the team. Balance in a team is not mentioned as frequently as it should be. It was a hugely important factor in how many of the great managers went about their work, from Herbert Chapman to Ernst Happel to Brian Clough.

After that sixth game in which Chelsea lost 0-3 at Arsenal they travelled to Hull for game number seven. Antonio Conte, unhappy with the loss and indeed with the team's form, decided upon a radical change. One of the oldest maxims in management is 'if it ain't broke, don't fix it.' Conte saw the other side of that coin in this case determining that something was certainly 'broke' at Chelsea. So Conte set about fixing it.

Deducing that neither Branislav Ivanovic nor John Terry was up to the task of defending at the highest level, he made a radical change. No longer would Chelsea play with a back-four. It would be a back three with wingbacks coming into the team. Marcus Alonso was one wingback selection but the other reflected sensationally well on Conte. Victor Moses, a forgotten player at the club, a man loaned out by Jose Mourinho, three seasons in succession, a winger all his career, was now converted and developed as a wingback by Conte. The player who had been widely expected to leave the club at the end of the season became a mainstay in the team signing a contract extension in March 2017.

Much has been made of the tactical switch but I like the suggestion made by one eminent pundit that it was a move forced on Conte, when he realised he did not have four defenders sufficiently good to achieve what he wanted for the team. The outcome was simply an example of brilliant maximisation of the resources which were available.

The tactical change had other dimensions. Edin Hazard, a sensation two seasons earlier had lost his way under Jose Mourinho. Now in a tactical structure which suited him perfectly he returned once again to become a key part of Chelsea's success. Players such as the former Barcelona duo of Cesc Fabregas and Pedro were also helped to rediscover missing form. Michy Batshusyi was under-used but came in to great effect in scoring the championship winning goal. Cesar Azpilicueta's role was changed and time will tell whether David Luiz became a better defender or Azpilicueta made him look better, with his diligent covering and superb, insightful defending. The new Footballer of The Year, N'golo Kante proved to be everything Chelsea had hoped he would.

Conte's handling of his playing squad was exemplary. One incident stood out above all others. In February it was claimed that Diego Costa, Chelsea's top scorer, was the subject of an approach from China which involved earnings beyond his wildest dreams. Costa became restless. This is a player so immature that one journalist claimed quite seriously that whatever else Antonio Conte achieved, managing Costa as he had done entitled him to the Manager of the Year accolade. The manager took on the player and when Costa threw what might be politely called a hissy fit, he was omitted from the squad for the next game. When questioned, the manager quietly declared the player unfit.

Chelsea went ahead and won the game and within a week the fuss had died down and a fit Diego Costa was back on board and fully functioning. To have won the league so convincingly in his first season is a remarkable achievement for Conte. To have managed all the other elements and to have so many previously underperforming players, again functioning effectively is further tribute to the Italian. The high standards of fitness were the subject of Conte's second comment after the league had been won. He paid tribute to his backroom team and to the minimal injuries suffered by the players saying this was no accident. He clearly believes, with good reason, his trainers know their business and as a result he has more players available to him more often than any other manager at this level.

Chelsea have the resources to build on this success. They have a strong squad which will be further strengthened during the transfer window. They have also chosen brilliantly when opting for Antonio Conte as manager. Conte, with his team of fellow southern Italians including his own brother, offers the club continued success as long as Chelsea can retain him and as long as he maintains the dynamism. That coupled with his intelligence, attention to detail as personified by the video recording of training sessions as a learning tool and his understanding of football makes him a truly formidable manager.

Jürgen Klopp
Liverpool

Liverpool under Jürgen Klopp have been the enigma of the football season 2016-17. They appear to find it easier to achieve results against the top teams than against the lesser teams. Their good form in early season was in no small way attributable to Philippe Coutinho's excellence. His injury-induced absence and predictably slow return to form was a setback.

Sadio Mane appeared an excellent signing and was scoring goals. He then departed for the African Cup of Nations leaving no obvious replacement indicating a lack of depth in goal scoring resources. Mane's return was marked by injury and further absence. During April and May it was hard to tell if Liverpool and the Manchester teams, were doing their level best to finish fifth rather than in the lucrative fourth place. A final day retention of fourth spot at Arsenal's expense, amounted to a good achievement. It was only the club's second time to qualify for the Champions League in the past eight seasons.

Competing in Europe while attempting improvement at home will be a huge challenge for Liverpool. As the season ends and they reflect on that top four place, some harsh truths need to be addressed. They don't have the squad for the forthcoming two-pronged assault. Transfer funds will be made available. Once again, how they are spent will be critical. The lack of depth in their panel proved problematic during the season and injuries and their frequency were an unwelcome issue. Their return to the Champions

League and a requirement on Klopp to improve their league position next time out, mean the club probably must buy better than any of their main competitors.

A squad with more depth, with more creative ability, better defence and some tactical adaptability would appear to be the requirements if Liverpool are to remain consistent contenders as they once were. Jürgen Klopp has brought about improvement but not to the degree expected by many Liverpool supporters. Returning to the big stage in Europe is a decent achievement. Dropping more points against mid and lower table teams than against their immediate rivals was a problem. Once the lesser teams decided to play defensively, the ability to break them down was too often absent. The noticeable difference in how they defended when compared with Chelsea and Manchester United raises questions to which Jürgen Klopp must find answers if his reign in Liverpool is to be a long one.

Liverpool football club has been an extraordinarily successful investment for its American owners. The club's value has soared since they acquired it relatively cheaply. They must now decide whether to cash in by selling the club or plough proper funding into strengthening the squad for the long haul. There has been no suggestion to date that Fenway will exit but the notion will not have escaped investors with their background. They have in place a much sought-after manager. They must support him to a degree far beyond that of recent times if he and the club are to return to the heights of the English and European game. But ultimately Klopp himself has to dictate and identify the additions he needs.

Pep Guardiola
Manchester City

Manchester City's Champions League exit to Monaco brought headlines such as the Times "Shambolic City crash out". There followed speculation that Guardiola would sell fifteen players as a result of the non-performance in both Europe and in the domestic league. Guardiola at Bayern Munich won three League titles but never looked like winning a Champions League, the yardstick by which all superstar managers are judged these days. Without Xavi and Iniesta in midfield, Carles Puyol providing leadership and Leo Messi up front, it was never likely to be as easy elsewhere as it had seemed at Barcelona. With Manchester City he is a further step down the European pecking order.

That City ended the season without a trophy played heavily on Guardiola who declared he could have been sacked as a failure. It was the first time in his short but very distinguished managerial career that his team finished empty handed. But perhaps he was being too hard on himself. The Premier League, despite the hype, is not the best league in the world. If it were, qualifying teams would do better in the Champions League. But it is competitive. The difference in standard between the best teams and those at the next level is such that the top teams are vulnerable if they are not properly focused. The facility to treat a good percentage of league games lightly exists in Germany, in Spain, in France and in Italy. In England it is a brave or foolish manager who underestimates league opponents.

Manchester City had played some excellent football at times. They showed flashes of what they might become but the consistency necessary for league success was never there. Nor was the defensive solidity without which Premier League success looks beyond them.

It was Guardiola's first season with an ageing team which will need and receive big investment ahead of the next season. As soon as the campaign had ended, news broke of the first step towards clearing out players over 30. Joe Hart's loan would end and instead his next move will be permanent. Willy Caballero who regularly had played instead of Claudio Bravo towards season end, would also go, as would Bacary Sagna, Jesus Navas and Gael Clichy. More would follow. A new side will likely be built around the outstanding Sergio Aguero and the promising Kevin de Bruyne.

This club has the resources to buy any player who becomes available, football governance limits permitting. It remains to be seen if Guardiola has the stomach or stamina for the battle to make City that which their owners and executives think they ought to be. Guardiola himself confirmed he felt the team had not been good enough to compete with Europe's best or to win the Premier league. Having finished third, 15 points behind Chelsea, he promised they would be better next season. Once further expensive additions have joined the squad, he will be judged more harshly on how City perform in 2017-18. He is said to be a fast learner. Time will tell.

Mauricio Pochettino
Tottenham Hotspur

The only manager in England to have been born in a town called Murphy, (in Santa Fe, Argentina) made a big impression when first he came into English football as manager of Southampton in 2013. After one season he was head-hunted by Tottenham and has worked energetically and constructively to improve the club. He is a believer in all Tottenham sides playing identically and has imposed this belief across the club. This was a principle of Herbert Chapman and of Bill Shankly and was most notably visible over many years in Europe at Ajax of Amsterdam. In 2015-16 Tottenham offered the only challenge to Leicester as the season reached a conclusion. Once the Championship was out of reach they tailed off badly finishing third behind Arsenal.

In 2016-17 again they offered the only viable challenge to the eventual winners, this time continuing with emphatic wins in the last few games even after the decisive moment had passed. Pochettino has built a young squad playing attractive football. The construction of a new stadium beside White Hart Lane offers long-term benefits and potential for the club. There remains a need to strengthen the current team, particularly in midfield. Most of the jigsaw pieces are in place. If the stadium construction project does not impinge on the need to complete the teambuilding, Mauricio Pochettino offers Tottenham a real possibility of returning to the glory days of more than a half century ago, the days of Bill Nicholson. In an increasingly competitive environment, it will not be sufficient to have the right manager in place. He will need to be supported unambiguously and unequivocally. The question is not whether Pochettino is capable of delivering. He is. The question is whether the club is capable of supporting him to the extent necessary.

Arsene Wenger
Arsenal

Arsenal and their at times beleaguered manager salvaged something from the season with a 2-0 FA Cup Final win over Chelsea. As Arsenal were the ones beset by injuries and suspensions while Chelsea had a full squad available it was a surprising result but a well-deserved win for the north Londoners. There had been regular protests at Emirates Stadium by an increasingly disenchanted group of supporters. Failure to qualify for the Champions League was seen as a further setback to a manager who felt, not unreasonably, that he was being shown little gratitude for his two decades of stewardship.

The problem was that the three League titles won were in his early days, 1998, 2002 and 2004 and there had been no serious challenge for the title for several years. His handling of a spat with Arsenal's best player, Alexis Sanchez, was seen as an example of weakness on Wenger's part. Unlike Antonio Conte's handling of Diego Costa in very similar circumstances, Wenger put Sanchez on the bench but once the game began to go wrong he brought on the sulking player, completely defeating the apparent objective of showing him he could be done without.

But the somewhat surprising defeat of an off-colour Chelsea meant Arsene Wenger has the record for the most FA Cups (7) won by any manager and Arsenal now have a record thirteen Cups.

The protesting fans believe Arsenal have been far too prudent in the transfer market and that a challenge for the title will require greater firepower than the club has had for some years. Their inability to progress to the latter stages in Europe since the 2006 Champions League Final defeat to Barcelona is evidence of their stagnation — a top four team, at least until the current league ended — but not a title contender. The manager still has support among the club's fan base as was demonstrated rather hilariously during the spring of 2017. The discontented fans organised a flyover of the stadium on match day by a small plane with a protest banner. This was countered by a second plane bearing a message of support. It was the Battle of Britain 21st century style.

The story of Arsenal in 2017 is not about the squad or who might be recruited for the next season. The story is about the manager. The question is whether he will be on board next season. He is reputed to have an excellent relationship with the controlling shareholder who is American and pleased with the prudent way the club is run and its profitability. The Chief Executive has suggested he would like a Director of Football appointed, something he knows is anathema to everything Wenger believes. The manager was not slow to ridicule this notion.

Whither Arsene Wenger and whither Arsenal are questions which remain to be answered at the time of writing but many objective observers believe Wenger brought much that was welcome into English football. His approach to team preparation and sports science demonstrated a degree of enlightenment and new thinking which served Arsenal magnificently but also served the Premier League very well. The man deserves to choose his time of departure. But this is football and few managers get such a privilege. Whatever happens — remember one thing. It's money that matters.

Elsewhere in 2016-17 in English football, the Premier League saw managerial change just as it always has done. Hull and Middlesbrough sacked their managers before eventually being relegated. The third side to go down was Sunderland. Their manager, David Moyes, went of his own accord, apparently, once the season had ended. The other Premier League clubs to change manager during the season, apart from the relegated three and Leicester City were Watford, Swansea (twice) and Crystal Palace.

Not all managers are equal

At the very bottom of the football food chain, Leyton Orient relinquished their place in League football after 112 years of continuous membership, their historical highpoint being their single year in the top flight when Johnny Carey got them promoted in season 1961-62. As a model for how not to manage your club they stand alone. In less than three years Leyton Orient have had nine managers. In the season 2016-17 they changed manager in October, in November, in January and in March, making it five different managers in one season. The protests against the Italian owner Sig. Francesco Becchetti continue while the team heads into non-league football. The discontented Arsenal supporters should thank their lucky stars they support what has been a well- run club from the days of the great Herbert Chapman to those of Arsene Wenger.

Managers have always been vulnerable to job loss. The mantra is that it is a results based business. However, in recent times an influx of foreign owners to clubs outside the top tier has had an impact, and not always in a good way. The 2016-17 season saw what was probably the worst decision in living memory of a managerial dismissal and replacement.

In December Birmingham City were outside the Championship (second tier) play-off positions on goal difference. Their manager, Gary Rowett, was sacked along with his coaching team. He was replaced by Gianfranco Zola. The explanation was that the owners wanted someone more high profile than Rowett. By April, Zola resigned having taken the club to the brink of the relegation zone, winning two of the twenty four games over which he had presided. Gary Rowett was appointed Derby County manager in March. That team finished a satisfactory ninth and next season will be watched with interest. Birmingham appointed Harry Redknapp to save them from relegation. Unfortunately he succeeded!

At the highest levels, managers in the modern age can afford to take breaks or be out of football management while they decide their future. Guardiola famously resigned from Barcelona, moving to New York for 12 months during which time he took tuition in German in preparation for the Bayern Munich job. Klopp quit Borussia Dortmund and had planned to take a year out. Liverpool made him an offer he couldn't refuse so he curtailed his sabbatical to just over five months. Mourinho, following his second enforced departure from Chelsea, was biding his time until he got to manage Manchester United, a job he had reputedly hankered after for some years.

Football has come a long way from the managers who had to work to keep a roof over their heads. Stan Cullis experienced hard times when his career was over. Alf Ramsey, Bill Shankly and their successful contemporaries never knew wealth and some of them came close to poverty. We are a long way from Rinus Michels, in Ruud Gullit's words, chasing the boys around the town on his bicycle, to make sure they were not out socialising.

Alex Ferguson and Brian Clough both found themselves having actively to sell the idea of supporting their clubs in their local communities, when first they entered the world of football management. They were managers, coaches, public relations officers and in Clough's case, team bus driver for a while. Football has changed beyond recognition. So has football management.

At the beginning of this book I made reference to the research of Professor Szymanski into English football and his conclusions that the team with the highest wage bill tends to come out on top while the worst paid playing squad will probably be relegated. In 2017 when everyone appears to have agreed, it's the money that matters, a table showing the cost per league point to each Premier League club makes fascinating reading. It reflects what Professor Szymanski claimed but presents the information in a slightly different way.

	Wages (£m)	Wages (£m)	Amount in £m paid per point
	2014-15	2015-16	2016-17
Manchester United	202.6	232.2	3.57
Sunderland	77.1	83.9	3.50
Liverpool	166.1	208.2	2.85
Manchester City	193.8	197.6	2.74
Chelsea	215.6	222.4	2.56
Swansea	82.5	81.8	2.15
West Ham United	72.7	84.6	2.01
Crystal Palace	68.0	80.6	1.96
Southampton	79.8	84.9	1.88
Leicester City	57.4	80.4	1.87
Stoke City	58.7	72.1	1.76
West Bromwich Albion	69.8	73.7	1.64
Watford	20.7	57.9	1.45
Everton	77.5	84.0	1.38
Bournemouth	29.6	59.6	1.32
Tottenham Hotspur	100.8	104.6	1.30

The chart confirms how much more the clubs of the big four managers pay in player wages compared with the rest of the Premier League. We see how relatively cheaply Leicester City got their league title and through Watford and Bournemouth, how big a jump there is in wages once a team is promoted to the promised land of Premier League. On a cost per point basis Tottenham are the best in their league operating as they are on wages which are half those at their top-of-the-table competitors, while Manchester United, on this calculation offer the worst value for money.

As far as the English Premier League is concerned the change is driven by gigantic TV revenues. An idea of the scale of the income to Premier League clubs may be gleaned from some figures released as the season ground to its unspectacular conclusion. The figures refer to the previous year and they show income from European games. It is purely TV income and excludes all gate receipts, match day revenues etc. Manchester City received €83.8m for reaching a Champions League semi-final. The clubs eliminated earlier such as Chelsea and Arsenal got €69m and €53m respectively, while Manchester United took home €38m having failed to make it out of the group stages.

Meanwhile the Premier League itself had a TV deal worth £5.1b over three years to 2016 which increased to £8.4b over the following three years. As long as that continues, this league will go on attracting top players and managers from all parts of the globe. And the demand for the best players and managers will become even more fierce as the stakes get higher and higher. The Championship promotion final in 2017 has been billed as the £170m game. Its money that matters.

Where all of this leaves the young trainees in development academies is a big question for those who govern football. When such vast sums are flowing into the game, club owners want the best readymade players and the best proven managers. The game is increasingly driven by money, increasingly influenced by agents and increasingly in need of proper governance. These are matters for another day. For now, please remember, however much your club spends on players and however much they pay their manager, only one team can win a Premier League in any given year.

Bibliography

BOOKS

Armitage Dave, Cloughie – The Inside Stories (Hot Air Publishers, 2009)

Ball Phil, Morbo The Story of Spanish Football (WSC Books 2001)

Barend Frits and Henk van Dorp, Ajax, Barcelona, Cruyff: The ABC of an Obstinate Maestro, translated by

David Winner and Lex den Dam (Bloomsbury, 1997)

Bellos Alex Futebol; The Brazilian Way of Life (Bloomsbury, 2003)

Bower Tom, Broken Dreams (Pocket Books, 2007)

Buchan Charles, A lifetime in Football (Mainstream Publishing, 2010)

Carson Mike, The Managers; Inside the Minds of Football's Leaders (Bloomsbury, 2013)

Carter Neil, The Football Manager; A History (Routledge, 2006)

Chapman Herbert, Herbert Chapman on Football (GCR Books, 2010)

Crick Michael, The Boss; The many Sides of Alex Ferguson (Pocket Books, 2003)

Crick Michael, Manchester United; The Betrayal of a Legend (Pelham Books, 1989)

Crouch Terry, The World Cup; The Complete History (Aurum Press, 2002)

Davies Hunter, The Glory Game (Mainstream, 1972)

De Bartolo Augusto, Tutti Gli Uomini Che Hanno Fatto Grande L'A.C. Milan (Ultra Sport 2011)

Edgerton Paul, William Garbutt; The Father of Italian Football (SportsBooks Ltd., 2009)

Edworthy Niall, The Second Most Important Job in the Country (Virgin 1999)

Foot John, Calcio; A History of Italian Football (Harper Perennial, 2007)

Fox Norman, Prophet or Traitor; The Jimmy Hogan Story (Parrs Wood Press, 2003)

Giles John with Declan Lynch, A Football Man (Hachette Books Ireland, 2010)

Giles John, The Great & The Good (Hachette Books Ireland, 2012)

Glanville Brian, Champions of Europe (Guinness Publishing, 1991)

Glanville Brian, England Managers; The Toughest Job in Football (Headline Publishing Group, 2007)

Goldblatt David, The Ball is Round, A Global History of Football (Viking, 2006)

Grant Michael and Rob Robertson, The Management (Birlinn, 2011)

Grimaldi Mauro, Vittorio Pozzo – Storia di un Italiano (Societa Stampa Sportiva 2001)

Guenzi Paolo and Dino Ruta, Leading Teams (John Wiley & Sons, 2013)

Guthrie Jimmy, Soccer Rebel (Pentagon 1956)

Hafer Andreas and Wolfgang Hafer, Hugo Meisl; Eine Biographie (Verlag Die Werkstatt GmbH 2007)

Hamilton Duncan, Provided you Don't Kiss Me; 20 Years with Brian Clough (Fourth Estate 2009)

Hermiston Roger, Clough and Revie (Mainstream, 2001)

Hesse-Lichtenberger Ulrich Tor! The Story of German Football (WSC Books 2003)

Hopcraft Arthur, The Football Man (Aurum Press, 2006)

Hughes John with Alex Gordon, Yogi Bare; The Life and Times of a Celtic Legend (John Hughes 2013)

Hunter Graham, Barca; The Making of the Greatest Team in the World (Back Page Press, 2012)

Hyne Ashley, George Raynor (The History Press, 2016)

Ibrahimovich Zlatan and David Lagercrantz, I am Zlatan Ibrahimovich (Penguin 2013)

Imlach Gary, My Father and Other Working Class Heroes (Yellow Jersey Press, 2006)

Keane Roy with Eamon Dunphy, Keane; The Autobigraphy (Michael Joseph, 2002)

Kuper Simon, Football Against the Enemy (Orion, 1994)

Lacy Josh, God is Brazilian; Charles Miller The Man Who Brought Football to Brazil (Tempus Publishing, 2005)

Lanfanchi Pierre, Eisenberg Christiane, Mason Tony, Wahl Alfred, 100 YEARS OF FOOTBALL (Weidenfeld & Nicolson 2004)

Liversedge Stan, The England Job (Soccer Book Publishing, 1996)

Marcotti Gabriele, Capello; Portrait of a Winner (Bantam Press 2008)

McKinstry Leo, Sir Alf (Harpersport, 2006)

Modeo Sandro, Il Barca (Isbn Edizioni S.r.l. 2011)

Morin Stephen R. The Munich Air Disaster (Gill & Macmillan, 2007)

Murray Les, The World Game (Hardie Grant Books, 2011)

Pawson Tony, The Observer on Soccer (Unwin Hyman, 1989)

Reade Brian, 44 Years With The Same Bird (Pan Books, 2009)

Reeves Jon, The Managers (New Holland Publishers, 2014)

Reng Ronald, A Life Too Short; The Tragedy of Robert Enke (Yellow Jersey Press, 2012)

Sadar Giuliano, EL PARON: Vita Di Nereo Rocco (Edizioni Lint Trieste, 1997)

St. John Ian with James Lawton, The Saint; My Autobiography (Hodder & Stoughton, 2006)

Studd Stephen, Herbert Chapman Football Emperor (Souvenir Press Ltd., 1998)

Turner Dennis and Alex White, The Breedon Book of Football Managers (Breedon Books, 1993)

Wagg Stephen, The Football World (The Harvester Press, 1984)

Walvin James, The People's Game (Mainstream Publishing, 1994)

Wangerin David, Soccer in a Football World (WSC Books 2006)

Whelan Ronnie, Walk On; My Life in Red (Simon & Schuster, 2011)

Williams John, Red Men; Liverpool Football Club, The Biography (Mainstream Publishing, 2010)

Wilson Jonathan, Inverting The Pyramid (Orion 2009)

Wilson Jonathan, Nobody Ever Says Thank You; Brian Clough The Biography (Orion Books, 2011)

Winner David, Brilliant Orange; The Neurotic Genius of Dutch Football (Bloomsbury, 2001)

WEBSITES

www.bundesliga.com

bundesligafanatic.com

www.espnfc.com

www.fifa.com

www.football-italia.net

www.transfermarket.com

www.uefa.com

www.worldfootball.net

outsideoftheboot.com

lfchistory.net

www.ABC.es

www.thehardtackle.com

www.storiedicalcio.altervista.org

truth-out.org

www.lequipe.fr

equaliserblog.wordpress.com

archiviostorico.corriere.it

www.gazzetta.it

MAGAZINES AND NEWSPAPERS

The Blizzard

Four Four Two

Guerin Sportivo

When Saturday Comes

World Soccer

Daily Mail

La Gazzetta dello Sport

The Guardian

Irish Examiner

Irish Times

Sunday Independent

Sunday Times

The Telegraph

The Times

T.V.

Sky

ITV Sports

BBC

Pitch International LLP

Index